BLAZE OF COLOUR:
EMBRACING CREATIVITY

Blaze of Colour: Embracing Creativity

Diane Eastham M. Ed.

Diane Eastham M.Ed

Blaze of Colour: Embracing Creativity

ISBN 978-0-9937560-1-6

Design and Layout
Karl Griffiths-Fulton

ACKNOWLEDGEMENTS

I would like to thank all those who have contributed to the making of this book. That includes the legion of proofreaders who encouraged me over the years and helped to refine my vision for my writing. I'm grateful to have had the support of such a talented circle of friends and colleagues, including just about every English teacher I've ever taught with. Shout-outs go to Rob Reid for his support and knowledge of the Arts community; Veronica Ross for assisting with editing; Muriel McMahon for her Jungian perspective; Dr. Judith Miller for tirelessly polishing the manuscript and Karl Griffiths-Fulton for producing the book design. Karl's work included the selection and reproduction of colour plates of my art work, no small task. Thank you to Chris Yellow at Pandora Press for taking the vision and turning it into this book.

TABLE OF CONTENTS

INTRODUCTION

The Dragonfly's Promise

I stand in the middle of the crowded art gallery early this February afternoon, soaking up energy from the blaze of colour on the walls and the buzz of conversation as viewers engage with the art and each other. Some make observations about the techniques, others about the body of work as a whole. Many, like me, simply enjoy the colour and spectacle, so welcome on this grey winter's day. The gallery is filled to capacity for this opening and the wine flows freely. The gallery's curator is smiling. He catches my eye and crosses the room to talk with me.

"We've set a record for attendance. 225 people today," he says.

We are both pleased with the turn out, due in no small part to some excellent advance publicity from the city newspaper including a feature on the artist. I survey the room, and take in the title of the exhibition, "String Theory." Stenciled in foot-high black letters, it stands out in stark contrast to the white wall. There's no missing it. Immediately under the exhibition's title is the name of the artist: mine. My sister, standing beside me, takes photographs.

This exhibition was a gift to me, an award for winning a competition held by our local art society two years earlier. When I began creating these works, I had no idea how much stretching and growing would be required. It has taken me two years to create the 24 works in this room: two years of hopes, dreams and struggle to say something of value that others might share. The moments of frustration, worry and despair that such a task was beyond my capacity are not easy to read at this moment but they are represented too—the ghosts in the frames. As so many of us do,

I juggled my work as an artist with my responsibilities elsewhere: family, home, and full time career. It often seemed there was little room for creativity within the confines of those responsibilities, that my creative work was relegated to whatever stray and fleeting minutes I could find in the corners of my life. Yet the work came together and the exhibition happened.

Shortly after this exhibition, at the age of 53, I became eligible for early retirement. After 32 years as a teacher and secondary school vice-principal, I realized that if I had the courage, I could make my creative dreams come true. I experienced moments of profound doubt as I contemplated trading in the chronic exhaustion and multi-tasking, heavily structured, overly scheduled life I had known for so long in the professional world. I wondered if I had enough talent to make life as an artist and writer anything more than a personal indulgence. I found myself suddenly unsure.

In my teaching career, I was immersed in a culture where the supports and incentives to keep working and do a good job were built in. The school board provided resources, rewards and opportunities to keep me motivated. I was surrounded by a cadre of like-minded people who offered me camaraderie and encouragement on a daily basis. I had developed the habits of thought and routine endemic to that particular lifestyle.

I wondered if I would be disciplined enough without such incentives to get up in the morning and go to work in my studio, or to sit at my computer and write the book I knew was waiting for me. Or being released to freedom after so many years, would I succumb to the temptation to do as I pleased… read all day lying on the couch, go out for lunch, visit with friends already living the good life? I would be a corporation of one working in the peace and sanctity of my home on my own terms. Was that enough? Was I enough? Would I be lonely on my own? And if so, what would I do about it?

I also had my finances to consider. I had just bought a modest house after living in an apartment for many years. I had mortgage payments, breaking one of the cardinal rules of retirement. Before I wrote my letter of resignation, I got out pencil, calculator and paper and crunched the numbers to make sure I could live on my pension. The news was not great. I would have enough to pay my bills, but not much beyond. I would have to adjust my lifestyle if I wanted to cover my mortgage. Which brought me back to the question of my own abilities. Was it worth pinching pennies and risking debt for the rest of my life to pursue the dream of developing my creative abilities? I had been working away at that dream in my spare time for more than 15 years, without much financial success to show for it. Could I supplement my income to a comfortable standard? Did I have what it took to be successful as a professional writer and artist? What defined success anyway?

As I looked at the numbers, I felt profound pension panic. I thought I would have to put my dreams on hold while I struggled to save more money. The thought of postponing or giving up my dream altogether threw me into depression. Recognizing I was stuck in an emotional quagmire, I consulted the people in my life who could offer expertise: my financial advisor and friends who had already taken the leap to pursue their dreams. In the last week of October, I sent the following e-mail to Muriel, a friend who had left teaching the year before to pursue her dream of becoming a Jungian analyst:

Dear Muriel,

Somewhat to my surprise, I have had a spell of Pension Panic this past week after crunching numbers. It means $1000 a month less than what I've been used to. My pension will cover all my monthly expenses but leaves little for anything else, which raises my fears about poverty. I don't want to be in a position of having to supply teach or get some other job just to survive in retirement. But I'm not sure the money is there comfortably at the moment. I have til the end of November to decide about it. Even though Halloween was a tempting date, I'm delaying putting in my resignation til my comfort level improves. I think my job is costing me my happiness and possibly my health, clear reasons why I want to leave. I would appreciate your perspective as one who has already made the leap.

Muriel wrote me this wonderful reply:

Dear Diane,

My heart tightens at the thought of you not following your beautiful and big creative heart. I will risk saying what I believe, trusting that you will do what is best for you. There are lots of ego voices you can listen to. Here is a raw soul voice. Get out! I watch your eyes sparkle and your energy buzz when you talk about your creative soul life. You are a good VP but you are a better creative woman. I have this image of your soul wanting to stretch to her full unfearful size. When your beautiful energy is not being swallowed up by your administrative job it can go to work for you.

And if your pension is not enough, it can work for you to make what you need. Spoken from a poor woman who wonders often what life under a bridge will really be like. Well, at least, it will be my bags I'm living with and not someone else's. A bag lady, but every inch a lady! So, if you were my client and not my friend, my supervisor would fire me from my program for giving raw soul advice. But, you are my friend so I risk it all and speak to that beautiful gutsy woman behind the fear. There is a gypsy in you waiting to dance. Listen to the music. The only way to wring out a saturated sponge is to wring it out into creative pursuits… "make from take." All that the demands of every day life take from our souls we MUST balance with making, creating, recreating… I know in my own work, I can't be creative with these souls entrusted to me unless I am creating with my own soul. Just felt like this might be worth both of us hearing…

Love,

Muriel[1]

You gotta love that raw soul voice. Muriel's reply bolstered my sagging confidence and gave me a truth I needed to hear. I needed to hear a great deal of truth from those around me as I sought to find it in my own life. I allowed my panic to motivate me to do an inventory of my life: would I be OK on my own living the life I believed I was meant to live, without an institutional safety net protecting me? That was the question I needed to answer.

From my inventory, I realized that having time free to work on my creative projects is more valuable to me than having a lot of money. I also realized I've developed my own internal resources over the years, and felt I was in a good place in my life to take this risk. I have reasonable financial habits. I've never carried credit-card debt and I've tucked away some savings that would carry me in a crisis. Furthermore, I realized there are some things it's not possible to know ahead of time. I would have to take them on faith and live them. By Halloween, I had come full circle back to "knowing" I needed to leave at the end of January, trusting my creative soul and my topside life to come into balance.

As I stepped out on my back deck into the sunshine of a late October day, a small red dragonfly appeared from nowhere and landed on my chest, right over my heart. I was so surprised I nearly stopped breathing. The dragonfly had no fear of me and remained where it was long enough for me to say, "Hello and welcome." In response, it lifted gently in flight and landed on my left wrist. I felt its actions were intentional but didn't "get" the message until after meditating and going for a walk. I intuitively understood the red dragonfly as a symbol of what I needed most: faith in the power of my heart to lead me, faith in my ability to express what is in my heart, to share it with others in the spirit of creativity, and courage to let go of the life I had led up to that moment.

This was a defining moment in my life, bringing together all the strands I had been working on for years: trying to decipher the desires of my heart, learning to recognize and listen to my intuition and honouring my deepest needs for creative expression. Would I act on what I knew and change my life so that it was more authentically my own or would I continue in the life I had—one that was useful, recognizably acceptable and rewarded, but not completely satisfying for me personally? Intuition, a key component of creativity, is like that dragonfly's kiss... easy to brush away, barely perceptible to the touch yet full of intent, shape, form—and essential to creativity. I was confident the message was meant for me to act on. I wrote in my journal,

> After more than 48 hours of anxiety, I feel deeply peaceful: I have found my direction and made my decision. I will cut the cord to my administrative life and leap in pursuit of my dreams.

It's taken me many years to develop the skills and self-confidence to tackle this life project and write this book, equal parts spiritual memoir and mirror. I plan to explore what creativity is, why it matters, how it is possible to lose touch with it and how pervasive is the process of loss in our culture. I will explore how to sustain creativity while living in relationships with others. I will also explore how to keep creativity intact while surviving the crises of everyday life, including the rigors of education and corporate life. It's possible to do so, but it does take work.

This book traces my personal journey: how I reached that moment standing fully-fledged as an artist with an exhibition of my work in a prestigious gallery. To realize my dream of giving full expression to my creativity, I had to discover and retrieve my nascent creative vision, then find and figure out how to articulate my creative voice. I spent years learning to listen to the messages I send myself, to trust them and to act on them.

Above all, I wish to share this journey into the creative realm, so that this becomes more than just a record of my struggles. Beginning in Chapter 1 and continuing throughout, exercises are provided to help the reader explore and develop creativity. I've used these exercises myself and professionally with clients in my creativity coaching practice. Each is designed to help develop creative ideas and give them expression—to find paths and nurture skills. Strategies are provided for identifying dreams, setting goals and taking the steps to achieve them. Exercises may be done whatever way seems appropriate. Impulse is to be trusted. Resonance or its inherent excitement is a good guide.

I have found journaling to be an invaluable tool in my own creative journey. As I work on my projects, I record and explore everything from ideas through attempts, to emotions and distractions along the way. I also use it to evaluate and reflect on whatever work I have completed. I recommend using a journal for many of the exercises in this book. A journal records the journey and, even inadvertently, captures ideas for future reference. A look back on musings will reveal growth and development and perhaps provide insights into process. It is as valuable to ask a question as it is to determine an answer. Noted Jungian author, Marion Woodman, advocates the importance of journaling:

> *The daily journal is like a mirror. When we first look into it, the blank pages stare back with ominous emptiness. But if we keep looking and trusting in what Rilke calls the 'possibility' of being' gradually we begin to see the face that is looking back at us...Journal writing is a way of taking responsibility for finding out who I AM.*[2]

And if already living a creative life, I trust that the reader will find affirmation and strategies to nurture and continue creative growth. There is good reason for doing so. The benefits of developing creativity include greater happiness and satisfaction from life, a better sense of identity, and a chance to help others as abilities develop.

All of us have the talent, abilities, ideas, time, and energy we need to live a satisfying creative life. This book can be seen as a blueprint to access individual gifts. Creative energy is effervescent and transmittable, capable of generating inspiration and ideas for anyone who comes in contact with it: ourselves, the people around us, society and the world at large. Goodness knows we can all benefit from that kind of energy.

ONE

Forward Into the Past

Somewhere along the way, towards the end of childhood, I lost track of my own creativity and many of the gifts with which I was born. I lost touch with a fundamental part of myself and it took more than 30 years to get "me" back. Since I believe creativity is innate, it is startling to chart how this loss can happen. Without my creative essence in hand or heart, I struggled for years with self-esteem and spent a lot of time searching for the answer to the question that is at once universal and personal: Who am I?

How does it happen that we stop listening to ourselves, lose key aspects of ourselves? There is no single, simple answer. Sometimes traumatic events can cause people to shut down parts of themselves as a matter of survival. Sometimes the shutdown is a response to abuse. But these traumas don't apply to my life, which has been pretty "normal," even privileged. There were no big events in my childhood, no traumatic accidents or major losses that caused me to lose track of myself in critical ways. Rather, it was a process that happened gradually over time as I grew up, a cultural erosion perhaps, rather than personal devastation.

I grew up the eldest of three children, born into a middle-class family in the 1950's. My father, Dr. Arthur Eastham, was a scientist with the National Research Council of Canada, and my mother, Marjorie, was a work-at-home mom who cared for me, my younger brother, David, and my sister, Jennifer. We lived in a bungalow in a pleasant suburb of Ottawa.

Creatively speaking, I had a good childhood. I was exposed to the arts early on. My mother enrolled me in art and ballet classes when I was five. Later came music classes after school. I learned embroidery, knitting, sewing and cooking—all forms of creative expression I have enjoyed throughout my life. My mother and my maternal grandmother encouraged my creative pursuits. I remember amusing myself for hours at my grandmother's, designing and cutting out clothes for paper dolls and creating knitted and sewn outfits using my own untaught techniques for the dolls my sister and I owned. I fantasized about being a fashion designer when I wasn't dreaming about being an underwater archaeologist with Jacques Cousteau.

My grandmother, Marjorie Frances Barrett Heward, was an artist in her own right. She worked in oil on canvas, painting realistic landscapes, beautiful scenes of the rural Laurentian countryside north of Montreal, Quebec where she lived with her husband, my grandfather, Charles Vivien Heward. Most mornings in the summers she would go off by herself carrying her gear to a location that inspired her and would return later in the day with works in various stages of completion. I grew up familiar with the aesthetics of art because she practiced them. By osmosis, I absorbed the smells, colours and uses of oil paint, turpentine, easels, brushes, board and canvas. I saw the process of creating from rough pencil sketch on white board to finished colourful painting. I learned that the white of walls, clouds and rapids was never just white, but an interesting combination of shadows and reflected colours from cream to rose to green to slate blue, depending on light and proximity to other objects.

My grandmother was talented enough to study with Adam Sherriff-Scott. Scott's name is a familiar one in Canadian art. His paintings are in the National Gallery and he was elected as a full member of the Royal Canadian Academy in 1944. Scott received his early training in Scotland, settling in Montreal in 1912. In 1938 he established the Adam Sherriff-Scott School of Fine Art, in Montreal, where he taught drawing and painting.[1] Despite the quality of her work, as far as I know, my grandmother never exhibited or sold any of her paintings. Instead, she gave them to family members, who extended the beautiful landscape paintings pride of place in their homes. I have some of her work in my own home.

My grandmother had good company in her artistic pursuits. Her husband's cousin, Prudence Heward, member of the Beaver Hall group along with Mary Cassatt, was painting in Montreal during the same period. In 1932, at a time when women artists were struggling for recognition, Prudence was given her first solo show at Scott's gallery in Montreal and was later invited to exhibit with the Group of Seven. Her work is in the National Gallery. She died young at the age of 49 in 1947.[2] I never met her, nor did I hear any conversation about her when I was growing up, but that was not unusual. Only the bare bones of family history were discussed *en famille*.

I think my grandmother tried to encourage her grandchildren in their creative pursuits as best she could. I remember a day when I was about 10 she offered to take my brother, my cousin and me on a painting expedition. She would have been about 70 at the time. She packed easels, brushes, boards and oil paints for each of us, set us up and invited us to paint what we saw. I was thrilled at the prospect. I remember a mass of pink flowers, so that's what I painted, using a lot of pink. I was pleased with my efforts until my grandmother commented that I needed to look more carefully and paint what I was seeing. This confused me as I thought I'd done that and told her so. She was adamant that I hadn't looked carefully enough. Perhaps my tendency to abstract expression was trying to surface even then. If so, it went unrecognized and there were no further painting excursions. I thought perhaps I was not a painter after all.

However, around the same time she presented me with a Brownie box-type camera that shot black and white film. I remember taking photos of the people in my life for a few years, but eventually lost interest, disappointed that the camera didn't have close-up capability. My grandmother died in 1970 at the age of 83, when I was 18. I loved her dearly and felt a profound loss. Though her creative gifts and journey were quite different from mine, and I didn't realize it at the time, we had much in common. Even though she painted realistic landscapes, colours like orange and turquoise found their way into houses and roof tops: evidence of her experimentation with colour. She, too, was a teacher who loved music, played piano and found life satisfaction through her art.

While my parents both appreciated art and spent spare moments doing some themselves, they saw creative work primarily as hobby, pastime and enjoyment: not something at which to make a living. Dad grew up without a lot of money and was always very careful with it. There was some family history of poverty. His dad's maternal grandfather had owned a hotel in a small town in British Columbia that burned to the ground around 1901. He lost everything and had to start over in his 70s. The only work he could get at that point was as a janitor. Growing up during the Depression affected my father's outlook when it came to money. He put himself through university on scholarships because his family couldn't afford to send him. Dad was determined to do better himself and to see his family better off financially than he had been growing up. He wanted each of his children to have job security, work they enjoyed and a good pension for old age. I'm sure that was partly behind my parents' desire to see me become a teacher.

Even so, both my parents pursued creative outlets occasionally. My dad liked to take photographs, carve wood and build things. Later in his life, he collected landscape paintings by Canadian artists. Mom enjoyed Ikebana, the Japanese art of flower arranging and also tried her hand at brush painting. She might have been quite good at it, but never pursued it. She preferred to have the company of women friends to take lessons with and wasn't always able to find it. As well, she had a busy, growing family to take care of and set her own creative needs aside—a pattern all too familiar in women's lives.

My family art heritage has proven a mixed blessing. In Grade 6, I entered the Humane Society poster contest for the city of Ottawa. My poster showed a black Labrador retriever waiting on the steps of a house with the caption, "Don't leave me out." My parents had encouraged me to paint a realistic landscape, as that's what they valued (as does a lot of the world, to the chagrin of my often abstract, non-representational artist self!) I remember spending hours painstakingly tracing pictures of dogs to get one that looked right—and that's what won. On the other hand, in Grade 7, my art teacher told me A.Y. Jackson had toured our art classes and had liked a piece I had created: a geometric abstract. Suffice it to say, my creative life was supported by my family, the school system (my marks in school were good) and the community during those years and there is not much in this background that would predict losing touch with my creativity.

For me, by the end of Grade 8 that precious time for unfettered expression of my creative voice was coming to an end. In our culture, "play" time is too often the preserve of childhood, and the dividing line occurs when we head off to high school. That is such a watershed. Though still young, at 13 or 14, we are expected to make choices that affect the course of our lives. During the Grade 9 course selection process, my parents made it clear I needed to concentrate on academic subjects. When I expressed an interest in taking home economics or art as options, I remember my mother telling me, "You can learn to cook and sew and draw on your own anytime, but you only get to go to university once." So Latin and conversational French landed on my timetable instead of the creative subjects I desired.

Though I was barely 13, at some level I knew this timetable did not suit me, but I accepted the authority of my parents' judgment. It was for the best and it was my job to do the work that would get me into university. Like so many others, my parents saw university as my route to a professional career with the stability of a regular salary, benefits and pension, worthwhile work, good working conditions and the opportunity for advancement. That's what they wanted for me and it was hard to argue against them.

From that year onward, doodling was confined to the margins of my life—and my notebooks—as the workload outside school became heavier. Like many teens at the time, I began babysitting for family and friends to earn spending money. In those adolescent years, I shifted my attention to the external world and looked to boys for the fun and excitement I was craving, placing an expectation on them they could never fulfill. The only creative outlet I kept through high school was music. I took piano lessons outside school, and I also played in the school band. I managed to squeeze music into my timetable by failing Grade 10 German. I was no longer the model student I had been—my soul was making itself known.

Sadly, even my favourite subjects, English and music, were becoming increasingly formal. Third-person writing replaced my first-person voice and essays replaced creative writing. I wrote poetry for a few years in high school, but gave up after Grade 11, as I didn't find much support. Sometimes when I was home alone, I would sit at my piano and compose spontaneously in unwritten form, expressing the emotions of my day. But for the most part, the freedom to play as I wanted was replaced by preparing for competition in the Kiwanis festivals and meeting the standards of Music Conservatory exams.

Spiritually, through my teens, I drifted. Though my parents drove their three kids to the neighbourhood church every Sunday, they did not attend with us and told us once we were confirmed in the Church (at the age of 13) we could choose to attend or not as we wished. I liked the hymns and the music in the services, especially for Christmas and Easter, and I even accepted the idea of God though perhaps not the image of him offered by the United Church at that time—a very patriarchal one. The God I learned about looked like Abraham Lincoln sitting on a throne in the sky, watching sparrows fall to their deaths, according to a popular children's hymn of the time. Sunday school classes seemed to emphasize rote memorization of scripture, something that never engaged me. Needless to say, I ceased to attend regularly after the age of 13.

By the age of 17, at the end of Grade 13, I was no longer certain God existed. In the space of those four years, John F. Kennedy, Robert Kennedy and Martin Luther King were assassinated and there was a war in Vietnam. These events contradicted my idea of what a God should allow. I designated myself "agnostic" and began to identify with the work of the Existentialists. The works of two Nobel Laureates in particular spoke to me: Samuel Becket's *Waiting for Godot*,[3] a work suggesting there is no salvation; and T.S. Eliot's poem, "The Love Song of J. Alfred Prufrock"[4] about the endless meaninglessness of everyday life.

It would take me three decades to reclaim my own spirituality and a belief in benevolence, abundance and a unifying force in the Universe. A Jungian would pick up on the words "assassination" and "war" and suggest I was defended against a truth: that my creative potential was being assassinated by my adapting ego, and there was a war within me. Certainly it felt that way for a long time.

When it became clear by Grade 12 that English was my best subject, my parents began screening universities in our area according to academic reputation. They offered me a choice of three: Carleton, University of Toronto or Queen's. I chose Queen's: close enough to go home for visits, and far enough away to offer independence. I left my piano behind and took a degree in English, learning to write essays about other writers. I expended my energy in the sanctioned outlets afforded by sports, student government and a busy social life. By the end of university, I had pretty much given up all recognizable expressions of my internal creative voice. I no longer worked with art materials, did any personal writing or played music. Without noticing it, I had lost or given up most of the creative outlets in my life along with the peaceful happiness I experienced when I was engaged in them.

I spent the summers through university working as a lifeguard and swimming instructor at summer camps and for the City of Ottawa. I had my first formal teaching experience with groups of young campers in the Beginners' Red Cross swim program. Some of the children were afraid of the water in the beginning, but all of them could swim their first lengths on their own by the end of the session. I discovered I loved teaching them, found the process satisfying and rewarding—and I got paid for it!

At the age of 21, when I graduated from university, teaching certificate in hand, I had successfully shifted my focus to receiving approval and winning accolades from the external world. As far as I knew, my years of formal schooling were complete and, by society's standards, I had a life worth living. For decades afterwards, I no longer knew I had a creative soul desperately craving expression. I had no idea I was capable of writing books or creating original art and photographic works dynamic enough to be exhibited, published and sold. My nascent self, like Sleeping Beauty, had fallen asleep.

Though I enjoyed university and was invited to continue my studies at the master's level, I had a younger brother coming up behind me. I didn't make a lot of money at my summer jobs and my father couldn't afford to support two children in university. I needed to earn a living and I had the skills, ability and desire to teach. By the time Queen's granted my teaching degree, I was already working. I had accepted a position teaching English and drama with a northern Ontario board of education when one of its teachers took a maternity leave. I accepted a permanent position with a southern Ontario board later that summer.

A complex weaving of dominant cultural influences, pragmatic family decisions and the whisper of personal choices directed my life path to teaching in the public school system. Clearly there was a broader patriarchal cultural ethos at work affecting my career choice. When I look back through my Queen's yearbooks for the early 1970s, I see the faces of women concentrated in the traditional professions of teaching and nursing. Both my grandmothers were teachers. I never met my paternal grandmother, Alberta Middleton Eastham, who died a couple of months after I was born. In her younger years, she taught school in rural Alberta. She rode a horse to get there and carried a derringer for safety, a gun that has since been donated to the Bow Valley Museum.

I had some natural ability as a teacher and my parents encouraged and supported this choice, feeling that it offered a good future: secure, personally fulfilling, financially safe and useful to society. They had no more idea than I did that I was capable of, and needed, greater creative expression. My own desires to please my parents, do well at university and earn my living combined to divert me from the path of pure creative expression to one that was "safer," more predictable and useful. Such is the story of an uninitiated collective leading the uninitiated.

Now I understand that much of the focus of academic work—studying and writing about the work of others, developing the technical skills to read, interpret and teach someone else's work—is a process that takes its impetus primarily from the external world. It can incorporate creativity, but differs from the innate creative endeavour that takes its impetus from, and honours, the self's eternal realm. To access this realm, one reaches deep inside, finds what's there, invites it forth and wrestles with it to find the form that gives it authentic expression. New and original work is the reward. For me it's the difference between teaching classic works of literature to students and writing this book. In my high school years I had begun the long process of shifting my focus from creating and expressing my internal world to working with the stuff of the external world. We call this process "growing up."

Professions in education, medicine and social work are often seen as desirable because they offer stable employment and a good salary, but they are called the "helping" professions for a reason. They demand the channeling of huge amounts of energy and time into assisting others. These days, psychologists caution that placing the needs of others ahead of our own is a sure route to losing ourselves. But that is the ethic I had been trained to, as were so many of us who grew up in the 1950s and 1960s.

As a teacher, I would be assisting future generations to achieve self-sufficiency and independence and to move forward in their chosen lives, as I already had. I would put my knowledge of writing to use, teaching my students and marking their work. My creativity would be directed into developing stimulating lessons for my classes. Unfortunately and unknown to me, while this approach poses as generativity and service, to the unrealized self it becomes a form of servitude.

I stayed with the same board for 32 years. In the early years, when it was new and challenging, I found great satisfaction in teaching. But after those first years, true happiness seemed increasingly elusive, and the servitude increasingly burdensome. As I became established in my career and was looking for new challenges, my dad encouraged me to become an English department head and to pursue administration, which I did. I carved out a good career for myself, which came with an excellent pay cheque. I travelled, had adventures, got married—and later divorced. I was living a respectable, provisional life.

The struggle to find, reclaim and keep one's authentic self is an archetypal journey that has been recorded in literature across the centuries. Two thousand years ago, Didymos Judas Thomas recorded Jesus as saying, "If you bring forth what is within you, what you have will save you. If you do not have that within you, what you do not have within you [will] kill you."[5] This text is from the Gnostic Gospel of Thomas, discovered just 50 years ago in the Egyptian desert. In William Shakespeare's Hamlet, Polonius counsels his son, Laertes, "To thine own self be true and it must follow, as the night the day, thou canst not then be false to any man."[6] Ironically, Polonius cannot follow his own advice, but that inability did not lessen the wisdom of his words. Contemporary biographies by highly successful people almost always record the struggles they faced to stay true to themselves: to find and keep true to their paths.

For a long time in my life, I didn't know if there was some path uniquely mine. I felt I wasn't using my talents and skills as I was meant to, that my life was out of balance. It took me a long time to work out the true problem: that I had masses of ideas, thoughts and feelings jumbled up inside me, crying out for expression in a healthy, positive, creative way. As Claudia Bepko and Jo-ann Krestan, family therapists and experts in gender issues and addiction, write in their book, *Singing at the Top of Our Lungs*, "It's clear that it's easy to get distracted and alienated from what moves us and that we don't often know how to reclaim our passions and shape our lives to suit us better."[7]

Without being aware of it, when I gave up working with my own forms of creative expression, I entered that dark night of the soul[8] which is the hallmark of the struggle to claim one's authentic vision and voice. I experienced chronic anxiety, guilt, resentment and bitterness. I developed a need for control and perfectionism that manifested as a critical negative voice, a constant need for accomplishment and external approval. I thought if I could just find the right job, lover, house—that perfect thing somewhere in the external world—I would be happier.

As many of us learn the hard way, when one's creative soul is thwarted or deprived of suitable means of expression, it will take any avenue it finds in life, causing disruption and dissatisfaction. This is the soul's attempt to make itself known and the struggle can only be ended by turning inward. Although not fully aware of it, I was being directed to do just that. To reclaim myself, to achieve satisfaction and find happiness, I had to find, explore and express the uncharted depths of my own creativity.

My experience suggests that knowledge of who we are can be trained out of us, just as knowing how to access and express our creativity can be. I was conditioned from earliest childhood to listen to and accept the authority of others in my life including my parents and teachers. The danger of listening exclusively to and following the instructions that come at us from the external world, as we are trained to do, is that we cease listening to and fully expressing our own ideas. If we do this long enough, it becomes a habit that impairs our ability to hear ourselves and express our ideas—the heart of our creativity.

Creativity is part of our essence so we can never truly lose it. Most of us retain a practical, down-to-earth level of creativity. It manifests itself every day whether we are conscious of it or not, as we decide what to do with the mundane information of our lives. We use it to improve our circumstances, and evaluate what we need to do to move forward. Creativity is there working in the background as we sort our thoughts and think about the people we are with, the directions we wish to pursue, the things we possess. We use it as we work out the schedule that allows us to drive our kids to practices, buy groceries and get to the dentist on time. At this level, it is mental and physical work that utilizes and develops problem-solving skills. This sorting, organizing and building process is creativity in action. We are all engaged in it most of the time. Creativity allows us to integrate into a coherent whole all the messages we send to and receive from the world.

But for many of us, this creativity yoked to function is not enough. When we lose touch with our core creative abilities, the ones that help us know, value and express what lies deep within, then the gifts and talents with which we are born are squandered. We search fruitlessly for a sense of purpose and direction in life. We lose the resources to conduct our lives as richly as we were intended to. We lose the depth and breadth of our experiences. We stagnate and feel trapped in the ruts of our existence. Quite literally, the colour goes out of our world.

So many of us find ourselves on different paths from the ones we dreamed of earlier in our lives—paths which somehow don't fully utilize our abilities, hold our interest or challenge us as we need to be challenged, irrespective of external rewards. The thoughts, feelings, emotions and dreams that make us unique are screened off from conscious awareness, and we stop pulling out from deep within that which is wholly and exclusively our own.

To stay true to ourselves, to maintain the power of our creativity, we need to commit and recommit to the things we know are true for ourselves as we make our way in our lives. Finding those missing pieces, claiming our truths and expressing them is something we can do for ourselves to live more fulfilling lives. If my experience is illustrative, the creative urge will keep knocking at the door, in the form of synchronicities and happy accidents, looking for expression until we welcome it. Even when we are not sure there is a place for them, we need to reach deeply within and pull our dreams and ideas to the surface, to work with them and mould them: offerings from our minds, hearts and souls to the world.

The health of our creativity affects what we bring to such basic tasks as building a home for ourselves and our families. When there's a disconnect, everything feels like a chore and we long for relief from the tediousness of existence. We experience an erosion of the quality of our lives. This feeling of disconnect is so universal as to be part of human experience. It is woven through the fabric of society. News broadcasts and talk shows are full of people disconnected from themselves, committing all kinds of physically and morally destructive acts.

Too often, in our market-driven economy, creative ideas are valued primarily as commodity for generating growth and prosperity, paving the way for new inventions, or "innovations" as they are frequently called, whether product or process. There is no doubt this kind of applied creativity allows us to revolutionize existing industries and create new ones. Yet as Richard Florida suggests in his book, *The Rise of The Creative Class*, we live in a world flooded by more information than we can process, or keep track of, and with not enough time or understanding to work out what to do with much of it. This abundance of data may be the backbone of the information economy we live in, he says, but it's our capacity to sift through the data and create something useable or new from it that is truly valuable.[9]

Valuing creativity only as something that drives the economic engine exacts a price from our souls, nature, and the planet. Being disconnected from the full power of our individual creativity leaves us less able collectively to marshal human resources, to solve economic and environmental problems—global warming, world poverty, hunger and war. The effect of the loss to society can be seen in the abundance of corporate scandals and the often less-than-effective response to devastation from natural and man-made disasters, whether fire, earthquake, hurricane or oil spill.

Awful events can sometimes bring out the best in individuals, even make heroes of us. But, too often the right kind of aid doesn't arrive where or when it is needed, increasing the suffering of those already in distress. Viewing this impotence, we experience an ennui that leaves us feeling depressed and overwhelmed. We doubt that we, as individuals, can exert impact on the world around us. But creativity is the gift that allows us to imagine and realize the "impossible," like sending spaceships to the moon, or Mars, and bringing them safely home again. Like getting the right kind of aid to those who need it in a timely and efficient manner.

Creativity is a deeply personal gift. Most of us have experienced those amazing flashes of creative energy whereby brilliant ideas spring to mind wholly formed, seemingly unrelated to anything we've experienced previously. This is grace. At this level, creativity together with our dreams and intuition is the passionate fire of our humanity, meant to guide our individual journey through life and help us find our original meaning and purpose. It's an esthetic for pleasure as much as for problem-solving and profit. Imagine if we tapped into that aspect of it. What then? What might the implications be for personal happiness?

I believe we are all born with the dreams and interests that match our creative abilities, ones that point the way to the paths we are capable of following when we live authentically, honoring and expressing the best in ourselves. The world needs what each of us has to offer from our authentic creative selves. We don't need to wait for happy accidents to begin recovering our creative voices. We need the courage to listen to ourselves, especially if what we hear runs counter to the advice given by those around us. When we exchange adapted servitude for service to our souls, we fan the creative spark that ignites the communal fire.

Exercise #1 Your Personal Creative History

a) Create a document on your computer or purchase and dedicate a notebook to use as a journal. In this journal, you will keep track of your own creative journey. Date your first entry.

b) In your journal list activities you enjoyed as a child. Do you still enjoy any of these activities?

c) When you were a child, was your creative life encouraged or not? Do you have specific memories of creative experiences and/or enjoyable activities? Describe them. What is it about them that you remember most vividly?

d) Were there any people who were instrumental in your own early creative development? Who were they and what did they offer you?

Exercise #2 Tilling the Soil: The High School Years

a) Did you enjoy high school? Were you able to take the subjects you enjoyed? What were your favorite subjects? Which ones did you do best in?

b) Were there subjects you disliked but had to take? If so, what were they. What was the reason you took them?

c) Was there a place for personal creative expression in your academic life in those years? How about in your personal life?

d) Looking back, can you trace the effect of these years on your personal creative development?

Exercise #3 Spirit of the Land

a) Were you exposed to any kind of religious or spiritual teachings in childhood? Did they accord with your own internal beliefs or was there a conflict? Has that background influenced your current beliefs, if any?

b) Is a spiritual connection important to you? If so, how do you foster it?

c) Do you see any connection between your spiritual beliefs and creativity?

Exercise #4 Rain-making: the Post-High School Years

a) What path did you pursue when you finished high school? Are/were you happy with this choice? Why or why not?

b) Do you feel you are on the right path in your life at the moment? If not where would you like to be?

c) Can you see any influences that might have been at work to direct your current path? (family, friends, finances etc.)

d) Do you currently make creative expression a priority in your life? Why or why not?

TWO

Eleven Creative Truths

Our society is rife with misconceptions about creativity, and we are influenced by them whether we wish to be or not; they are in the air we breathe. These include the limiting ideas that creativity means artistic ability, that it is linked to personal suffering, and that it is only as useful as the market value it produces. A lot of people say they are not creative because they aren't blessed with the ability to draw or paint, play the flute or write stories. Artistic, musical and writing abilities are all specialized branches on the tree of creativity, but creativity is the forest. The word "creativity" literally means to bring forth that which is new, to produce through imaginative skill.[1] Creativity can be exercised in any field of endeavour.

We are all familiar with stories about great artists who suffered profound distress in their lives. Vincent Van Gogh cut off part of his ear. Jackson Pollock was an alcoholic. Virginia Woolf, Anne Sexton and Sylvia Plath, all twentieth century writers, committed suicide as did fashion designer Alexander McQueen, singer-songwriter Kurt Cobain, and indirectly, Amy Winehouse. Countless others across the centuries have died in poverty and obscurity. These are historical facts. However, as medical research sheds light on the afflictions some of these artists suffered, we learn it was not their talents or chosen professions per se that caused their suffering. It is believed Van Gogh suffered a mental illness. Alcoholism is a disease. The misconception about creativity being the cause of torment does not necessarily hold true, but fallibility does not stop it from being pervasive in our culture.

Such examples are used to support the idea that it's only if a person's blessed with considerable talent that it is possible to enjoy success pursuing a creative path in life—that this kind of talent is something one is born with and cannot be otherwise generated or cultivated. Furthermore, we often believe that only a limited few are born with innate talent and they do not need any assistance from the rest of us. Their rise to the top will be natural and automatic. The force of their talent will somehow overcome all obstacles and suffering to leave a legacy for the rest of us, who are unable to do anything but dream about such accomplishments.

These days, studies of those who achieve creative success are revealing a different picture. Both Geoff Colvin, senior editor-at-large at *Fortune* magazine, and author Malcolm Gladwell provide evidence that factors such as early exposure, excellent instruction, perseverance and deliberate practice contribute to achievement.[2] Gladwell writes in his book, *The Outliers*, "The idea that excellence at performing a complex task requires a critical minimum level of practice surfaces again and again in studies of expertise."[3]

Another reason many of us hesitate to be creative is that we fear having to meet some elusive standard of perfection predetermined by our competitive market economy and the culture at large. In this view, the goal is commercial success, which happens when we create and sell a product with a value that can be measured in dollars and cents. Such a view does not allow us to determine our own measures of success or to choose what is worthwhile for ourselves.

Check the following statements. If you've thought or given voice to any of them, chances are you've been influenced by these misconceptions.

- I'm not creative. I can't write, paint, compose, build, sing, dance... because I'm too old, it's too late, I don't have the talent, energy, ideas.

- I wasn't born with the creativity gene and I don't have an original thought in my head.

- You're either born with it or you're not. If you're born with it, you will be successful, no matter what.

- What you see is what you get. There are no second chances in life; suck it up.

- I'd love to be more creative but I don't have enough time to get everything done as it is… I never have the time and solitude necessary to create anything worthwhile. There are always more pressing tasks requiring my attention.

- I wouldn't know where to start.

- I don't have the money and equipment I need to be successful.

- I'd do it but I'd have to give up my day job.

- What if I failed? My husband, lover, family… would disown me and I'd end up alone and lonely.

- I'm too stressed to create anything.

- No one would want what I create anyway; there's no market for that kind of work. It's already been tried.

These misconceptions are damaging for all of us because they foster doubt about the value of pursuing creative ventures. That places us in the double bind of wanting more from life, yet not knowing how to create it from within ourselves, and being afraid to even if we know how. I am no exception. Through the decades of my twenties, thirties and forties, I was a consummate consumer, engaged in the distraction of endless "retail therapy," scoring energy from every bargain I purchased. I enjoyed shopping and my "habit" was encouraged by the consumer culture. I took pride in helping to fuel the economy and I made enough money to do so.

I was buying colour and texture with every household item and article of clothing I purchased, not realizing I was literally trying to put back into my life the colour and texture I had lost when I stopped working creatively somewhere back in my high school years. No one pointed out to me that I could use my money in ways that might make me happier. Instead of renting an apartment, I could have bought a home and paid down the mortgage, yet such thoughts never occurred to me. I might have gone on like this forever, except fate had other plans.

When I was 42 years old, I re-discovered my creative dreams and abilities quite by accident. That year, feeling a need for a break from an endless routine, three women friends and I, all twenty years or more into our careers and looking for adventure, took a leave of absence from our jobs and travelled around the world together. As I was packing to leave, I came across a point-and-shoot camera my ex-husband had left behind after we separated. Though I hadn't owned a camera or taken photos in more than 25 years, I tossed it into my luggage, thinking I would take some photos to remember our travels.

I mailed each completed roll of film home from around the world, so didn't see the results for several months. When I finally did, I was surprised to discover the pictures were quite good: clear, well composed, with good use of light. It was a life-changing realization for me. Until that point, I'd never had an interest in photography. Suddenly, I found myself wondering if this was something for which I had talent, yet I doubted the possibility. I still had a few months left of my leave of absence, and at this point, I got quite lucky. My partner at the time, Greg, got hold of a beautiful Nikon AF (film) camera. (Interesting how cameras kept showing up in my life!) With the camera and his encouragement, I discovered the world of close-up photography by focusing—literally—on flowers.

There are lots of gardeners in my family and I have always loved flowers. For me, gardening—planting and shaping a riot of colour, rooting around in the earth and coaxing things to grow—is a creative activity. My paternal grandfather, John W. Eastham, was the plant pathologist for the province of British Columbia. My dad was a gardener and used to tell the story of how I could name all the flowers in his garden by the time I was three years old. Though I later forgot their names, I still love to have flowers around me. When I got my first apartment, I filled it with potted plants and put bouquets on my dining room table. Now, with the aid of the camera, I could give myself a hit of colour, capture the beauty and pattern of fragile petals and freeze a moment in time. My photos turned flowers into permanent visual reminders that beauty is everywhere in the world. More important, they showed me what I was capable of creating… that I could create something new, beautiful and original by observing what was in front of me, using the rudimentary photography skills I possessed, exercising my imagination, and becoming engaged in the process. And it was fun.

This was a watershed moment in my life. Intuitively, I understood my creativity held the key to a richer, happier life. I knew I needed to reclaim it by exploring my abilities and I felt the need for some support to do so. The local camera store came to my rescue. One day when I took a roll of film in to be developed, I discovered the store was selling tickets for an evening with Freeman Patterson who would be giving a presentation and speaking about his books. I'd never heard of him, but the clerk said he was one of Canada's great photographers and tickets would sell out fast. I bought one and attended the presentation.

That evening was a revelation. I experienced first-hand the power of exceptional photographs. I bought his books and dreamed of taking my own beautiful photographs. I found a camera club and joined. Other members encouraged me to frame and show my photos and I did so hesitantly, assailed by nerves at every step of the process. My internal critic was pressed into overdrive by all this new activity, and pretty soon I came up against my own perfectionism. I found myself constantly comparing my work to those around me. I had to adopt that Nike motto, "Just do it," like a mantra each time a doubt surfaced in my mind. It's a strategy I still use and recommend.

I have come to know my internal critic well over the years. In those days, he would shout such things as, "You don't even own your own camera! You know nothing about the basics of shutter speed and focal length. Who are you kidding?" or "Your photos are only colour print, not the professional slide photos of real photographers. No one's going to be interested in your conventional photos. That's already been done. If you want to get noticed you have to be cutting-edge, take serious, gritty photos of war and poverty." My internal critic was ruthless. Despite my strong interest and early success, it caused me to have doubts about the whole venture.

At this point, my leave of absence was almost done and I was set to return to my demanding, full-time career. I was an English teacher set to assume my first hard-earned administrative position as vice-principal of a secondary school. I had more than enough to keep me busy and I had neither the skills nor the training to be a professional photographer. I didn't want to do it if I couldn't be "perfect." I still had a lot to learn about the importance of process and of being willing to take risks.

Support can come from surprising places. As I wondered how I would find the time to pursue photography and worried about who would be interested in my pictures, my mom told me she loved my photos. I had placed a couple on some cards for her and she asked for more. She thought her friends would love them. She can be pretty finicky about what she likes, so her support meant a lot to me. My mom became a staunch supporter, telling me I should sell my cards; that they were nicer than the ones she'd seen in stores. So I mounted photos on cards and began giving them away as presents. Reaction from others was positive, and I made the commitment to buy a good second-hand camera of my own, one that would allow me to experiment with different types of lenses.

Then one day, I was offered an opportunity to sell my cards locally. Though I had no retail experience and did not believe anyone would pay for my work, some of it sold. That boosted my confidence. That part of myself influenced by the misconception that something is only valuable if people are willing to pay for it found what it had been looking for: approval and confirmation from the wider world. I feel profoundly grateful to those unmet friends who bought my early photos. Though some of my photos were quite good, I also see that some of them were not, at least to me. Maybe the adage is true: beauty is indeed in the eye of the beholder.

I returned to work, but continued to shoot photos in spare minutes, sometimes on the balcony of my apartment, sometimes in other people's gardens, usually on weekends. This made me happier and softened the blow of Monday and the work-week. I was still dealing with the same job issues, but I was no longer the same person. I had something energizing that was all mine: the beauty of the world I saw through the lens of my camera. I was able to capture this beauty, to preserve it in photos as a reminder for myself and others. Seeing that beauty altered my perception of the world around me, taught me to appreciate the richness of the world in which I live, to see and feel more than the daily grind. I was beginning to have some balance in my life, but my secret doubts were profound. Even though my internal critic was having a field day, I decided to trust that photography was an interest I should pursue.

As I look back on the photos I've taken over the past dozen years, I see a body of work that I feel good about. I can see that my skills have developed and I've made progress. Following my interest proved worthwhile. When I set out I had little idea what I was doing or where I was going. It will perhaps come as no surprise that I suddenly lost interest in shopping: I no longer had the time for it and I began to set other priorities for my hard-earned money.

I learned that whatever my creative interest, the process of a creative endeavour can work the same way. When I exercised a talent or followed an interest, it grew with me, as did the power and scope of my imagination. I needed enough faith, even a blind faith, in my own interests and abilities to make a start. I would now say, "take this leap of faith and see where the creative process leads." When I do that, the world is likely to meet me at least halfway. Yes, there are thousands of photographers out there who are better than I am. And my internal critic still wonders how I can possibly "compete." That competitive-market ethos is deeply ingrained in my psyche as it is in our wider western culture. The rise in popularity of reality TV shows pitting individuals and teams against each other for prizes is yet one more incarnation of this ethos.

I have to consistently remind myself that I can carve out my own niche in the world. There is a place for my particular creative sensibilities and my work in the universe is required, though I may not know why. This is enough to encourage me to exercise my creativity. I didn't set out with a plan to accomplish anything with my photography, yet a plan had either been there for me or evolved as I took the steps in pursuit of my interest. Both the process and the results give me pleasure.

There's been a digital revolution since I began taking photographs. The saturation point where digital cameras outsold single lens reflex (SLR's) happened fairly quickly. When I took a week-long photography class with Freeman Patterson and Andre Gallant in New Brunswick in 2004, we were instructed to bring and use slide film. Without exception, everyone in the class used SLR (film) cameras and shot slides. In the summer of 2006, students who took the course arrived with computers and digital cameras: photography had gone digital, and I needed to learn a new set of photographic skills to participate in the global conversation.

By the time this happened, I'd already had several one-woman shows, and my work had appeared in newspapers and magazines. When I thought about the money, time, energy and work I would have to invest to learn this new medium, I found myself thrown back once again to that place of doubt and discouragement where I felt too old to learn a new way of doing things. I wondered if I should just let the technological revolution pass me by. My internal critic was dancing on hot coals shouting with glee, "Here we go again; this girl never learns." The advantage I had at that point was that I had some consciousness of my internal critic. Even though its message sounded negative, I knew it was directing my attention past inertia and fear—prompting me to move forward and learn new stuff. I began my transition by purchasing a relatively inexpensive point-and-shoot digital camera and reading the manual accompanying it. Then, as before, I took the camera and went shooting. I also enrolled in a night school class in Photoshop.

The world does not stay in one place forever and creative fields are not fallow: they grow. Through evolution, we are challenged to adapt and keep growing. Companies like Kodak have faced this struggle. Photographers like Freeman Patterson and Andre Gallant have changed how they produce their work. I will also. I know my internal critic is missing the mark when he tells me, "You never learn." I am a learner, even though learning doesn't seem to get any easier. I have learned to move consciously through my fears by reminding myself of my achievements. I wrestle my way through the process of new learning, taking one step and overcoming one doubt at a time. Having taken the risk once, twice, three times and survived, I have the confidence to do it again, and again and again.

History shows us that we evolve, that consciousness evolves. It is time for our notions about creativity to evolve as well. There are creative truths waiting for us. Our task is to listen with ears, eyes, mind, heart and soul wide open. Our creative truths look like this:

- Creativity is innate. We are all born with this gift and we exercise creativity all the time, every day of our lives.

- No two minds are alike. We all have thoughts original to us.

- Accessing, nurturing and expressing our creativity—finding our creative voice and developing habits that support it— keep us healthy and give meaning to our lives.

- Creativity doesn't happen in a vacuum. It utilizes the stuff of life… all our experiences.

- Creativity is multi-faceted and multi-dimensional.

- Progress can be made in several directions at once, and they may seem divergent or unrelated at first. Eventually, they converge.

- Creativity can happen in small steps in short snippets of time, so you can keep your day job. Money is not always the answer or the obstacle.

- Family, relationships, marriage and children will allow time for your creative urges. Make time to follow them.

- Creativity is not necessarily linear, bound by time, isolation or failure. What we call "failure" is a natural part of the process and there are second chances.

- It isn't necessary to feel creative before setting out to do creative work. You can often start the creative juices flowing just by getting to work.

- If you create it, there's a need for it somewhere.

Embracing these truths and nurturing our creativity is what allows us to give full expression to the creativity harboured within our souls. Once we embrace these truths, there are specific steps we must take to nurture our nascent creativity.

Exercise #1 Personal Mythology

a) Do any of the creative "myths' resonate for you? Which, if any, have influenced you and how?

b) Can you think of others not listed here that have had an effect on you? What might they be and how have they influenced you?

Exercise #2 Weeds or flowers?

a) Do you have any habits or patterns of behaviour that work against being more creative?

b) Do you have any habits that might be the creative urge working in disguise?

Exercise #3 Internal Voices and External Support

a) Do you recognize the voice of your internal critic? What words does it say and what effect do they have on your self-confidence?

b) Are there people in your life you would trust to support your dreams and creative work? Who are they?

THREE

Priming the Creative Pump

To begin our creative journey, we identify our area(s) of interest and then we take one step at a time. The first step sets in motion creative energy to fuel our journey. We require self-discipline to avoid excuses and the temptation to procrastinate. But there is no substitute for taking that first step. As Thomas Edison, once said, "Opportunity is missed by most people because it is dressed in overalls and looks like work."[1] He should know. He tried out thousands of filaments before discovering the one that lit up the world.

Once we get to work, we must trust our process. We need to learn to respond to what presents itself and to work with it instead of trying to control the outcome every step of the way. We can teach ourselves what we need to know, and the process we need to follow will reveal itself as we explore our path. Creativity benefits from spontaneity as well as planning. We must learn to trust that solutions to creative challenges will emerge if we persist.

We must also learn to recognize and trust intuition. Intuitive messages, however softly they whisper, are powerful and can guide the creative journey. An intuitive message can be as simple and straight-forward as the one I experienced to toss that point-and-shoot camera into my luggage. By doing so, I found something of value unexpectedly and my photographic journey followed from that one action. However, intuitive guidance is not always linear or fathomable. Sometimes, we have to follow the impulse to take a particular step, then wait for intuitive guidance for the next.

Even when we have lots of experience with the creative process, we can still get bogged down. It helps to know that even in these fallow times chances are that creativity is gestating though you may not have recognized it yet. You can nurture these seeds to sprout and harvest by asking and tracking the answers to two critical questions: "Who am I?" and "What are my dreams for myself and my life?"

Here's a key to beginning: if we wait for a good idea to appear before we start, we may wait forever. Sometimes, beginning comes first; ideas and concepts follow. It may seem counterintuitive, and it may feel like working backwards—setting out with no clear idea of what to accomplish or how to go about doing it. It's a weird aspect of the creative process that picking up a paintbrush and mucking around with paints, makes ideas begin to flow. Or sitting at a keyboard and typing something—anything at all—pops up a thought to work with. Ideas begin to percolate. There seems to be creative synergy, reciprocity between engaging the work and inspiration for the project. We know more about how to be creative than we think. Actively applying creativity in life means becoming more conscious and intentional about process.

Despite research into brain activity and creativity in recent years, the creative process still retains mystery. According to Richard Florida, "...creative thinking is a four-step process: preparation, incubation, illumination and testing or revision." Preparation is "consciously studying a task and thinking about it, perhaps using logic"; incubation is the "mystical step where consciousness and the subconscious mull over the problem" in ways we are not aware; illumination is a "new synthesis", when the mind suddenly presents a key to understanding the problem...the famous "Eureka" moment Archimedes experienced as he sat in his bath. The fourth step includes "all the work that comes after," as we work with, check out and revise what we have learned or discovered.[2]

When I first took my camera to go shooting, I did not think in such formalized terms. But looking back, I can see I cycled through each of these steps repeatedly. The first few times I took my borrowed camera into a garden to shoot a roll of film I was shaking with nerves. I feared the camera wouldn't work. I worried I wouldn't be able to get the film into the camera. There wouldn't be anything to shoot. If I got into trouble, there would be nobody to rescue me. I didn't know how to take reasonable pictures. I was afraid the whole thing would be a waste of time and film. It was strange to me that going into a garden could be so scary! Muriel, my Jungian friend, comments: "Maybe you were feeling excitement that your creative energy was finally waking up. I wonder if we sometimes misinterpret anxiety and miss our capacity to experience excitement. In the body, they can feel the same."

As part of my preparation, I learned to talk myself consciously and logically through the task at hand. I reminded myself that I had nothing to lose except the cost of a roll of film. (Those were pre-digital days!) Even if my worst fears came true, I would still be ahead. I would have spent time in a garden, which I enjoy doing with or without a camera, and I would have gained experience looking through the viewfinder, learning to compose and frame photos. My time would not have been wasted.

As it turned out, once I got into the garden and began working with my camera, my anxiety faded, as I immersed myself in the images I saw through the viewfinder. The images filled my awareness and nothing else mattered. There wasn't time, or need, or brain space for any other thought. Through this experience I began to understand what it means to "live in the moment." And often, as I immersed myself, I experienced that "Eureka" moment when a flower leapt into brilliant focus through the lens of my camera. When that happened, I knew intuitively the photograph would be good—that the image I saw through the viewfinder when I clicked the shutter would match the image in the photograph once it was developed—a kind of magic had happened.

Even at the time of those early shoots, I was hard at work, learning to "see" as a photographer, creating new habits of thought and routine for myself. Each time I reviewed those early rolls of film I found two or three photographs I felt were good enough to keep. Studying the photos helped me learn what I liked and to see what was good technically. This is a natural "do it-review it" process and it kept me growing once I gave myself permission to work with it.

It is not necessary to be perfect. I remember delivering one of my early rolls of film to the camera store for developing and having a discussion with the owner about how many good photos a professional photographer might get on a roll. He surprised me by telling me that most photographers are happy if they get three or four good pictures per roll of 24 photos. Perfectionist that I am, I'd been thinking the goal was to shoot a perfect 24! But I was happy to revise my expectations, free myself from pressure and "shoot" for a more achievable goal.

The territory we enter as we become more creative may be new and uncharted, and that can stir up anxiety, fear and resistance. We need to remember: the greater the fear, the greater, and more important, the mystery. When we have performance anxiety, the soul knows there's a gift to be found. Hence the advice often given by psychologists to move into fear rather than avoid it. As it turned out, there were amazing blooms for me in gardens of my delight. One was the beautiful flowers and time to appreciate them, to be reminded how much beauty there is in the world. Another was capturing the images and freezing them for a moment of time, recording evidence of my experience in the tangible form of beautiful photographs.

One of my fears as I was beginning my creative journey was that there would come a day when I would run out of ideas. I was afraid of the question: "Now what?" I have learned that what comes next in the creative process is often contained in the work that is already completed. As I looked back at those early photos, I saw compositions that were blurry but showed promise, so I learned about the importance of depth of field. Some of my photos had beautiful lighting but had been taken from the wrong angle. I learned to watch where I stood relative to my subject. Others had telephone poles and wires mucking up otherwise gorgeous views. This taught me to check all aspects of an image and its background before I clicked the shutter. Each bit of knowledge I picked up by studying my photos helped me pinpoint what kind of photos I liked to take, where I could go next to take good ones and how to improve the quality. My internal critic had found his calling in the service of my creative self and was now gainfully employed. His voice seemed to soften and become a helpful discerning function.

I discovered I could teach myself a lot of what I needed to learn about my own creative process. We inherently know what pleases us and we know good results when we experience them. These criteria are sufficient to guide us for much of our journey. Each of us has the ability to assess our own work, though many of us have been discouraged from trusting our own judgment. As we get into the habit of trusting our judgment, we nurture our natural abilities and our confidence grows.

"Do something everyday which scares you," wrote Eleanor Roosevelt, U.S diplomat and reformer.[3] One of the scariest things I ever signed on for was a week-long class in New Brunswick with master photographers Freeman Patterson and Andre Gallant. I was pretty sure I wasn't good enough to take that class, but when a friend suggested doing so, I took the chance. There were some challenging moments. The class took place in rural New Brunswick during black fly season in May. I hate being bitten by anything and I suffer an allergic reaction to black flies that makes their bites a misery, so there were a lot of moments when I had to have that "just do it" talk with myself.

As it turned out, despite my anxiety, I didn't get bitten once that week. We were shooting outdoors in natural light, so weather-wise, I had to learn to work irrespective of conditions. There were days when I got down on my belly in the mud to shoot ferns sprouting in a spring rain. Through trial and error, time and experience, I learned that I prefer shooting on slightly overcast days, away from direct sun, as colors came through more vibrantly when exposed under those conditions.

The final project for that class was to create a show of 24 images from the week and present them to the class on the last day. There were some challenges. Freeman and Andre assigned each of us a topic based on our interests and our weaknesses. My topic was "Delicacy." We were given our topics about 12 hours ahead of time, so we had to work fast. Though I looked forward to seeing the work of the other students, I'd never created this kind of presentation before and I was nervous. It took me hours to sort through hundreds of images, many of which didn't seem very interesting. I found I had to trust that something worthwhile would emerge and it did. I now have a beautiful photo book made from the photos I used in that project.

Challenging myself to keep growing, and making a point of going into my creative fears daily, has given me additional unexpected gifts. I feel good about the body of my photographic work and good about myself for meeting the challenges. I have developed confidence in myself, my abilities and my process. I have learned that creativity benefits from spontaneity—that, in fact, it's difficult, and even undesirable to control and predict everything as I am working. Needless to say, that recognition has challenged me to acknowledge and deal with my tendency to be a control freak in other areas of my life.

Somehow, somewhere along the way, to keep chaos at bay and my life safely ordered, I became an expert at control. Being out of touch with an essential part of myself—my creativity and my emotions, I wasn't particularly aware I was living in control mode. As children, we are given the message that we need to "control ourselves." This message permeates our psyches. We learn that we have to control both physical and metaphysical processes, from our bowels to our appetites, from our tempers to our creativity and our desires.

I remember being a fairly emotional child and that often got me into trouble. I had explosive outbursts of temper and was punished for them. I remember being brought to tears too often to count in response to criticism. By my early teen years, I was so tired of crying that I kept a tight rein on my emotions. This ability proved useful in the classroom and the boardroom. However, always controlling things took time and energy, leaving me drained and exhausted. A need for control can also negatively impact creativity in that it means we don't trust or feel safe to respond. We need to be able to respond to those creative urges and work with them when they show up in life. Responding to what presents itself is a different way of being in the world. It takes less energy, but requires trust and faith that I will be able to handle whatever happens.

Whatever a person's issues, they will surface in the creative journey. Issues of control and emotional expression surfaced in mine. Emotion and our access to it are essential to the creative process. One way or another, what emerges from the creative process is a reflection of the creator and his or her feelings. Part of my journey as an artist has been to make space for my emotions and relate to them in a positive way.[4]

Writing this book has been instrumental in opening my heart and teaching me about the power of creative work. I am happier and more grounded for articulating and subsequently owning it. Not surprisingly, I experienced an emotional roller coaster writing this book. Every time I began a new chapter, I alternated between hope and fear about whether I was up to the challenge. I rode this roller coaster even during the revision stage, after I already had a draft of the book completed. I have had to get used to rolling between optimism, despair and every nuance of emotion in between. I have learned not to let any mood become an excuse for avoiding my creative work. I have stayed with the process, through the dry periods when the challenges seemed greater than my skill, determined to move forward. I have had to remind myself over and over again to trust that I would find my way once I sat down at my computer and began to type. Eventually, even the most difficult chapters got written.

Living creatively means identifying what is important to us, bringing that into our lives and allowing ourselves to dream about what else might be possible. There is a channel for creativity and it takes effort to keep it from getting clogged with the debris of everyday life. When we put forward the effort, we are usually rewarded. When we take the first step and the ones that follow, the accumulation of steps leads us to develop our skills, abilities and a body of work we can respect. A kind of magic happens when we trust in our process and follow it to the completion of a project. We are transformed by it, just as it is transformed by us.

Exercise #1 Gathering the tools

a) Think about your current hobbies and pastimes. Is there already something creative in your life that you enjoy? Are there projects you've begun and not had time to finish? Do they still hold your interest? Be honest. Record them all!

b) Do you have a new idea you'd like to explore, something that beckons you? Have you heard others speak about something that piques your creative interest?

c) Do you have a stash of materials somewhere... articles, books, magazines, knitting needles, unusedfabric, tubes of watercolour, equipment you've purchased, meaning to use one day? Unearth your stash of materials and review it. What does this stash tell you about your interests?

d) Do these materials still appeal to you? Are you prepared to work with them, even if the thought of doing so is a little scary? Or is it time to make room for something new?

e) Write out your thoughts as honestly as you can.

Exercise #2 Plant the Seeds: Begin Your Creative Work.

a) This week, begin working on the creative project of your choice. It could be something you've already started, something you have identified in one of the exercises above. Or it could be something new. What is one step you could take this week to welcome this creative project into your life? For example, if you like to work with fabric, you might decide to use some scraps to make a doll. It doesn't have to be a big project or take a lot of time. You just want to make a start—to begin engaging with ideas and materials.

b) Look at your calendar. If your schedule is pretty full, slot the idea in wherever you can carve out space, even if it's just ten minutes and all you do is look at some books or materials. The idea here is to begin the habit of making time for yourself and your creative work on a regular basis. Living creatively means identifying what is important and making a place for it in our lives. Get in the habit of making a creativity date with yourself at least once a week.

Exercise #3 Weeding the Garden: Self-reflection

a) Are you a perfectionist, a procrastinator or a control freak? Do you have other issues that interfere with your creative work?

b) Are there things that scare you about your creative work or projects? What are they? Write about them in your journal.

c) What is your payoff for giving into your fear(s)? What would be your reward(s) if you overcame them?

Exercise #4 Watering the Garden: Generate Some Creative Energy

a) Identify something you could do for yourself this week to welcome fun and spontaneity into your life. Create some positive energy as you begin your journey. Give your ideas room to flow. If what you are doing is not destructive to yourself or others, give yourself permission to follow your heart.

FOUR

Inspiration and Vision

Where do creative ideas and inspiration come from? What is creative vision? How does one begin that great novel, that famous painting? Inspiration happens when the mind becomes interested in something, perhaps an activity or idea. Inspiration can also be a product of creative thinking or a sudden intuition as part of solving a problem.[1] It's that burst of energy or pulse of an idea that zings through the mind, capturing and engaging attention in a positive way. It can be as simple as suddenly knowing what movie to see, or what to have for dinner. Or we have an idea for a creative project we'd like to try. Inspiration opens up new possibilities. Thinking about a situation we'd like to change, we wonder aloud, "What if…" and allow ourselves to daydream. Suddenly our perspective shifts and we see a problem in a new way.

There are strategies to encourage inspiration. One is to develop the habit of "idea capture" and use it to build an inventory of ideas and inspirations to draw on for creative work. I keep a notebook beside my bed, another one in my purse and a document on the desktop of my laptop and use them to jot down ideas as they flit through my mind. A number of these jots have worked their way into this manuscript. Sometimes my jots take the form of small drawings that I will experiment with later in my art studio.

These days there are lots of portable devices that can be used to record ideas (tablets, digital phones with photographic capabilities, video recorders etc.) so we are not limited to paper. We need to use what we are comfortable with so the focus stays on capturing the moment of inspiration, not fussing with the method of doing so and possibly losing the moment itself. Often these "jots" contain wisdom, which would otherwise be lost. By doing this activity on a regular basis we learn what kinds of things appeal to us, capture our attention and inspire us. These things can form the basis of vision.

Vision is the bigger picture. When it comes to individual creative projects, vision is the idea, the concept or intention that can give form to inspiration. Though we may find the notion of artistic vision a bit scary and overwhelming, we do not need a brilliant level of inspiration or vision to undertake our creative work. Whatever we already have in our minds will provide sufficient inspiration, and brilliance may emerge from our efforts.

When I get angry about the clear-cutting of arboreal forests, or the over-fishing of the oceans, I realize I could take photos or make a documentary film exposing the issue. That is vision. When I watch the Olympics and am inspired by an athlete's struggle to overcome the odds, I realize I could write that athlete's story. That is vision. When I understand that the medium of dance can be used to portray joy, that is vision.

Vision is how we see the world today and how we wish things could be tomorrow. It includes that which antagonizes and outrages us as much as what pleases; it can take the form of anguished protest or rhapsodic love song. It is both cipher and filter for conscious and unconscious thought. Intellect, mind, body and spirit have an amazing capacity to absorb things from our daily lives and the external world, integrate them into our lived experience and generate a response to our perceptions. Even the simplest vision involves a complex interweaving of talents and abilities along with the dreams, thoughts, beliefs, skills and experiences we acquire through daily living.

Vision is dynamic. It shifts and grows over time as we are inspired by new things and re-inspired by familiar ones. As we get a sense of our vision, and claim it, we can take steps to express and shape it creatively, one step at a time, one routine at a time. When our work is guided by that internal vision unique to each of us, it is authentic. There will be a resonance between our thoughts and ideas (our inspiration), what we express (our vision) and the form that expression takes—our creative work.

Some gifted individuals throughout history seem to have arrived on Earth inspired with a vision of what their life's work is and how to complete it. Their time is spent realizing these gifts, shaping their vision and inspiring the rest of us. Tom Thomson and the Group of Seven showed us the beauty of the Canadian landscape and new ways to see and portray it, influencing generations of artists[2].

It is easy to laud such inspirational artists and wish we could be like them. But it's also comforting to know that their vision is part of our heritage: their ideas are embedded in our Canadian culture. We absorb, are influenced by and have access to them both consciously and unconsciously. This means we are never working in an idea vacuum and we never have to invent completely from scratch. And lots of us will spend our creative time wrestling with ideas in the culture, trying to free ourselves from boundaries established in the past.

I think we are lucky in Canada because there is an openness to cultural influences and forms from around the world that means creatively we can turn our hands to whatever inspires us. There is a never-ending stream of influences in the culture, a never-ending source of inspiration. We are permeable to the culture, as it is to us. The Canadian landscape is in my soul and at some level, my work may well be influenced by the Group of Seven, perhaps in my preference for strong colour and unusual colour combinations. The English poet, William Blake, with his vision of heaven and hell[3] leads me to try my hand at poetry. The American, Frank Lloyd Wright, who inspired a more organic style of architecture for buildings in the Western world,[4] and the towering office structures soaring above my head in downtown Toronto prompt me to take photographs of interesting architectural structures. When I move from photographing the landscape to painting what I imagine, my vision shifts and my work becomes more abstract, charting my inner terrain.

Sometimes we are lucky and inspiration arrives complete with the vision to shape it, giving us a sense of what medium to use and what steps to take. This has happened for me, even at the beginning of my creative career. In the year of my travels when I explored photography for the first time, I also discovered the beauty of illuminated letters in the medieval manuscripts I saw in various museums. I wanted to try and create them myself so when I returned home, I signed up for a lettering workshop and bought a book showing how to construct such letters. I spent many happy hours working on my own with simple tools like markers, coloured pencils and paper trying to produce these letters.

I didn't know it at the time, but my quest to make perfect illuminated letters, though later abandoned, set me on the path to extending my artistic expression. That interest in illuminated letters led me to join a calligraphy guild. I took lettering workshops that were instrumental in teaching me the fundamentals of drawing, as all letters are made from combinations of straight and curved lines. Making letters trained my hands and eyes to make intricate shapes and laid the base for some of the sweeping curves that are now part of my "artistic handprint."

Calligraphy is a very disciplined art and I realized a few years in that I didn't really have the temperament for it. Though I love the look of beautifully lettered pieces, I longed for more abstract shapes and sweeping gestures. Here again I was lucky. Beautiful lettering is often accentuated by interesting painted backgrounds, and learning to make the backgrounds is part of the calligraphic journey. The calligraphy guild offered workshops in watercolour, acrylics, printmaking and a host of other art forms. I took many of them, and realized in fairly short order that was where my true interest lay. I discovered a world of colour and texture and began my journey to become a multi-media artist.

Inspiration and vision for a particular project do not always arrive complete or even partially complete. Inspiration may begin as a tiny inkling, an idea that might hold appeal or be worth exploring further. And it will require work on our part to elucidate a vision for it. Sometimes it takes years of research and thinking about a subject to arrive at that vision. This has proven true for me in my fabric work. I love painting cloth as much as I love painting paper, and have taken a number of workshops in that medium over the course of many years. However, for the longest time, I had no idea what to do with those bits of painted material. For years, my stash of materials grew, along with my despair about ever using them.

Then one summer, I took a week-long fabric painting workshop where the last day was spent actually assembling and sewing a piece from the painted materials. I was so tired by that last day, I wasn't sure I could make anything, but I used the energy of those years of frustration to force myself to take that next step. I took three pieces of painted fabric and randomly cut, pinned and stitched them together into a piece that was about 16 by 30 inches. I hardly cared what the piece looked like; assembling it was all that mattered. I finished stitching the piece together at 3:30 pm, Friday afternoon. At that point, time ran out and I had to pack the piece away.

Later at home, when I examined what I had done, the piece felt unfinished but workable. I realized I could give it unity by quilting and topstitching with black thread, so that's what I did. In looking at the newly-stitched and suddenly finished piece, I recognized I had taken a major leap forward in my journey as a visual artist. I now knew how to use the materials I had been creating for all those years. I will never be a traditional quilter, but instinctively, I know how to translate quilting techniques into a more abstract and contemporary art form, stitching hand-painted pieces together to make canvases that can be mounted over stretcher bars and hung on walls. The vision had finally emerged and I recognized it when I saw it—not before.

Sometimes I have a sense of what I'd like to create without feeling the least bit inspired. I lack motivation, that burst of energy and self-discipline, to get creating. And so some of my creative work gets left undone. My experience is that if I can just get myself moving, inspiration and vision will emerge and my work will take concrete form.

John C. Maxwell, American entrepreneur, motivational speaker and author says,

> *The whole idea of motivation is a trap. Forget motivation. Just do it. Exercise, lose weight, test your blood sugar, or whatever. Do it without motivation. And then, guess what? After you start doing the thing, that's when the motivation comes and makes it easy for you to keep on doing it.*[5]

Vision can and will alter as we work. This has proven true for me with the writing of the chapters of this book. Originally, I thought this chapter was about "vision." But in attempting to clarify the term, I discovered vision is closely tied to inspiration and voice. As I wrote, it became clear that I needed to separate and deconstruct the three concepts, then "voice" requested its own chapter—not part of my original vision! I had to restructure the book as my vision for it altered. The unexpected changes in direction meant I had to keep seeking fresh inspiration for my writing. And I only received it by doing the painstaking work of trying to string together words and ideas into sentences and paragraphs.

Fortunately, when it comes to inspiration and vision, we can be proactive. We can open our minds and allow ourselves to be inspired by any number of things in the world around us. There is inspiration to be gained by immersing ourselves in the creative energy to be found in galleries, libraries, and great buildings. Learning about the work of others can inspire us. If we've already begun a project, studying the work of others can help us see solutions to problems and directions to pursue in our own work.

Many people find inspiration in nature and work directly from it—with sounds, colours, patterns, textures and landscapes.

Nature has inspired all manner of creative work from symphonies and songs to paintings and sculptures, poetry, books and movies, architectural design, quilts, fabrics and fashion design. And these things, once created, also serve to inspire us. I am one who is inspired by beautiful flowers and magnificent sunsets. When I was first starting out, other people's close-up photos of flowers inspired me to try my hand at macro-photography. Flowers proved an excellent subject for me because they appealed to my idea of beauty and stayed in one place long enough for me to try and capture what I saw and felt: my vision.

Similarly, the stuff of the urban world—sounds, colours, patterns, textures and landscapes—can provide inspiration. Imagine we are in a restaurant and witness a scene between an irate customer and the wait staff. The situation escalates. The manager is called over and escorts the irate customer to the front door. As creative people, we note the dialogue and details of the setting. Later we use them as prompts for some scene-writing of our own. Depending on our vision and what we are creating, we can slant the encounter to suit any number of genres from mystery to comedy. We can also choose from multiple points of view. The manager, the wait staff, the irate customer and an outside observer will each have a unique perspective. As we are creating the scene, elements of our personality will work in combination with the real-life experience to generate work that is unique to us.

The stuff of one's internal world can also provide inspiration for creative work. Our thoughts, feelings, fantasies, daydreams, night dreams and desires can all serve as inspiration. Artists through history have splashed their emotions across canvas in great swathes of colour. Composers empty their grief into songs and music that span the centuries. Writers turn the stuff of their dreams and nightmares into fiction and non-fiction in equal measure. The psychoanalyst C. G. Jung began dictating his autobiography when he was 81 years old and called it *Memories, Dreams, Reflections*, because that is what he devoted his life to studying. He said of his life, "My life is a story of the self-realization of the unconscious."[6]

It's a life-long journey to gain as much knowledge as possible about who we are, to understand what is important to us, what inspires us. Consciously looking into ourselves, learning our own minds and hearts, as well as our anxieties and fears—acknowledging what's there however fragmented, fragile, underdeveloped or disavowed—is essential to claiming our creativity. These are elements of our over-all vision of life.

As we become cognizant of the information fed to us by our senses, we become more aware of why we do things and how we are influenced. We become clearer about who we are, how we want to live and what we wish to create. We begin to truly inhabit our own lives. As we develop a sense of what we want our creative work to be, we take the steps to shape our vision one step at a time.

A design wall is a useful tool for shaping vision of creative work under construction. Even a bulletin board will work. I first read about design walls in quilting magazines, which advertised portable, collapsible versions to save on storage space. I liked the idea so much, I had a permanent one built in my art studio. It's 7' tall and 6' wide, because that's the amount of wall space I had. I worked with a carpenter friend to construct it out of flannel-covered corkboard and wood molding trim for very little money.

When I'm not sure how to finish a piece and need inspiration, or when I want to study my work further, I pin it to my board. Depending on the type of project, pieces can be pinned or taped to the wall and auditioned for inclusion before a final decision is made. Pieces stay there for varying amounts of time depending on how quickly inspiration arrives. And always, something does.

Some writers use a similar technique to build and keep track of the ideas for their novels. They will draw time and plot lines and create character sheets all of which get taped or pinned up on the wall of the room where they write. Creating a work-in-progress blueprint for a project helps develop vision. Terry Fallis, winner of the Leacock Award for his novel, *The Best Laid Plans*[7], kept his plan for the book in a separate document on his computer. That way he could keep it on the computer screen beside the manuscript page as he was writing. The film-maker's equivalent is a story board.

When we see (or "envision") what we are creating, we measure progress as we go. We get a sense of what elements are working, whether something's missing and where there's room for improvement, leading us to fresh inspiration. Each problem we solve in a new way strengthens our vision. Then we dream about what else might be possible.

Exercise #1 Identifying Vision

In your journal write the following questions one at a time. Listen carefully for the answers and record whatever surfaces, free of censorship.

a) Who am I?

b) What are my dreams for myself and my life?

c) What inspires me?

d) Who do I care about and why?

e) What do I care about and why?

f) What do I dislike and why?

g) What would I like to create?

Return to these questions regularly and add any thoughts that come to mind, so you build a picture over time.

Exercise #2 Build a Portfolio For Inspiration

Are you an urban or rural person? Are you inspired by city life or do you prefer nature? Perhaps you prefer the stuff of your own interior world? Maybe it depends on your mood at the moment. Begin to build a reference collection of images and ideas that appeal to you. These could be your own photos or clippings from websites, books and magazines.

Exercise #3 Using Your Portfolio

a) Try some journal writing to explore images that inspire you and your thoughts about them. Pay attention to the mood a particular image calls up for you? Do you prefer light and bright or dark and somber? Are you drawn to edgier treatments of a subject or peaceful, harmonious ones?

b) What steps might your images prompt you to take next?

c) What might they inspire you to create?

Exercise #4 Idea Capture

a) For the next 7 days, carry a small notebook or digital device with you. Practise noting anything you observe in the external world or your internal one: ideas of interest that cross your mind.

b) At the end of the week, review the ideas you have listed. Take one of the items and write about it in your journal. How might it connect to your creative work?

c) Review your idea capture list over time. You will likely find items worthy of further exploration.

Exercise #5 Create a Visual Display of Your Work

a) Dedicate a space or create a design wall or equivalent that suits your particular type of work.

b) Try displaying your work to see what it looks like.

Exercise #6 For Further Inspiration

a) Take yourself to an interesting place: a museum, gallery, movie—whatever catches your fancy. Allow your imagination to roam.

b) Browse through a book, the library or your corner newsstand. Pick up a book, magazine or video about something that appeals to you. It could be one of your favorite subjects or something you know nothing about. Learn about someone else's truth and see the world from a new point of view. That slight shift in perspective can spark greater clarity in your own thinking. Or try reading contemporary psychology, literature, philosophy and history to discover what others think about life, death, relationships, money—the big questions.

c) Listen to music and allow your mind to drift and daydream. Imagination and creativity can be inspired by music. Record any ideas that surface.

d) Go into a home improvement or paint or fabric store and check out colours, designs, interesting textures, whatever speaks to your imagination. Make notes as you go.

e) As you are doing the activity, notice what captures your attention. What might you do to follow up your interest? Brainstorm. List other options. Ask the all-important question: "What if?" and allow yourself to spin out the answer. Then make this a reference list for inspiration by adding your own ideas to the list.

Exercise #7 Inspiration With Others

a) Have a conversation with someone where you really dig into some of the questions on your mind. Incorporating positive input and inspiration from others can move you closer to what you want in your own life.

b) Join a creativity group. Or a group that suits your interests and talents.

FIVE

Dreams and Creative Vision

Another way to foster creative vision is by tuning into and tracking our daydreams, night dreams and secret desires. These can provide information about who we are, what we'd like our lives to be and what we dream of creating. By allowing ourselves to dream, and recording our dreams, we can generate a map to guide us on our path of creative self-discovery. We often tell others about our dreams: the things we wish we were doing; the things we dislike; the things we wish were different. Yet we are surprisingly good at tuning out this information about ourselves. It's time to pay attention to all our dreams. Some dreams speak softly and make their appearance gently, while others speak loudly and dramatically. Sometimes a dream will come with its own imperative, dictating the mode of expression it must take. I have learned firsthand about the power of this type of dream.

In 2001, my partner Greg died unexpectedly. That experience from beginning to end was profoundly shocking. Yet from it came the idea for this book. It arrived in a dream the night of Greg's funeral. I saw an image of a book complete with title, The Gatekeepers, and a plot for the book downloaded itself to me spontaneously. I awoke to a powerful sense that Greg was in the room with me. I felt he was sending me a strong message to write this book and I felt in my body that it would change my life. The vision was compelling, unlike any dream I have had before or since. Shocked as I was, and only half-awake, I got out pen and paper and wrote down as much information as I could while it was still fresh. I was already in the habit of recording my dreams, so I didn't worry about it; I just wrote it down to consider later.

At that time, there was such a gap between the dream and where I was in my life, I couldn't conceive of writing a book. I already had a full time job and more than enough to keep me busy. I wondered if Greg might have meant for me to pass the idea along to his son (a film maker) and daughter (a writer). That actually made more sense to me than writing it myself, so the following day, I told them about the dream in as much detail as possible. I could read in their faces that the dream didn't resonate for them. Most often, the messages we dream are meant for us, however difficult they are to decipher.

The impact of this dream, and the vision for this book, stayed with me through the following weeks. Gradually, I came to believe the dream message was Greg's final gift to me. I was to write a book and even though I couldn't fathom how, I would receive the help I needed. The confusion I felt was more than I could handle and I knew I needed to get help. I connected with a Jungian analyst and began a two-year journey into myself, a journey that taught me a great deal about my powers of intuition, helped me to come to terms with Greg's death, and eventually allowed me to make sense of the dream.

During the course of my analytical work, two distinct types of dream images informed my process and guided me. First, transcendent visual images (like the book) appeared spontaneously and complete in both my night dreams and my waking consciousness at various stages of the analytical process. For example, an image of the Titanic recurred regularly in my mind. Initially, it came to me during the day and the message was that changing the direction of my life was as difficult for me as changing course to avoid the iceberg was for the doomed ocean liner. Eventually, towards the end of my analysis, my Titanic sailed safely into harbor for a retrofit to make it more seaworthy. These images acted as map and compass for the changes my psyche was directing me to make, letting me know I was on course as I traveled.

The second type of image, equally important to my process, emerged kinesthetically as I worked with the tools of my art and photography to give visual form to my emerging thoughts and feelings. As I set out to express an idea or clarify my mood in the moment, I never knew ahead of time what my finished image would look like or have to say. I simply created freely, allowing psyche space to manifest. Images came in graphic form, catalyst and crucible, articulating problems and solutions—a process that was surprisingly efficient at connecting me to myself.

Would I have understood these images on my own? The meaning of some of them was clear almost immediately. Others were more challenging to understand and I found it reassuring to have help. Working with the images through meditation, journaling and analytical discussion, I came to understand that I was bone-weary from my job as a high school administrator and that stress was taking its toll on my body in the form of osteoporosis. My psyche made it clear I had a soul craving creative expression but I had no idea how to write a book. The amount of work involved was intimidating. Though I was apprehensive, something inside me knew I had to honor the imperative of this gift that seemed to appear from nowhere. Doing so was intrinsic to who I am and, once revealed, meant making a choice to live differently.

Despite the initial clarity of my dream about writing a book, I remained confused for many months about what shape this book was meant to take. Initially, I thought I was supposed to write a novel using the story of my life with Greg as the basis for the plot, but I hadn't written fiction in more than 40 years. My writing to that point had been non-fiction and poetry. Eventually, deciding to go with the energy of the dream, I enrolled in a fiction-writing class. To my surprise, I turned out to be quite good at it and began work on two novels during the time of the class. I doubt I would have discovered this ability without the prompting of the dream.

At the same time, I began to pay serious attention to a document sitting on my computer desk-top which held a collection of unsorted thoughts about creativity. I had started it a couple of years earlier and, from time to time, I recorded thoughts and ideas in this document with no idea what I was going to do with them. I had never read through the document or tried to organize it. While working on my computer one weekend, I opened the document, read through the material, and saw that it could be divided into ten topics. As I worked with the material, it began to shift shape, sorting itself into blocks of text under various headings. It took me about an hour to do this and when I was done, I discovered I had the outline for a non-fiction book on creativity.

I decided to print it out and make a home for it in a binder. The blueprint for my book had emerged. Within an hour, I had the "bones" of a manuscript sitting on my desk. It was in rough form, but a manuscript nevertheless. That was a life-changing moment: the dream image had proved true. I had found the book I was meant to write. Once the form of it lay in a document on my computer desktop, I understood that I would be writing creative non-fiction, a kind of autobiography about my creative life. The book would be driven by narrative and provide guidance for the development of creativity.

Almost immediately, I could feel the rest of the story wanting to get out of my head onto the page. But to write it, I would have to change my life. I had to make time to write and I had to make it a priority in my life. Hence my decision to take early retirement so I could choose a new creative life as artist, photographer and writer.

Five years later, I have no regrets. I know deep in my soul that the work of writing this book is mine. Honouring the work of writing has changed the shape of my life. It has freed up some part of me that was buried deep within and for the first time in my life, I have clarity about who I am and where I stand. I feel my life moving toward wholeness. I feel I'm where I'm meant to be. For the first time in many years, I am happy and my life is an adventure. I feel a deep-seated confidence in myself, that by doing this work I have strengthened my own spine and ceased to be so much at the mercy of the world. That's the power of dreams and the way they work.

Carolyn Myss writes in *The Castle: An Inner Path to God and Your Soul,*

> *The journey into your soul can begin with a dream. You may not realize it at the time, but that dream may be telling you that you are about to come home again, to return to yourself in some essential way.[1]*

At the time of my dream, although I was unaware of it as such, the "bones" of this manuscript already existed as a word processing document on my computer desktop. Making the discovery of its substance, becoming conscious of what was already there, was one of the biggest surprises of my life. Puzzling out the dream brought me here. You are holding in your hands the concrete evidence of one of my dreams.

Dreams are a remarkable and mysterious function of our minds and bodies. They offer deeply personal guidance we don't receive from any other source. My experience with this guidance confirms it can be gentle, insistent and healing. One night when I couldn't sleep, I got up after midnight and went into my studio to paint. Often, if I put some brilliant colour on paper, it releases whatever tension I hold and then I can sleep. Later that night, I had a vivid sequence of dreams about Greg.

In the first one, he appeared semi-opaque, almost transparent. He was standing at the edge of a lake in the woods and said he wanted to take me to his favourite place, a hill in the woods where you can sit and see clearly into the distance. We needed to get there by canoe. I then became aware of a yellow canoe floating upside down just under the water by the bank of the lake. There was a message in the canoe for me, but I couldn't quite get it before it was gone. Then Greg and I were suddenly in a canoe paddling to the place he called Faith Hill. At the end of the dream, Greg died and I was alone on the hill, which was a very peaceful place.

Immediately following this dream came a second one where Greg and I were both at his friend Doug's house. Once again, he died. I wrote in my dream journal afterwards,

> The place was different, but he died in both cases. His time was clearly up regardless of the circumstances. His death was sudden and peaceful—not a mistake, not simply random, and not alterable. One purpose of my life with him was to learn faith.

I am in awe of the authority of these dream images. In the face of the unpredictability and fragility of life, they offered me the greatest gift of guidance imaginable. Trusting and working with my own images restored my faith both in myself and in the universe as a positive place to enact the transformational and healing process. These transcendent and emergent images embody more than the mystery of the creative process; they show the hand of the Unseen at work in the soul, fostering an abundant flow of life.

My images allowed me to "see" that my old way of life needed to "die." They aided me in my struggle to come to terms with Greg's death and reconstruct my life, bridging my conscious and unconscious, incorporating lived experience and reconciling my need for healing and desire for growth. Despite the gravity of some of the images, they enabled me to understand and trust deeply that, though I might feel alone and afraid, I had an internal wisdom steering my course.

One of my creativity clients has an interesting story to tell about the importance of dreams and desires in her life. Kamil, in her twenties, is the mother of four children. She has a daughter with her husband, Raould, and together, they brought his three older children by a previous marriage to Canada from Africa. Kamil also works full time in her family's business. Despite being busy with her responsibilities, she made time for her creative work because there was an issue she needed to explore. When her daughter turned two, she experienced a strong desire to have another baby. She loved being pregnant and having babies. She didn't feel adding a fifth child to the family would be a good idea but she experienced grief at the thought of not having another baby and had a hard time letting go of this dream.

More than a year later, she had the opportunity to travel by herself to a conference in California. She used the time to do some deep thinking about her life and was surprised to discover that it wasn't a child she wanted: it was babies. From her teen years, she had been fascinated by midwifery and had amassed a library of books on the subject. She was surprised to discover her desire to have a baby was really a call to take up this career. It will be quite an undertaking for her to make this change. She has to complete high school science credits before she can enroll in the undergraduate program that will lead to her becoming a midwife. It will take years to complete the training and she has to balance this with caring for her family and continuing for the time being in the family business. Yet she feels the desire strongly enough that she has already begun the journey. That's the power of dreams: they change our lives if we make an effort to let them show us our way.

Dreaming is a fascinating part of the sleep cycle. We all do it whether we remember or not. Marion Woodman writes of the importance of dreams to the soul and the development of creativity:

> The dialogue must go on between consciousness and unconsciousness if we are to live creatively... if we watch our dreams long enough, themes are repeated, symbols reappear with variations. And if we contemplate these emerging patterns, gradually we begin to see some order in the chaos. We begin to see our own individual symbols weaving themselves, or being woven into some greater pattern. In that dialogue is soul-making. The dialogue between the ego and the self creates the Soul... changes life from a meaningless puzzle into an awesome journey.[2]

It's possible to tap into our dreams, to get to know our individual patterns, by developing the habit of tracking them. It's good to keep a notepad and pencil by your bed for this purpose, as so many dreams flee conscious memory with the light of day.

Sometimes our dreams have a connection to the events of the day preceding the dream. Sometimes they are trying to give us messages about ourselves. The imagery can be startling and embarrassing. I used to have "public toilet" dreams on a regular basis. Apparently, I am not alone. Woodman clarifies the message:

> *Our bodies have become so rigid and so plugged with unexpressed emotion that there is no room in them for creativity. If you doubt this, think of how many toilet dreams you have—plugged toilets, overflowing toilets, toilets you can't get to, toilets in the middle of the living room, toilets with outrageous contents... Blocked expression leads to depression, and depression ultimately to collapse.*[3]

Eventually, I worked out that the toilet imagery in my dreams had something to tell me about process and flow in my life, and the conflict I often felt between my external world responsibilities and the call of my own internal world:

I am in a cloister-style dormitory in an old stone house somewhere in Europe. The dorm rooms are small, with cots and desks for four girls, and one toilet out in the open that I can't use, even though I need to, because someone else is already on it.

When I looked at what was going on in my life, I realized I was feeling anxious because my job was keeping me too busy to find some much needed time and space to process my own thoughts and ideas. Literally, there was always something preventing me from doing what I needed to do.

Later: I am in a large public washroom sitting on a white toilet. A girl I attend school with is on another toilet beside me. At first I am constipated, but eventually I am able to "let go." I flush the toilet but it doesn't flush properly, so I have to flush a second time. This time the toilet overflows and the contents go all over the floor. I have to get a custodian to assist with the clean up.

After this dream, I realized I had been feeling anxious and blocked creatively. Things weren't flowing well in my life. Furthermore, I was afraid everyone could see what a mess I was making in my life. In my dream, I was going to have to get somebody to clean up after me, but in real life, I realized I had an inner custodian who could be called on to help clean up my mess.

These dreams helped put me in touch with myself so I began recognizing the signs when I needed some down time. I haven't had a public toilet dream since I deciphered the core idea. I have also learned how to "enter" my dreams to direct the action towards a satisfactory ending, so if I did have one, I could probably work with it while dreaming it. Muriel thinks it's better to let the dream unfold as it wishes.

Daydreams have as much to offer as night dreams: they often contain threads of our interests and passions in life. As already noted, following such a thread, my interest in illuminated letters led me to my career as an artist, separate from writing and photography. One Saturday, I came across an ad in a local newspaper for a workshop in illuminated letters. (Chance meeting the prepared mind!) When I called the number in the ad, I discovered the workshop was being offered by the local calligraphy guild—something I'd never heard of before. The woman I spoke to was warm and welcoming. She registered me for the workshop, gave me directions about finding it and explained about the guild. She then invited me to join if I enjoyed the workshop.

She was the first person I met the day of the workshop, and that workshop proved to be an amazing experience. I knew from my first moments there that I had found a place I belonged; here was a group that could support my interest in art and help me develop as an artist. I joined and have belonged ever since. Though I no longer pursue illuminated letters as an art form, my work with the guild has taken me in other directions I enjoy more, such as art journaling. I believe my interest in illuminated letters served its purpose by leading me to join the guild. I can't imagine my life without it.

Poets have written through the ages about what happens when dreams die. When we abandon our dreams without exploring their potential, or what they mean for us, our creativity has fewer places to go and we slump into a place where we are less than we have the potential to be. We don't take the steps that free our own creative expression; we refuse even the tiniest one that can kick-start our creative process. We become reluctant to walk towards the healthy self-expression that makes our lives deeper and richer.

Instead, we spend our lives distracted by the world and turn our attention to everyone else's business, squandering our time, energy and focus looking to the larger world for answers that only exist internally. When we hold no possibility of knowing what our dreams are, no possibility of having them fulfilled, we suffer emptiness in our lives and our souls. This emptiness seems the norm and we accept it. We can actually be unaware of it though we express it in the trench humour we use with each other as we go through our days. "Life's a bitch and then you die," we say or "Would you like fries with that?" as if we see a glimmer of something better lying just outside our immediate perception. Then we turn away from our inner knowing and self-medicate or reach for an anti-depressant to fill the void and dull our anxiety.

Our abundantly excessive world offers a host of addictions to tempt us away from feeling our anxiety rather than dealing with it. It is no stretch to see violence, itself a kind of personal expression, result from the thwarting of a more positive creative outlet. It seems to me we would live in a happier, more peaceful world if we knew how to turn inwards and reach deep within ourselves to bring forth our dreams—and let them motivate us in positive creative ways.

Note: The following exercises will help you focus on yourself and your dreams. You can do these exercises on your own through meditation and/or a journal or you can do them with a partner. If you are puzzled by the meaning of a dream, don't worry. If you are patient, stay open to your dreams and ask for answers, they will eventually reveal themselves. My own experience is that it can take some time for ideas and answers to surface. Many times I've put my journal away, gone on to do some other task and suddenly had a thought pop into my head, which I recognize as being the answer to a question I had asked in my journal. As these are often valuable thoughts, I now try to capture them, either by going back to my journal or jotting them down on scratch pads I keep around the house.

Alternatively, you can join a dream group or consult someone about what your dreams and ideas are telling you. I believe you are the best authority on your dreams, but sometimes talking to someone who is experienced working with dreams can help you get the hang of listening to them, unpacking them and their instructive wisdom.[4]

Exercise #1 Dreams From Childhood

This Exercise takes you back into the past to recall what dreams you held as a child.

a) Sit quietly in a comfortable chair where you won't be interrupted for 10 or 15 minutes. Close your eyes and allow yourself to relax. Let your mind drift back to your childhood. Do you remember your childhood wishes? Don't worry if nothing comes to mind; just ask the question and sit with it. What you are doing is opening yourself to possibilities. The child who had those dreams is still a part of you.

b) Record any thoughts that occurred to you, whether they are related to childhood dreams or not.

c) If you are working with a partner, have him or her repeat back to you what you said. If you are writing in a journal, read what you have written out loud, so you can pay attention to the words.

Exercise # 2 What Gives You Pleasure?

a) Think about what made you happy in the past. What did you long to do before you grew up and became responsible? Whatever it is, it's a piece of you and you probably won't be complete without it in some form, which may not mean quitting your day job and moving to paradise. Remember, even Albert Einstein created his theories while working full time.

b) Record these thoughts or share them with a partner.

Exercise #3 The Dreams of Your Heart

This exercise moves us into the present.

a) Close your eyes and allow yourself to relax. Quiet your mind. Think about yourself and your life now. What are the dreams in your heart? Don't worry if nothing comes. Just allow the question to float to the surface of your mind.

b) Open your eyes. As before, if you are working with a partner, tell him or her what came into your mind and have him or her repeat back to you what you said. If you are writing in a journal, read what you have written out loud, so you can hear the words.

Exercise #4 Just For FunThis exercise moves us into the future.

a) What's the wildest dream you can think of that appeals to you? This can be an escape fantasy. It doesn't have to be something you'd actually do.

b) Record it and then look carefully at it. Is there some element of it that you might be longing to put into your life? Something you could safely incorporate?

Exercise #5 Keep a Dream Journal

a) Start by paying attention to the basics. Do you dream in colour or black and white? In images or words or feelings?

b) Try tracking the content of specific dreams. If you can do this over time, you will likely notice certain types of images or events recurring.

Exercise #6 Seed Your Dreams

a) Try asking a question out loud before you go to sleep and see if an answer comes through in a dream.

b) Exercise the self-discipline necessary to wake up and record ideas in a notebook. See what they tell you.

Exercise #7 Follow Your Dreams

a) Close your eyes for a moment and think about your life. What do you enjoy, love, feel passionate about? What is something simple that excites your interest? When was the last time you took time to follow the thread of that interest, that spark of curiosity about something in your world, something that caught your eye, however briefly. It might have been something simple, like trying that new recipe you saw in a magazine, baking a cake, going to a movie. These are all creative acts. Note the ideas that pop into your mind.

b) Open your eyes and talk to your partner, or write the ideas down.

Exercise 8 Check In With Yourself

a) In your journal list the projects and creative work you dream of completing.

b) Evaluate the progress you have made in your creative work this week.

SIX

Articulating Voice

Where vision guides the creation of a project and suggests form for inspiration, voice articulates that form. It is the instrument or medium of expression[1] that allows us to give physical shape and substance to dreams so we are able to complete our projects. It's critical to find and utilize the voice unique to us that speaks our truth. To do this, we must learn to recognize and articulate honestly what's on our minds and in our hearts. We feed ourselves creatively when we speak honestly—when we realize we can't take on any more, and we say so. We feed ourselves creatively when we speak truth to ourselves as well. We feel better when we complete those tasks we've been saying we will, and sign up for that class we've been talking about. When we follow through, we are exercising our voice authentically.

We are not necessarily in the habit of listening to our inner voice. From early on we are trained by our parents, our teachers and society to listen to others at the expense of our own vision and voice. This makes us vulnerable to the habit of putting other people and priorities first. A lifetime of misplaced priorities and we can experience a cognitive dissonance[2] that prevents us from holding a clear vision and speaking in our own voice. We are taught to watch what we say, and we are reminded, perhaps wisely, that what has been said cannot be unsaid. Most of us rehearse ahead of time when there's a chance we will be judged by what we say and how we say it, for example in an interview situation. Speaking what we truly think can be risky in such situations.

Yet ask anyone who uses her voice to make a living and she will say a voice needs to be cared for, exercised and nurtured, or it falls into disrepair. Think of Whitney Houston and what the world lost with her death. Like plants, when we get good growing conditions—enough water, sun and fertile ground—we thrive. We need essential "creativity" nutrients: the opportunity to express ourselves honestly, encouragement to do so, an audience receptive to what we have to say—or we can lose confidence in ourselves and wither. When that happens, awareness of our dreams, talents and abilities gets buried in our psyche and we lose track of ourselves. This regrettable loss has an impact on our ability to access and express our creativity.

We can find our vision by exploring our voice and, in the process, chart our creative direction. A journal is useful for exploring voice and recording the ideas from which we elucidate vision. It offers a safe page to dump the most outrageous thoughts and feelings, free of censorship. It's available any time of day or night. We can scrawl down what's important to us, and scroll through it as often as we like. Keeping a journal is like emptying our pockets or our purses: once we see what we've accumulated, we can determine what to keep and what to discard. If something's missing, we can take steps to find or replace it. A journal allows us to walk away from an idea and come back to it later, to seek clarity over time. Or ask a question. Answers don't have to emerge immediately. Sitting with a question and waiting to see what answer emerges is a valuable creative exercise. As Caroline Myss writes in *The Castle: An Inner Path to God and Your Soul*,

> *Self-examination is the practice of accountability to your soul. You review how well you live in congruence with the truths that you know and believe most deeply... self-examination is the process of becoming your truth.*[3]

I journal every day to track my dreams, thoughts and interests: my truth. I've done this for more than thirty years. I find it especially helpful during times of great stress. I have written my way through all the big events of my life one page at a time, one day at a time. When Greg died, I wrote through my grief day and night. I found it helped me to sleep if I exorcised that wild landscape of emotion and recorded it on a page. Journaling also helped me track my thoughts about writing this book, taking early retirement and making the transition to my creative career. Now that I'm in that career, it helps me keep track of where I am, and where I want to go. On days when everything's right with my world, journaling keeps me grounded and serves as a kind of mental housecleaning.

We can expand the definition of a journal. We are not restricted to pen and paper or proper writing structure. We can write or dictate whatever words come to mind in whatever order they appear, even if they seem to make no sense. We can paint, record in audio or video mode, even construct something out of wood or glass. Let imagination play. We can check the results and leave as is or use them as a springboard for additional composing.

Even a list can be a kind of journal. Making lists gets trivial stuff out of one's head: a kind of simplifying and decluttering process for the mind. It's difficult for me to settle down to my creative work in the morning when I've got a lot of things to take care of in the afternoon. If I jot the list down on a piece of paper I can consult later and place it on my dining room table, I'll see it when I have lunch. That way, I know I won't forget anything and my mind is clear to focus on my creative work.

Another fruitful way of finding voice is to have a conversation with a trusted other who pays close attention. Though it is possible to map personal vision and trace voice by listening carefully and really hearing what we are saying to ourselves, the habit has to be cultivated. I found it easier to do this with another person when I first set out on my creative journey. I didn't realize I had a lot of good ideas worthy of further exploration until I heard another person say them back to me. I learned to record them from these conversations so I didn't forget or lose them. Over time, this process taught me to access and pay attention to my ideas as they occurred. I began to "see" (and hear!) what they looked like.

It is essential for our creative development to learn to listen to ourselves, to heed the messages we send ourselves. Over the past decade, I've noticed a strange phenomenon: most of us know in our hearts what our creative vision is and how to give it a voice. We know what we need to do to be more creative, to live happier, more fulfilling lives. We can even share our vision clearly with other people. Yet somehow, we don't pay attention to what we are saying.

An especially vivid example of this happened in a conversation I had with my real estate agent when I went to buy my house. Sherri, my agent, grew up with an alcoholic father who was violent at times. Consequently, she left home when she was 12, was married by 18 and divorced a couple of years later with no children. When I first met her, we got to know each other by exchanging details about ourselves. She had just separated from her long-time partner because she no longer felt she had much in common with him. Earlier in the year, her sister, to whom she was very close, had died. She told me she didn't need a man in her life at the moment; she needed time to heal. She wasn't happy in her own house; she had outgrown it.

On learning that I was an artist, she said she wanted something creative, possibly drawing, in her life. No love interest at the moment, time to heal, a new house and drawing classes: if ever there was a blueprint for a new life—one which she would find more rewarding—that was it. Yet as our conversation continued, it became clear she hadn't really heard or understood the directions she was giving herself. She was aware of saying the words, but had somehow missed their significance. I asked her what she thought her dream house might look like. We enjoyed discussing the possibilities and looked at some great houses she thought might work for her. Six months later, we both had new houses, homes for our blossoming creative selves.

We can learn much about our vision and voice from the negatives we are saying quietly to ourselves, and loudly to others. The "tapes" in our heads use up energy. If we become conscious of the messages and deal with the issue(s), we can redirect that energy to use more creatively in life.[4] Though in the past I have sometimes been afraid to hear my own thoughts, over time I have discovered really listening to myself, even through something as overwhelming as my shock and grief at Greg's death, can prove gentle, instructive and transformative.

What kind of voice do we use when we are talking with ourselves? Our minds are busy places, working constantly, burning energy whether we want them to or not. They are like companions with libraries full of books stored from our earliest beginnings. They talk to us in an on-going dialogue and constantly play old film clips of our behaviour. We have to learn to listen carefully to this dialogue and determine what it is we are really thinking and saying. We burn up a lot of energy giving space to those worn out, negative habits and self-defeating patterns of thought that originate in our early years. As creative people, we need to exchange this re-iterative monologue for our own internal dialogue. We must let go of this "debris," free up energy, and develop our creative voice.

In our relationship with the unconscious, there is a give and take. We don't just say to our creativity, "Give me a beautiful picture!" and expect it to appear automatically, though sometimes we are lucky and that happens. More often, we offer our struggle and angst in exchange for that beautiful work. Many times I have struggled with a trial and error process as I sought to create a work of art that I found satisfying. I ask myself, "Is this what it looks like? Or this?" as I try out different colours and textures. "What do I need to do next to complete this work?" is a question I am always asking my unconscious self. And I listen for the answers, which tend to come over time in the process, rather than all at once. Many times those answers have come out of the blue while I'm doing something else entirely, and I've had to scramble to make note of the answer so I don't lose or forget it.

We are made of energy, so it should be no surprise that our bodies and brains are energized by positive thoughts and drained by negative ones. If we use precious stores of energy to engage in negative self-talk, we will kill creative projects before they ever get off the ground. We want to keep our energy available to explore opportunities that further our creative development.

We can use cognitive dissonance to our advantage. It's difficult and uncomfortable to hold two competing thoughts in consciousness at the same time. Given a choice, we will seek to ease the level of discomfort. We can interrupt a thought that is causing us tension by consciously substituting a more pleasant one. There are a number of ways to do this. One method I use is to count out loud to 10 forwards and backwards, saying the numbers clearly each time. I do this repetitiously to interrupt the train of thought I want to derail. If I'm really steamed or upset, I'll do this in co-ordination with my breathing. Over time, I have gotten to the point where I can just count to two over and over again, and my mind will calm. I've found this especially helpful in traffic: no more road rage!

I can recall my parents and grandparents advising me, "Just don't think about it!" when I was worried about something as a child. Based on brain research by neuroscientists like Dr. Donald Hebb[5] and Dr. Wilder Penfield[6], and those who came after them, that turns out to be good advice. Repetition of a thought creates a dominant brain path. The more we think about something, the more we will continue to think about it, and if it's negative or anxiety-provoking, that's what we will experience. But the neuro-plasticity of the brain means rewiring is possible.[7] To break out of the cycle, we have to break the thought pattern. A good strategy is to consciously and deliberately substitute a happy thought for the annoying one, saying it out loud so we can hear it.

Other suggestions: we can choose an affirmation or mantra to concentrate on and repeat over and over for this purpose. Yoga or Tai Chi or other exercise postures have the advantage of engaging the body as well as the mind, not leaving room for a lot of unwanted thoughts. Breathing out—exhaling—is one of the body's built-in stress-reduction systems. So is going for a walk and appreciating the day. An offending thought can be sealed in a box and placed on a shelf in a storage room in the mind, so it can be re-directed to what's important. If that's too much clutter, it can be written it onto a piece of paper, then released by burning or burying it. We can choose thoughts that are grounded in reality and uplifting. Gardening is a very creative act. There's nothing like digging in the dirt to really "ground" a person, and the plants benefit too.

If none of these strategies work, we need to consider getting support. Sometimes it takes a skilled other to help sort out, make sense of, and act on what we hear ourselves saying: a coach, mentor, or counsellor. Though I value in-person conversation, in my mentorship practice, I have talked to others who live at a distance via phone, e-mail and VoIP (Voice over Internet Protocol such as Skype). There is no cost for some of these technologies, and they offer the advantage of being able to see who I am talking with, allowing me to read body and facial expressions. They also offer the freedom to choose a time that best suits and to converse from the comfort and privacy of home.

Counsellors usually have access to personality inventories that can also help us work out who we are and what kind of life might be most satisfying for us. This can be particularly helpful after a major disconnect in life, even one as "simple" as being born left-handed and being forced to live right-handed. Living a disconnect over time can habituate us to shutting down who we are until we lose ourselves.

One of the biggest challenges we have in life is creating and offering to the world what is ours alone. When we act in a way that aligns the dreams of our hearts—who we dream of being and what we dream of creating—with who we are and how we live, we experience congruence. It's the sense that we are where we are supposed to be and doing what we are meant to be doing. We live creatively with confidence. When we allow ourselves to create the life that suits us best, we speak our lives in our own authentic voices. We explore our voices and begin to live more creatively when we step outside the box just a little: we decide six cloves of garlic make the recipe tastier than the single clove it calls for. Suddenly we "own" this recipe and it will be made to our specifications. If it's a success, we get the credit. If it's a flop, we get credit for experimenting and will know how to do it better next time.

We are the gatekeepers of our own souls and we have work to do. The better we understand who we are, the more easily we are able to harness our creative gifts and offer them to the world. All life experience can feed creativity and become the raw material for what we long to express. What we create authentically gives the world form, colour and diversity, enriching human experience. When we voice our perspective to the world, human understanding improves and the store of human knowledge increases. This exchange is the basis for the evolution of society and our best hope for improvement in the human condition on this mysterious planet we call home.

Exercise #1 Exercise Your Voice

a) At least once this week, say out loud something you really think, feel, or believe to another person. If you are not used to being candid, pick a situation that is relatively low-risk. Write it out ahead of time in your journal or rehearse with yourself ahead of time.

b) If you're good at candour, increase the risk level. Practise the honesty habit until you are comfortable

Exercise #2 Exercise Your Creative Voice.

a) What's on your mind at the moment about your creative work? Do you have any unresolved issues? Things you'd really like to talk over with someone? Or are you having a really good day?

b) Either way, write it out.

Exercise #3 Giving Shape and Form to Voice

a) What concrete form would best identify and express the many threads and ideas that run through your mind?

b) What process would help you find and explore issues that interest you?

Exercise #4 Reflective Listening

a) Find a partner who understands what reflective listening is, someone who listens carefully and attentively. Have a conversation with this trusted creative soul friend. Have her tell you what she heard you say, free of all judgment, and check to see if you were heard correctly.

b) What clues about yourself do you hear? Of course, you can return the favour as well.

Exercise #5 Personal Manifesto

a) Make use of a tablet or other technological device, or keep a little book in a pocket or purse for the next week and write down thoughts as you notice yourself saying them silently to yourself or loudly to others.

b) Learn to ask yourself: am I telling myself and others what I really think, feel and believe, or is there is a disconnect between what I am thinking and saying?

Exercise #6 Check Those Repetitive Messages

a) Listen to what's in those repetitive messages playing in your head. For the next week, give them voice by writing them down in a daily diary or recording them so you can play them back.

b) Review them at the end of the week. Notice anything interesting? Is any of your energy tied up in negative thinking? Do you see a sense of direction emerging? If not, keep tuning into yourself and recording your thoughts.

c) Give yourself the peace, space, solitude, time and freedom to do these exercises. It only takes a couple of minutes. Sooner or later, you will find the messages worthy of your attention. When you give them time and attention, you are paying the rent for the real estate of your castle.

Exercise #7 Creative Work Check-in

a) What steps have you taken on your creative project so far? How's it going? Is your creative voice emerging?

b) Identify one issue that emerges from the work you've done so far and write about it. Is there a message trying to come through? Ask yourself these key questions about your own internal dialogue: Does it serve my creative work? Is it energizing or draining me? How does my body feel when I think this way?

SEVEN

Cultivating the Spirit of Creativity

Oliver Wendell Holmes, an American physician and poet, regarded by his peers as one of the best writers in the 19th century, wrote, "Many people die with their music still in them. Why is this so? Too often it is because they are always getting ready to live. Before they know it, time runs out."[1] One of the most important lessons we have to learn in life is that the perfect time to begin a creative project may not exist. If we wait to experience this mythical perfection before we begin, we may wait forever. However busy we are at the moment, there is no guarantee things will be easier in the future. The same is true for inspiration. The present moment is enough to work with. Being willing to move forward with our creative work ensures we will use the time we have: now.

Early in my art career, I used some of my weekend days and holidays to have a kind of art boot-camp at my house. I planned ahead so I could immerse myself in creative activity for a day. This was a time for me to do something I loved, uninterrupted by anything or anyone. Here is what two of the days looked like.

Creative Day #1: Creating Marbled Paint Papers

My activities for this creative day actually began the night before as there is a lot of preparation to be done ahead of time. I diluted paints with water and put each colour in its own jar to sit overnight so the paint and water could combine properly. I then mixed up the methyl cellulose size as it needs to sit for several hours. I laid out eye-droppers to use for each colour, containers for the size, pattern-making tools and papers, so everything was ready to go in the morning.

After breakfast the next day, I spread out sheets of plastic on the floor to hold the wet marbled pages for drying. Once my set up was complete, I began making the papers. About 3 hours later, I took a break for lunch and surveyed the pieces I had created. I replaced the size I had used in the morning with some clean stuff and embarked on my afternoon session. This session lasted about 2 hours, as I began to run out of paint and space to put the paper to dry. This process is quite physical and intense. I was tired by that point and still had to do quite a bit of clean up. Once this was done, I checked my papers again and stacked the dry ones. I was pleased with myself for making the effort to do this activity. The papers were very colourful and satisfying to make and I knew I would have use for them in the future.

I've also had Creative Days where I haven't planned too much ahead of time. I simply promised myself I would do something creative. I got up when I woke up and followed my whims from moment to moment. Here is what one of these days looked like.

Creative Day #2

7-8:30 am Rise and shine. Journal writing, listening to music and breakfast

8:45-10:30 am Creative work… painting

10:30-11 am Break: snack and reading an art book

11:00 am-12 noon Shovel the driveway

12-1:30 pm Cook lunch and read

1:30-2:15 pm Meditation

2:30-4 pm walk. Bought newspaper. Read some of it when I got home

4-5 pm Completed a double-page art journal spread

5-6 pm Finished paper; mopped the floor

6-7 pm Watched the news; prepared and ate dinner

7-7:45 pm Filed mail and paid bills

8 pm Watched a movie.

Though as written here, the day seems laid out with specific tasks at specific times, I did not know ahead of time that's what I would do. As the day progressed, it emerged that those tasks suited my mood at those times on that day. Only we can determine what such a day will look like. To save time, we can make food ahead and freeze it so all we have to do is warm it up or make sandwiches first thing in the morning. Then we don't have to stop what we are doing later when we are caught up in creative activities. I tell myself: remember to eat.

There are still housekeeping tasks during the day. There are always things needing to be done in real life and there is room for them, even in a creative day—if I feel like doing them. Otherwise, they'll keep. If I'm doing a lot of creative work, I find a shift to routine tasks or physical activity provides an excellent break. A little "breathing" space helps my creative work. The mind needs to relax, to be allowed time to mull things over consciously and unconsciously. Sometimes I have to step away and switch gears for a while. Clean up the kitchen, do the laundry, go for a walk, do something fun, work on another project. Spend time doing nothing, allow myself time to catch up with myself. Inspiration emerges from the struggle; it can't be forced.

The Creative Day exercise is important for several reasons. It imprints creativity as a habit and ensures that we will express our "music" rather than keep it hidden away. Creating a new habit takes some self-discipline and commitment. It's much easier to continue something that has become a habit than it is to initiate it in the first place. This kind of Creative Day also gives us opportunity to be inspired by what moves us, to exercise and explore personal vision and articulate voice. It means that whatever else may be going on in our lives, we are committed to honouring our creativity and learning more about ourselves.

I know the creative day exercise is manageable, because it's how I made creativity a part of my life when I was working full-time as a vice-principal, living with Greg and juggling various family responsibilities. When I was working full-time, I would try to build one of these days into my life at least once a month. Though I didn't always succeed, I looked forward to them as something to be treasured because they allowed me to do my own work, or play if I felt like it.

Creative Days allow us to actively participate in our own creative process and discover how we like to work. We begin to give some of our ideas concrete form as we experiment with the tools and materials of our chosen activity. We learn what aspects of the creative process we enjoy, which come easiest and which are more challenging. We learn where our natural talents and abilities lie and where it might be useful to seek out further instruction. We determine the aspects of projects that appeal most, which is important in developing creative perception. We develop skills as we work with our tools and materials. We begin to build a body of work and portfolio of ideas for future work. As you can see, though the creative day plan doesn't take a whole lot of time, there is nothing "small" about the exercise. When something's important, we make the time to do it. We, and the world, are richer for it.

When the thought of starting anything creative is overwhelming and stirring up fears, it's time to meet the Internal Critic. We all have one. In Jungian psychology that critical voice can be an aspect of the negative anima for men and the negative animus for women.[2] It's the energy of the opposite gender, the yin to our yang. We can experience the voice as chronic anxiety, doubt, guilt, resentment, bitterness, and the need for control. It can manifest as a constant need for accomplishment and external approval... the feeling we will never be "good enough." It's that feeling so many of us have acquired that somehow it's not okay to be who we are. This voice can reverberate in our minds, driving us crazy.

I have had my share of struggles with my internal critic and have learned a thing or two about working with it. The first thing is to acknowledge its existence. Then we need to develop a relationship with this important internal voice. Some people give him/her a name. "Oh, hi Frank," they'll say when they begin to hear the doubts whispering.[3] Identifying and acknowledging our personal "anima" or "animus" can help to lessen its negative impact.

For a woman, the animus in its negative attitude elicits the left-brain functions. It can be overly detail-oriented, logical and ruled by facts. The animus is meant to serve a woman's desires, not take over. As various stages of the project are completed, a softening and relatedness to these functions allow the animus in its positive attitude to emerge. For example, it can be utilized to perform an editorial function, offering suggestions to improve work and helping refine it so it's closer to an initial vision. Conversely, for a man, the anima in its negative attitude elicits the right-brain functions. It is often emotionally laden and a man may become moody if he's feeling swamped by those emotions. In a man, the anima is meant to give meaning to his desires. His critic can be invited to colour an idea with eros.

It's helpful to know this voice has a useful role to play in creative work. It's especially good at editing, but it needs something to work with first to soften or mediate its impact. The problem for each of us creatively is that listening to that critical (editing) voice too early in the process can make us afraid to do any work. As we begin a project, what we need is courage to take one step—any step—in the spirit of imagination. We need to be willing to be beginners in our chosen fields and to make mistakes—to experience the messiness of the process as we create. Editing does not belong at this stage.

I had a surprising experience with my own critic, or animus image, recently in the form of a dream. Turns out he's a shape shifter. In this dream, he appeared to me as the best quarterback in the premier National Football League in the States, and we were on the same team. What an image! He is a brilliant strategist, throws the ball with unerring accuracy, knows how to pull the team together and march it down the field to score a touchdown every time. He's in incredible physical shape, respects himself and others, appreciates his gifts, and is skilled at using them. It was clear in the dream that he is also a gentle man and knows how to listen and respond... to me.

This dream transformed my thinking about the critic. Until this point I had visualized it as holding negative energy. Now I see that it holds critical energy—a substantial difference. Critical animus energy can just as easily be positive. I see also that the critic can assume all kinds of personas. It is possible to get to know this voice in all its guises and in time, transform it. And be transformed by it. I am aware that working with my own creativity over time, I have become optimistic about life. I see this dream as offering visual and imagistic confirmation of the shift.

Whatever the creative mode of expression, a finished project is a set of solved problems. Every time we set up a problem in our work and then attempt to solve it, we are exercising creative voice and refining vision. It is the job of the internal critic to help us solve the problems at each stage in the creative process. The trick is to use the imaginative brain to create something substantial but unresolved, and then invite the critic in as a detective to help find solution(s). For example, sometimes I paint fairly quickly, perhaps intuitively, without thinking a lot about it. I put a series of marks or colours on a canvas without worrying about balance, perspective etc. Or I put some words on a page, capture some ideas, and turn them into words however improbable and grammatically incorrect.

Once the problem is created, I invite the critic in to evaluate what's on the canvas or paper and make suggestions. I can take the critic's advice or not, as my mood and imagination dictate. Sometimes the critic's advice will provide a key to finishing the work. Other times, that advice will contain a nugget of information that will spur my right brain on to fresh ideas and I will add more to my canvas or paper. Either way, I am refining my vision. If at any time the negative critic starts to censor imaginative ideas, it's probably time for me to kick it back to the curb and get on with capturing imaginative ideas. When I capture those ideas, I ensure that I will have something of value for the critic to work with later.[4]

Learning to solve problems as they arise in my projects is one of the aspects of creative work that has transformed my life. First of all, I learned that a problem is not an insoluble crisis: it doesn't have to trigger an anxiety attack because... problems can be solved! Sometimes they are solved simply, sometimes with effort. In both writing and making art, I have learned to hold the tension of a problem, to stay with conflict long enough to gain an understanding of it. I still have moments when a difficulty in my creative work will cause me to lose confidence. For example, sometimes when a chapter in the draft of this book seemed hopelessly muddled and confused, it would make me feel I wasn't a good enough writer to fix the problems.

By taking on the challenge of problems in my creative work over and over again, I have learned that I can trust my process and my abilities. I just have to keep faith that if I stay with the challenge, I can work it out, or alternatively, find a teacher who can help me do so. In my creative work, I've had the experience of being able to work out solutions to even the most challenging problems as they arise. I don't have to know what the problems or solutions are ahead of time. Solving problems on an ongoing basis has helped me to develop patience, and instilled confidence that I can handle whatever comes up in this work. The creative process itself has restored my faith in my ability to solve problems.

Over time, I realized that what was true for me in my studio was true in life: I could solve problems by staying with them and working through them. That's one of the things that's been truly transformative for me. I also learned that problems often have more than one solution. And as I worked with the possibilities, I got better at finding fresh solutions. I became less anxious and less of a perfectionist. I no longer needed to spend so much energy controlling the outcome of any situation; I could let a situation evolve rather than rushing to "fix" it immediately. As I began to trust my process, I began to have faith that I could shape what happened in my life, one step at a time, one decision at a time. I began to feel grounded in myself. I still valued the advice and assistance of others, but had learned to stand on my own two feet even in challenging circumstances.

One of the problems I faced when I finished this book was how to write a query letter that might interest an agent or publisher. You would think writing a single page letter would be easy after writing 18 chapters, but actually, I found it a very intimidating exercise. So much so, that I got stalled and couldn't seem to move forward on my own. I asked a friend and fellow writer for help, and together we drafted a letter. I sent it off to an agent and received my first very nicely-worded rejection letter.

Of course that was discouraging, but I also felt dissatisfied with the query letter. Somehow, I didn't feel it truly summed up my book. So I wrote and revised many more drafts until I thought I had one that better reflected my work. I then took it to a writers' circle for feedback. As it turned out, few of the writers in the group had experience with query letters. The feedback was positive, and I felt I was on the right track, but still lacked confidence in my letter. What to do?

I happen to belong to an authors' organization that provides a number of services for writers including a list of editors and their contact information. Who better to evaluate my letter than an actual editor? After sending off a couple of inquiry e-mails, I found an editor who would evaluate my letter for a small fee. This letter was important enough to me that I paid the fee. The result was a query letter that accurately reflected my work and the confidence to send it out to agents and publishers. It took persistence, trial and error to solve this problem but doing so was critical in moving forward with my work.

It requires courage to take the steps in the creative process when we haven't had a lot of experience with it. And even when we have, it still takes courage each time we start a new project, or a new aspect of a big one. Exercising creativity means stepping into the unknown, being uncertain what we are going to accomplish even when we have a plan in mind. It's difficult to predict where the process will take us. Creative work can transform us by providing opportunities to practice courage, faith and persistence. As Alexander Graham Bell advised, "Leave the beaten track behind occasionally and dive into the woods. Every time you do you will be certain to find something you have never seen before."[5]

I speak from experience when I say the struggle is worth it. Creative work is an exercise in faith. Opening myself to the creative process has transformed me spiritually. Somehow, I came away from my childhood church experiences with the dissatisfying idea that God sat on his throne in the sky, looking like Abraham Lincoln and acting like a punitive father. So as I have written earlier, it is not surprising that in my late teens, I declared myself agnostic.

Searching for something to believe in that felt positive and helpful, I did a lot of reading: explored Buddhism, meditation, the tenets of New Age spirituality and the precepts of quantum physics with its concept of the unified field. Though all of these explorations were helpful, it was my work with the creative process that ultimately restored my optimism and belief in myself, and a force or energy beyond me. Solving problems to create beautiful work shows me something important about who I am. It gives me tangible evidence that there is more to me than I am often aware of, and supports a vision of the universe that is life-affirming and pleasing to me.

Just about anything that happens in life can throw us off a creative path. Big events such as being involved in an accident, a major loss of some kind including the death of a loved one, betrayals—each can cause us to lose track of creative work. But so can the little things. Day to day disruptions and hurts can cause injuries to the creative soul and what it's trying to express. Living in a family or relationship that is damaging causes pain that can dull the senses. So can being trapped in a limiting job, one that doesn't offer opportunity for growth.

Over time, we can become habituated to the pain of being less than who we can be and having less than we need to grow and prosper. The slow erosion caused by unfavourable living conditions can make us lose touch with ourselves—abandon parts of ourselves there doesn't seem to be room for. Without faith, life becomes a series of sinkholes we fall into and can stay in for years. The Greek myth of Orpheus and Eurydice makes this point vividly.[6] Despite instructions not to look behind him, Orpheus had a moment of doubt, looked back into the underworld, and lost his wife. Perhaps this story is about the need for faith as we move forward, and the challenge to overcome our doubt and fear because they cost us our dreams. Adhering to our path, we learn that taking one step at a time will carry us forward in our creative process even when we feel the storm winds of everyday life blowing. The steps on the path keep us anchored. We weather the storms, affirm ourselves and exercise faith in the process.

To bring a project to successful completion, it helps to have faith that, over time, each step brings us closer to the place where solutions will be found. There will be surprises along the way. We can pretty much count on that. Whatever we are trying to create will have its own internal integrity and it's our task to discover, uncover and work with it. Michelangelo said of his statues that they were already there in the marble. His task was to free them.[7] Marble is a hard rock that can be fractured by one wrong stroke. Michelangelo took astonishing risks with that first chisel stroke and each one after. And because he was willing to do so, he left a remarkable legacy. Each of us has it in us to exercise courage, and the work we do as a result will shape our own legacy.

When we exercise our creativity, we are expressing our authenticity. We are on track in our lives, or getting there. Our lives feel full of possibilities and accomplishment. We learn more about who we are. We feel whole–who we are meant to be. Although it can stir up our doubts, fears and anxieties, this work has much to teach us. We learn about commitment, self-discipline, risk, courage, patience, faith, persistence and problem solving—all while doing something we love. Ultimately it is satisfying work because living creatively restores energy. Creative work is soul work because it has the power to transform.

Exercise# I Incorporating Creative Days Into Your Life

Note: Give yourself the whole day to do this if you can manage it. Make no plans in advance and have no other people around. If time is tight, choose a morning, afternoon or evening. It could be a Saturday or Sunday, when everyone else is busy or the kids are with your ex. Turn off your cell phone and ditch the day planner. Put aside all the usual commitments, stop multi-tasking and tune into yourself. The point is to allow yourself to do the things you enjoy when you feel like doing them instead of having to jam them in on top of everything else the way you try to during the work week.

a) What might a creative day look like for you?

b) When you've got a couple of them under your belt, consider making them a regular part of your life. If your life is busy, try for one morning or afternoon a month. Then build to a day a month, a day every two weeks, one day a week.

Exercise #2 Identify Your Critic

a) In your journal, identify the forms your critical voice takes. List the comments you hear in your head that inform you the critic is active.

b) Give him or her a name if that is helpful. If the critic is interfering, address it directly. Ask it to be patient. Embrace your critic so that it works for you rather than against you.

c) Inform your critic you will be calling on him/her for input later. Then put it firmly on Hold. Assert, "It's okay to be who I am and right now, this is what I'm doing."

Exercise #3 Image Make-over For the Critic

Create or visualize your own positive critic or animus image. Think Olympic team captain, brilliant analyst: whatever will be useful to you in your work and your life. It's all part of cultivating your creative self.

Exercise #4 Practice Problem-solving Skills

a) Identify a simple problem in your life.

b) Determine and take the steps to solve it.

c) How does it feel to solve it? Just getting something simple crossed off your To Do list gives you a lift and frees up some energy.

d) Alternatively, tackle a problem you are experiencing with your creative work. Think about ways to solve it and try out some of the possibilities.

Exercise #5 Take a Risk

What is one thing you could do today either in your creative work or elsewhere in your life that would take you outside your comfort zone and carry you a step forward in your life? If it's something that won't cause harm to yourself or others, take that step.

EIGHT

From Dreams to Priorities and Plans

When it comes to creative work, I frequently hear people say, "I just need a good idea. I'm waiting for inspiration." However, the creative process does not necessarily work that way. If you wait for a good idea to come along or until you are in the right frame of mind, you may never start. This is the conundrum of creative work: ideas often follow action. You have to get the body moving to engage the mind. Make a place for inspiration to show up by beginning your work and don't worry whether what you're doing is "right."

Even when we have a clear vision of the work we wish to create and a voice willing to give it expression, pulling an idea into concrete reality can be demanding physical and mental work. Though we dream of long stretches of unbroken time to work on our creative dreams and projects, what we often have available to us is short bursts of time. We need to learn to use our bits and pieces of time. We will never have more time than we do right now. Or as I tell myself: write now.

There are benefits to learning to work in whatever time is available. Doing things in steps and stages allows time for us to absorb what we have created. It allows us to step back and look at the whole picture, so our creations can tell us where they would like to go next. When we are willing to enter the process and respond to our creations in this way, integrity and congruence inform our work in a way that is not possible when we simply impose solutions using only left-brain logic and rationality.

A little planning helps us allocate our energy, attention and whatever time we have available to what is most important. It improves our efficiency and keeps us focused on our goals. The number of hours in a day is finite and we need to use time wisely, as we strive to balance our creative tasks with the rest of our lives. Which of our dream projects will we choose to work on now and which will we take on down the road? There is a limit to what we may accomplish in any given time period and it's good to be realistic about the amount of time we have to commit to a project.

Sometimes creative projects take longer than we think they will (or should, my internal critic carps!). The vision of the completed work we see in our minds may look easy to create, so it can be surprising how much time it takes to move from idea to finished work.[1] When I sit down to write, the words don't always flow as smoothly as I would like, and sometimes I have to backtrack. In art, I forget to envision the more mundane tasks such as mixing paint or allowing drying time as part of my process, and I often struggle to recognize them as legitimate creative work and necessary steps. Many times I have ruined a strong beginning by not allowing time for the piece to dry. Sometimes, just when things are going well creatively, a household crisis arises and I have to put my creative work on hold.

The good news is that we can accomplish the work we dream of one step at a time. It's amazing what can be accomplished in ten minutes of focused creative work. Those ten-minute periods over the course of a week or month can be enough to complete a dream project. I have built portfolios of work using ten-minute blocks of time over the course of a year. The critical step is to ensure we utilize that ten minutes—and a little planning will help.

A quick and simple method of planning is to make a list. There is a truism in life that it doesn't matter where we start, what matters is that we start. Making a list is a way of doing that: we pick an item and jot it down. Doing so begins the process of going where we wish to go. Some dreams will take years to achieve. Making a list of them helps us keep our dreams in our line of vision and work towards them. Even taking one step at a time means we stand a good chance of bringing them to fruition.

I write lists of tasks on little coloured slips of paper and stick them all over the place: on my dining room table, the sides of my computer, in my day planner…I am always revising my lists, crossing things off and adding new ones. I often cross-reference my list with dates in my calendar. This can take as little as five minutes, first thing in the morning or at the end of the day.

I have found list-making to be a powerful planning tool, one which I have used to identify my creative priorities. To begin, I asked myself two questions: "Which are the projects that mean the most… the ones I most wish to accomplish? Which would I most regret leaving unfinished?" My answers determine what goes at the top of the list. Here is one of my earliest lists.

First Dream List:
- Great Art, Calligraphy and Photo opportunities and instruction
- Perfect photo and computer equipment
- A powerful computer and accessories that work perfectly including but not limited to Internet, tablet, photo programs and scanner
- Perfect shelving-Prosperity from a variety of sources and investments
- Travel opportunities
- Visits with family and friends
- Exercise and fitness

(Oops! I see I've used the word "perfect" in the above list. What can I say? It takes vigilance to root out old habits.)

When I created that list, I hadn't done enough visual art or photography to know what skills I needed to develop or what equipment to acquire. I couldn't articulate the specifics of what I needed. I thought that if I could take some classes and observe other artists at work, I would be able to figure out what to do next. That is why "opportunities and instruction" are at the top of this list. At the same time, I was aware my computer was not powerful enough to handle working with photographs. I didn't know what type of computer or camera I needed. I required information so I could make these purchases. I was living in an apartment and didn't have enough storage space for a lot of equipment so shelving was on the list. And money was on my list because I knew I had to work out a budget to make these purchases. I didn't realize it at the time, but I was beginning to re-think all aspects of my life.

To begin, I took a photography class at the local library and through it I discovered a good camera store and a camera club. I learned basic camera skills, joined the club, met other photographers and viewed their work. I discovered the world of macro photography and started hanging out at the camera store, where the staff mentored me about equipment. I also took a calligraphy class, began to learn those skills, joined an art group and discovered acrylic paint. Such is the domino effect of lists— one thing leads to another. That is the flow of life and the creative process. I found my new activities absorbing and I was happy, albeit there was a huge learning curve for me that year. The focus of my life had shifted and now I had to re-jig my routines to free up the time I was spending at classes and clubs in addition to my job.

The following year I had a better sense of the direction I wished to pursue and how to proceed. I began to dream of having room to work at home, so I expanded my list to include three categories. The big purchases were still on the list. I was still learning my way around equipment and wasn't ready to make the purchases that first year. And I was still saving money.

Second Dream List:

- Things I'd like to do: attend art classes and art conferences

- Things I'd like to have: excellent photo/computer equipment; a powerful computer and accessories that work including but not limited to Internet, tablet, photo programs and scanner; suitable shelving; my own home(?)

- Places I'd like to go: art classes and retreats; ocean (Caribbean in the winter?) New York City; New Mexico.

Some of the items on these lists have a question mark beside them. For example, I thought it would be fun to take photos while travelling, but I didn't really have the money to do it at that point. It's a dream I have since accomplished. When I created this second list, the notion of owning my own home was just surfacing in my consciousness. It was something I thought I'd like to do but I didn't see it as being immediately achievable. It took six years before I purchased my dream home, but it has happened and I am now living here. I have my camera and computer equipment all properly stored. And it wasn't necessary to break the bank to do any of it.

Writing the lists and doing the tasks on them has carried me a long way creatively. As I write this, I have completed many, but not all of the tasks on my most recent lists. I have purchased my own home and had it renovated slightly to provide shelving and storage. I then purchased a great computer. I took early retirement so the pace and rhythm of my life are more under my control. This in turn allowed me to spend more time with my family and friends and to take advantage of some of the international conferences and art workshops I dreamed about for so long. I spent a week one winter on a beach by the ocean in the Caribbean.

These things, which began as dreams, took time, energy and work to achieve. They have altered the shape of my life. They have helped me grow personally and professionally in ways I have dreamed. This progress in my life has also affirmed for me the value and power of articulating dreams and keeping lists where we can see them regularly so we are reminded of what matters to us and can measure our progress. My creative work, my mentorship practice and my journal writing have taught me that it can take work to stay organized and focused on creative goals and to make the best use of my time.

These days my planning process is more comprehensive because I have three creative fields in which I wish to make progress, (art, photography and writing). Since I also teach each of them, juggling my professional obligations with time for my creative work, not to mention the rest of my life, has proven challenging. I found I needed to get clear about my commitment to my personal creative work and put it on my calendar to ensure it got done, as it seemed to be the first thing sacrificed when the rest of my life came calling.

After using lists for a couple of years, I realized I had a lot more I wanted to accomplish and found myself getting anxious about when I was going to get around to everything. At this point, I happened to come across a corporate strategic planning document at work,[2] and realized it would be simple to apply the same type of planning to my individual creative work. A strategic plan for the year, or even five years ahead, is reflective, proactive and visionary. It looks at where we are now in life, articulates where we think we need to go and sets out strategies to get us moving in the right direction. It's a kind of map, embodying our dreams and giving them a time line, transforming them into achievable goals to increase our creativity and to provide an overall sense of direction.

Strategic planning is useful whether creative projects are great or small. Whatever the creative project, it is helpful to articulate goals and the process we will use to achieve the goals—both short and long-term. Planning the steps familiarizes us with the process and helps us articulate the tasks. We can also plan individual sessions of creative work. Planning saves time and energy by keeping us focused when the creative process itself and the demands of our lives push us off course.

My strategic planning arises from my journal work. Each morning, and sometimes in the evening, I do some reflective journal writing where I record my thoughts about what I am working on and how it's going. At the end of the month, I make a summary page for that month by highlighting and tracking my accomplishments. This tracking allows me to see my progress and grapple with issues that have arisen. At this point, I can accommodate shifts in direction, incorporate new deadlines and projects and update my plan for projects in which I'm already engaged. This process keeps me focused, and moving forward.

In December of each year, I review the monthly summaries and create a Strategic Plan for the coming year. I outline the projects I wish to accomplish, a process that works much better than making New Year's resolutions, because everything on my list has grown out of my work of the previous year. I review my strategic plan every few months and update it as needed.

As it turns out, planning my work for a year at a time is simpler than I expected. I just look at my list of priorities and flip through my journal writing from the past year. Then I think about the work I want to achieve. I identify what I want to work on immediately and where I think I want to go next. Then I make a more comprehensive list with more categories. I did this at the end of the year and this plan took the place of any New Year's resolutions. A birthday is also a good time to make plans.

Here is what my first Strategic Plan looked like:

Year One Creative Work Plan

Photography
- Create 3 photo books: The Red Shoes; Dot Com Dysfunction; Delicacy

- Begin work on subsequent books… Christmas, Best of, Flowers, Stairs etc.

- Future plan:
  - ~ Work on special techniques for photography… montages; multiple exposures.
  - ~ Submit photos for exhibitions and publishing

Art
- Continue journal work
- Future plan:
    - ~ Create cards, articles and examples of calligraphic/ decorated papers
    - ~ Create canvas/material paint work… hangings… abstract quilting(?)
    - ~ Create large-scale calligraphic/weaving/ journal pieces
    - ~ Submit for exhibition/sales/publishing
    - ~ Present: reclaim framed photos and take new work into the Working Centre.

Writing
- Send poems to magazines; attend writers' club
- Future plan: Edit book of poems already written for publication
    - ~ Create new poems
    - ~ Write Creativity Guide
    - ~ Write novel
    - ~ Art

Business
- Future plan
    - ~ Establish Creative Arts consultancy
    - ~ Go Digital: Purchase new computer, scanner, printer, Digital Camera. Learn to use this new equipment effectively to facilitate my creative work.

It is interesting to look back on this plan now and see what happened. That year, I did create my three photo books. The following year, I set up my Creativity Coaching business.[3] However, I changed directions dramatically with my writing when I realized I had the material for this book already waiting for me on my computer desktop. I gave up writing poetry altogether as

I no longer had the time for it. And a number of other project possibilities, such as a novel, got put on hold as I began writing this book. There is only one of me and there may well be a lifetime's worth of work and direction in this plan. That is why it is so important to prioritize creative projects. If we aren't going to be able to do them all, we must choose the ones we really want to accomplish and focus on them.

There are no dates beside the items on my list. I didn't really know how long the things on my list would take and since it was my choice to work on them, I had no specific deadlines. Some of the items were thoughts for the future. With creative work, I find I need a plan that has some flexibility, so that I can change directions once I've accomplished some of my goals and discarded others. I'm usually self-disciplined enough to work without specific dates in mind, unless I have to meet a deadline of some sort. Then I put them in.

We know ourselves best. If we have deadlines, we incorporate them and allow some breathing space or wiggle room in case something comes up. If we work best by specifying dates, we do so. We can revise our timelines down the road, if necessary.

Here is another of the paradoxes of creative life. It helps to keep us focused if we have an overall plan, yet the work that happens on any given day can be tricky to mandate. In creative work, the process is one of discovery, unique to ourselves and the specific project. We may wander off course in interesting directions. We may find that we are working backwards. When that happens, we trust our instincts, follow them, allow them to guide us. For example, as we begin our creative journey with a specific project in mind, we might do a little reading or research to see what ideas are already out there. We might go to the library or the bookstore to see what's available… and discover a world we didn't know existed. And that world will somehow figure into our completed project. If we need particular tools, we might go shopping and find all kinds of other promising tools. So our plan needs to incorporate room for lateral shifts and creative detours in the framework of linear progress. Just remember that following endless tangents is another way to keep ourselves distracted from doing our work.

Once my strategic plan is in place, I create a monthly calendar listing obligations and events by date. I keep this calendar on my computer desktop and revise it throughout the month as necessary. And because I am visual, I keep three paper calendars... one in my office, one in my kitchen, and one in my purse, which I cross-reference and update regularly. Most days I create a To Do list for the day. This strategy keeps me on track and keeps me from forgetting things I want to accomplish. Crossing things off my To Do lists, tearing them up and creating new ones gives me great satisfaction. It confirms I am making progress. When I am engaged in a creative process like writing a book where I don't necessarily see much progress some days, or even weeks, despite my best efforts, this visual reminder can be enough to keep me going.

Sometimes, the decision about which project I will work on is pragmatic. While I was working on the revisions for this book, I was also trying to finish up an art quilt and do some new art pieces. I realized the only way I could really make progress was to focus on my book and one other project. Otherwise, my time and energy became too fragmented. Since I wished to exhibit the art quilt in a show that was a couple of months away, and I really wanted to get that project finished, that's what I decided to work on. I was much more peaceful once I'd made that decision, and I began to see progress in my work. When we hold a specific creative goal in mind, whether it's a big one such as writing a book or creating a body of art work, or a smaller one such as completing an individual project, we can determine what steps to take, what skills we must have and what habits we need to develop. We can break the project down into manageable tasks. Doing so gives us a better sense of what the work is that we have to accomplish to pull a particular dream into concrete form. This kind of thinking and planning provides a framework within which to be creative.

For example, my friend, Jayne, is passionate about baking. She loves the look of fancy, decorated cakes and dreams of being able to create them. Eventually, she'd like to design her own cakes and sell them through her own catering company. She realizes she has many skills to master on the way to achieving her dream, so for the moment, her priority is to learn, practice and polish her cake-making and decorating skills. Her dream of owning a catering company is one she will work towards over time as she does this.

Jayne's list looks like this:

- Experiment and develop a classic butter cream frosting and cupcake recipe and try them out on family and friends. (This is an easy first step for her. She knows how to go about it and it doesn't require any new equipment or materials. She also knows her family and friends will appreciate her efforts. Her children might even be able to help her here and there.)

- Enroll in a class that teaches how to work with rolled fondant and design fancy cakes.

- Build her own reference library of recipes and materials related to her dream by collecting inspiring photos, recipes to try, reference books and magazines and articles about people already working in her field.

- Visit a cake store(s) in town and talk with the staff to find a (business) mentor.

By identifying the steps we have to take, the skills we need to learn and the habits we need to foster, we are essentially making an action plan that shows us where to begin and how to accomplish our creative dreams. In the example above, Jayne is a single mother who has a full time career and two daughters, 8 and 10. Her girls have busy lives and she has to take into account their schedules when she's planning her own. In looking over the calendar for the week, she sees they have some time free Sunday afternoon, so she and the girls will do some baking. She had already planned to take them to the library during the week, and while she's there, she will browse through recipe books and magazines. On one of her lunch hours or coffee breaks, she will research what classes are available in her area and get the registration information. That will be an excellent accomplishment for the week.

Once we've identified our goal(s), we require the self-discipline to take that first step. The only answer to the question, "How to begin a creative project?" is "Just do it." If we wait for the right time, proper equipment, brilliant inspiration, knowledge to do it correctly, our work will not get done. There is only now and we will never have a better opportunity than we do—right now—so we might as well get to it. We eliminate distractions, putting away the electronic devices, turning off the phone, ignoring e-mails and housework. We begin.[4] We get out the cook book, pots and pans, or our paints. We boot up the computer and put some words on the page. We start to work without really thinking a lot about it. That may be the most important step we'll take in the process. It's how we turn on the creative tap.

Everything flows from that first step. Until we pick up the brush and start to paint, until we sit down to write, we may not know exactly what it is we want to accomplish or what we need to know to do it. When I began photography, I just took my camera and went out looking for things to shoot. I went for half an hour at a time. I learned not to think too much about it, or worry about how good the photos were. Beginning is that simple. You have to take the risk, get out your equipment, go where you need to go, and get started. One step at a time is all you need to take. But you have to take it. This is the step where you really need a little burst of energy, and enough self-discipline to overcome inertia and procrastination. I can't emphasize that enough. There is no magic bullet. There is just getting on with it.

It could be that the work from our first session is good and we will refer to it or use it in our next session. It's also possible that we won't like what seems to have happened. And sometimes we like it later. Doesn't matter. What matters is that we made a start and tried things out. Taking physical steps to do the work, even when we aren't sure what we are doing comes first. Ideas follow. It's backwards and counter-intuitive, but that seems to be how creativity works.

Trial and error are as much a part of the planning process as making lists and taking steps. While some creative types seem to be able to plan chapter by chapter, or stroke by stroke so to speak, many of us, especially those of us who work intuitively, don't know exactly what our book or painting or cake will look like until it's completed. We work "backwards," and only find what we set out to create when we reach the end point of our process. Our intuitive guidance, a process that is often less than completely conscious, steers us in the right direction one hint at a time: "Hmm… I might have to sand down that rough spot," we will think to ourselves, or "That sentence will work better at the end of this paragraph." Strange as it is, this process can be trusted to take us where we need to go, even though the exact form our creation will take may not be clear to us for a while.

As we seek to accomplish our goals, some tasks might prove difficult. We might experience being out of the comfort of our routines and we might struggle with issues of control and surrender. That is the nature of creative work. The key is to keep our goals in mind. As our creation emerges, we might give our heads a shake and say, "Well if I'd known that's where I was going, I'd have done it differently." But I couldn't have because I didn't know ahead of time. It had to emerge through process and actions. That is why there can be no "one size fits all" linear plan for creative work. When I look at my process, a lot of times it's a matter of doing the step that comes next.

Here is an example of this process from the journal I have kept as I have been writing this book:

> Monday, the first week after New Year's. The day I marked to get back to my manuscript. I'm finding it tough to get going again after a three-week break, especially to take on the writing of a new chapter. I have a topic: goal setting and

strategic planning, but that's all. Once again I fear I have nothing to say and don't know how to begin.

It's been tough sitting down at the computer and bringing up the manuscript. I realize after a quick glance at it, that I am going to have to go back and read the whole thing from the beginning as I've lost my sense of what I'm trying to say and what I've already said. At the moment, this task (writing this book) feels way too big for me. I'm overwhelmed again. I go back to my original idea manuscript, find a small section with some ideas about goals and plans. Copy and paste it into the document called Chapter 9 as a place to start.

I take my copy of the manuscript as it exists thus far downstairs and read through it, to refresh my mind about it. See places where it needs some editing… the beginning chapters don't have any headings, which would help the reader—and writer! I see there are no exercises in the first chapters, so the format is different than the later chapters. I missed that when I was editing previously. The three-week break helped me to see with fresh eyes. My first task is to fix the problems that already exist.

Holding to a course and accomplishing a goal is a big thing in life, and a major source of self-esteem. Working on something as big as a book, I learned to take satisfaction in the process, because the thing took so darned long to create. Deferred gratification is not an easy concept in this world of "instant," but in the end, our plan becomes a guide and affirms our process as we work to pull something new into existence.

Once you've determined your goal and made the list of steps to make it happen, consider making a contract to keep yourself on track. A contract is a visual and graphic reminder of a promise made to ourselves. I first came across the idea of making contracts for individual purposes as a vice principal in my work with high school students who had behaviours they wished to change.[5]

I have found contracts very helpful in my own creative work. For three years, I told myself I wanted to get my book written. Yet, so often I allowed myself to be distracted from it by other things. The book wasn't getting written and I wasn't happy with myself. Recognizing the source of my unhappiness, I created a contract with myself to finish my book. At the same time, I felt I was not on the right track with my artwork: I said I wanted to use brilliantly intense colour, yet I wasn't doing so. The contract I made honours these two desires and looked like this:

> **For the next three months:**
> I will write my book and finish it this coming spring. I will experiment with strong use of colour, texture, depth and visual interest in my art.I will take good care of myself in that time and keep distractions to a minimum.
>
> Date............. Signature................................

This contract covers a specific time period. Three months is not a long time and I felt I could live my promise to myself for that long. If I wanted to renew it at the end of three months I could. An interesting thing happened once I had the contract written and printed out. I felt better: like I had got my priorities straight and made a commitment to myself. The contract provided a kind of shield between me and the rest of the world, giving me permission to guard my creative energies and use them for the things that are important to me. It offered protection against those distractions I am so prone to and kept me focused on priorities in my creative work. Reviewing it daily reminded me to stay on my path, to stay true and say "Yes" to myself. In fact, I was so happy with the contract I renewed it at the end of three months. And kept doing so through the year it took me to finish the first draft of my book. In that time I grew comfortable with my writing and art routines. I was making better use of my time and progress in my creative work.

The types of planning in this chapter keep us on track creatively. We are willing to allocate time to our creative work and we are willing to complete it one step at a time. We make a plan and we stick to it, revising as necessary because we know that to be afraid of our creative work and to avoid it, is to be afraid of ourselves and to settle for less than who we can be. We know that when we say we are going to do something and don't follow through, we are breaking a promise to ourselves, and creating a gap in our internal authenticity. We know that emergencies will arise and have to be dealt with. We deal with them and then get right back to our plan. We will hold to our plan and build creative energy that sustains us for however long it takes to complete our project. Doing this work, we affirm ourselves and create with confidence.

Whether we are just beginning our own creative work, are already well-established in it or wish to change directions in life, the kind of planning discussed above, even in its simplest form, is invaluable because it helps us get organized and stay on track even when there is a lot to balance in our lives. It defines a clear and distinct place in our schedules for our creative work, even makes a date for it on the calendar. Making ourselves and our work a priority gives us a head start at getting our projects completed, and gives us the satisfaction of owning our creative process.

Meeting the challenges of the creative process as we move from dreams to goals, priorities, tasks and completed projects is the journey into wholeness. There is a Buddhist saying that the most beautiful lotus grows in the deepest mud. Whatever the circumstances, no matter how deep the mud, if we nurture it, the lotus will bloom. How we meet the challenges, overcome obstacles that present themselves along the way and integrate them into our work—that is the sound of a particular voice articulating and giving concrete form to a dream.

Exercise #1 Project Priority

a) Identify the creative project(s) you'd most like to complete in the coming months. For some of us, there can be an advantage to having more than one project on the go. That way, when one needs some incubation time, you can work on another. However, some of us get overwhelmed if we try too many things at once. In that case, choose one and work on it. You know yourself best.

b) If you can't decide between a couple of projects and have the time and desire for only one, try this. For each project, draw two columns on a piece of blank paper. Make a heading at the top of the first column indicating what interests you and what you stand to gain by completing the project. At the top of the second, make a heading that indicates the problems and drawbacks of the project. Ask yourself what you have to lose by taking it on. When done, compare the two pages. Evaluate which column is longer, has more weight. According to your lists, which project interests and offers you the most?

Exercise #2 Identifying Steps and Tasks to Complete the Project

a) On a blank sheet of paper, put a heading that identifies your dream or goal from #1 above. List the steps you must take to make immediate progress. Don't worry too much at this point about accuracy or getting the steps in the right order. Just mark down everything that comes to mind that you will need to do. Sometimes your list will be short and sweet and sometimes writing one step down will prompt you to think of another. Allow some free flow to the process.

b) Are there skills you need to learn or acquire in order to complete this project? What are they? List them.

c) Are there habits you need to develop to facilitate your work? What are they? List them. What steps will you take to develop them?

d) Are there materials you need to buy or borrow?

e) Do you need some assistance with this project? Where can you get it?

f) Do you need to do some research?

Exercise #3 Prioritize the Tasks

a) Once you have your comprehensive list, prioritize the tasks according to what needs to be done first.

b) Decide which of the steps in your plan you will work on this week. Get out your calendar and mark each step on a day of the week.

c) Make any necessary appointments. You can do this week by week, or you can work ahead a month at a time. Keep in mind you may have to revise your list and dates as you work.

Exercise #4 Creative Work Contract

Make a contract for yourself and your creative project.

Exercise #5 Doing the Work

On the day you have marked on your calendar, get where you need to be (office, kitchen, studio...) and do the work. Don't wait for inspiration or a "good idea" to show up before you begin.

Exercise #6 Cues For Staying on Track

a) Post visual reminders (Post-its, calendars, to-do lists) and consult them regularly (daily, weekly) to keep yourself on track.

b) Cross each step off your To Do list as you accomplish it.

c) Acknowledge and celebrate your accomplishment(s) as they happen.

d) Update and revise your lists as you accomplish the tasks.

Exercise #7 Strategic and Longer-term Planning

Looking ahead, make a strategic plan for your creative work, prioritizing the things you'd like to accomplish in the coming weeks, months, years. You can use the list(s) you created in Chapter 6 as a basis for your plan, or you can evolve a plan through daily journal work.

NINE

Ascending the Curve

Creatively speaking, the shortest distance between two points—where we are now and where we want to go—is not always a straight line. However confident we are, no matter how well we plan, as we work there will be problems to solve and obstacles to overcome. We may find ourselves getting muddled about what to do or where to go next. That is the nature of the work, so it's helpful to be prepared with some strategies when this happens. The places where we are stuck can absorb a lot of our energy if we let them. If we've made a start and find ourselves stumped about what to do next, the good news is there's often more than one way to move forward.

Breaking big projects down into smaller tasks, listing and prioritizing them gives us a game plan that makes the project easier to tackle. It also keeps us from feeling overwhelmed. When I decided to create my first (non-digital) books of photo essays, I broke the process down into the following steps:

- buy black photo albums
- get prints developed from my slides
- pick up prints and review for quality
- type up text; create text pages
- print pages on laser printer for durability

- create master text page to ensure uniform size
- cut to fit on black album pages
- insert photos using double-sided tape

If I'd been under a deadline to create these books, I'd have assigned dates to each step, so that I finished in good time.

Once the first three books were completed, I liked the results so much that I created a series of fifteen photo essay books on different themes using this process. I discovered the books made a kind of portfolio of my work, showcasing it and making it very portable, easy to show to others. This is the kind of experience that has taught me to trust my process: when I make the leap of faith, the work I do will produce beautiful, interesting, and useful results.

These days it's possible to create such books on-line. The tasks are digitized, and the planning process has to be adapted accordingly. Whatever the creative work, showcase it well.

Sometimes we can solve a problem by asking the right question. When I was trying to sort out my confusion about this particular chapter, I asked myself what information needed to come after what I had written in Chapter Eight. I realized I needed to write about the next step…overcoming the obstacles that inevitably surface during the creative process. I felt a bit stuck, as you can see from the following journal entry:

Tues. Jan 8

Is the material in this chapter in the wrong place? Should it be Chapter 4 rather than Chapter 10? After the chapter on dreams… taking your dreams and making them a reality? Looks like I'll be restructuring the book again. How confusing!

I had to use a couple of strategies to help me move forward: decided to double-space and format the material so it looks better and gives me a sense of progress even if none of the material is very useful. I now have 12 pages of this chapter, which makes me feel so much better! I know how to edit material already on the page, even if writing and creating anything still feels beyond me. And maybe that's enough for today... maybe inspiration will come as I begin to work with what's there. I hope so: fear of creating and the blank page is ever-present.

As I worked, solutions emerged: Hey, the process of just beginning by writing down words and ideas related to my topic on the blank page as a way to start–is working! Went back to my manuscript to take another look after writing this and all of a sudden the beginning started to make sense to me... I could see what the first three exercises need to be... just like that! Congratulations, self! Suddenly, the structure the chapter needed to take had become clear.

It would seem good to have a lot of ideas to work creatively, but having too many flooding the brain all at once can be paralyzing. There are too many places to start and no single clear idea to pursue. This happens frequently to me: I often feel overwhelmed by choices. It helps to release some energy so that the flow becomes manageable, like tapping maple trees in the Spring. There's all that sap running through the trunk, but it drips out of the spigot one drop at a time. Every drop is valued and collected carefully. Ideas are like that: valuable and worth capturing one at a time using the Idea Capture strategy, (Exercise 4, Chapter 4.)

When my brain feels agitated, I try writing out what's on my mind first, and then do a meditation to focus myself on the work I wish to do. Sometimes I take a walk or get some exercise to burn off some excess energy. I tidy up my art space, or finish a project that's already underway. As always, the rule is don't worry about where to begin. Just begin. I've learned that "what to do next" can often be hidden under or behind "what to do now." As we take the first step creatively, the second step reveals itself. The trick is to take one small step to capture and use some of the high-octane energy for the projects that are most important to us.

Being stuck and having no idea how to proceed can be about fear, especially fear of the unknown. Clarissa Pinkola Estes, author of *Women Who Run With the Wolves*, reminds us: "Fear is a poor excuse for not doing the work. We are all afraid. It is nothing new. If you are alive, you are fearful."[1] Starting this book paralyzed me with fear, and fear was a regular companion as I wrote, as was my internal critic. Who was I to think I had anything worthwhile to say or that I was capable of writing a book? I'd never written one before.

One day as I sat down to banish my internal critic for the time being by writing him out in my morning pages, I decided to light some candles for inspiration. One of the candles needed replacing, but it was firmly melted in to the holder. I had to chip it out using a screwdriver and hammer. The message to me was clear: when things get stuck, as they invariably will, look around for the tools to solve the problem. Then take the action necessary to solve it one step at a time. Purging or clearing something in any area of life can be a symbolic act to start a move forward creatively.

Procrastination can keep us stuck and sabotage our creative process, if we let it. This particular energy-draining project-killer can also be about fear. We fear that what we do will not be good enough, let alone perfect. We fear making a mistake, being permanently tied to a wrong choice. One of the good things to know about the creative process is that there are very few "mistakes." There are choices that work and choices that don't work so well. Sometimes the latter can be fixed. Then they become choices that will require additional work.

We can use the tools of our trade to make repairs. In art, that's what paint and gesso are for. When I first began working with art materials, I used the trashcan to solve a lot of problems. I threw out a lot of "failed" paintings before I realized I could salvage the paper by painting over or cutting it into smaller pieces to use elsewhere. Some writers keep an "out-takes" file. Instead of just deleting passages of words that don't work, they cut and paste them into a new document. Sometimes those "out takes" combine into interesting new passages.

The universe is an efficient place: very little is wasted in creative work. The skills we exercise in a project will prove useful elsewhere in our creative work. The work we create and then discard may well have a place in another project. As creative people, we know we learn something from each of our attempts. We refuse to allow procrastination to stymie our learning. We don't allow our family responsibilities or social commitments to be our means of procrastination. We kick our critic to the curb and commit to our creative time. We keep that creative date on our calendar. We say aloud: "I will begin my work in 10 minutes…" and we do. We promise ourselves, "I will work for 30 minutes before I take a break"…and we do. Then we agree to take a break for 15 minutes and we set a timer, returning promptly to our work. We do this because we know we have to supply the effort and self-discipline. That is how our work gets done.

Sometimes the best way past being stuck is to pick up the tools of a project and get working. We articulate creative intention and hold it firmly in place. We persist. Then we write, paint, or hammer out our "stuckness." We don't worry what it looks like. We just do it. Sometimes, energy and ideas begin to flow as we work, not before. I keep this famous poem by Johan Wolfgang Goethe on a bulletin board in my studio as a reminder:

> Lose the day loitering, 'twill be the same story
> Tomorrow, and the next more dilatory,
> For indecision brings its own delays,
> And days are lost lamenting o'er lost days.
> Are you in earnest? Seize this very minute!
> What you can do, or think you can, begin it!
> Only engage, and then the mind grows heated;
> Begin it and the work will be completed. [2]

Creatively, we can get stuck if we are trying to move too quickly or accomplish too much too fast. We like instant gratification and in our culture we admire and reward those who are driven to succeed. But equating speed and accomplishment can drive us to multi-tasking distraction. We scramble to get everything done and our blood pressure rises accordingly. We judge ourselves harshly when we don't succeed. This is fertile ground for my critic who bullies me if I let him, saying things like: "You need to get this done. Now!" and "If you don't work fast, it won't get done!" and "Your time is limited; use it or lose it!"

When this happens, I have to step back and ask: what is it I'm afraid will happen if I don't accomplish this now...or ever? What is it I really wish to accomplish? What am I afraid of? Usually, I find I'm afraid of failure, or of not being good enough, complicated by the fact that I have a lot of ideas, skills and abilities clamouring to be used. But here's my truth: my work is better when I'm in my creative zone. I can usually get there by slowing down, immersing myself in my work, completing one task at a time and losing my awareness of time. I have one small human body to accomplish my creative work. If I burn myself out multi-tasking, none of it will get done.

We may get stuck if our ideas need more time to grow and bloom. Gestation requires patience. Allow it. I work in several creative spheres so if one is not going well, I can work in another. Within each sphere I often have a couple of projects I'm working on, so when one needs drying or developing time I work on another one. I find this strategy extremely helpful. My pieces get the time they need to set and I am able to get on with my work. Sometimes I will do household tasks that require my attention or go for a walk in these moments. I do whatever works and come back to the work later. The time away can be just enough of a break to incubate ideas.

Sometimes, our process may take us to a nice-looking dead end. We know intuitively we aren't finished, but we seem to have run out of options. When this happens, we have to set the piece aside for a time or be willing to go into the problem and risk wrecking what we've already created. Stephen King has a passage in his book, *A Memoir of the Craft On Writing*, where he says:

> *...let me reiterate that it's all on the table, all up for grabs. Isn't that an intoxicating thought? I think it is. Try any goddam thing you like, no matter how boringly normal or outrageous. If it works, fine. If it doesn't, toss it. Toss it even if you love it. Sir Arthur Quiller Couch once said, "Murder your darlings," and he was right.*[3]

To keep building or moving forward, we have to risk what we've already created. This advice holds true in all creative work. To get movement in a painting, we may have to paint a slash of blue over those beautiful yellows. I've just thrown out a stack of failed prints that have been haunting my studio for a couple of years because I thought it would be a waste of paper to get rid of them. I planned to cut them up and use them in collage, but I never seemed to get around to it. The truth is these prints didn't excite me and I couldn't see a way to make them better. I got tired of being haunted by work I'm never going to improve or finish. Better just to admit that and move on.

In photography, I've thrown out or deleted unpromising photos and re-photographed the same image countless times to get one that looks right. This is a place in the creative process where risk-taking and courage matter. I've scrapped page after page in this book. Many times, I've been discouraged by my lack of progress, confused about the structure of this book and the chapters in it. But I've never lost sight of my overall goal: to write a book about creativity that will spell out what worked for me that might help others on their creative journey.

When we discard creative work that doesn't "work," it's easy to feel we've wasted our time and energy. It may look like failure according to the old way of seeing. We have to remind ourselves that solutions to problems arrive in their own time: quickly or slowly, whole and fully formed or just as tentative glimpses. It can take years for solutions to emerge for some projects, and there may be skills we have to learn before we know how to complete our work. Sometimes, time runs out on a project before we feel satisfied that we resolved it. It's comforting to know that even the great Leonardo DaVinci wrestled with this issue. He once remarked, "Art is never finished—only abandoned."[4]

When we get to a difficult place where things don't seem to be going well, it's important to stay with the process and work through it as best we can. We may have to walk away more than once. Experience with the struggle over time teaches us that solutions emerge eventually, though they may not be the ones we were anticipating. The tide of ideas is infinite, as is the sea they come from. As with the sea, there is an ebb and flow. We will discover the rhythm of our ideas as we work with them.

The key is to keep our goals in mind. If we are patient and persist, though it may take longer than we expected to finish a project, we will eventually get there. Deferred gratification is not an easy concept in this world of 'instant.' Staying with the struggle is one of the ways we gain faith and confidence in our process. We build self-esteem as we hold to a course, overcoming obstacles on the way to accomplishing our goals, and the creative process offers a safe place to do this. Simply affirm: "I am good enough. I do enough. I approve of myself. I am talented, accomplished and creative. I support myself fully and so does the universe."

Another strategy I use when I get stuck or my energy is running low, is to show and/or tell about whatever I have been working on to a trusted other. There is value in having the process witnessed, and there are things for all of us to learn from one another about the process. We pick up tips that are integral to our work. A group, or a circle of friends who work creatively can become a 'tribe' and source of support. Such a group can provide a shared, sacred space where it's okay to experiment and push the envelope (and that may involve risk and failed attempts as part of the process). A group can re-energize us and help us gain clarity when we are struggling. It can support, affirm and provide encouragement that others close to us may not be able to. It can also provide some of that so-valuable group energy that is greater than any one of us possesses individually. The wisdom of the group can inspire all participants and we need to pay attention when we feel inspired. Those impulses and glimmers of ideas can be fleeting, so we need to capture them as they arise.

I belong to such a group; we call it the Tuesday Art Group. There are five of us who met when we took art classes at a local art school. We get together at the home of the woman who has the largest studio space. Since we work in different media, we spend the morning working on our own projects. Then we break for lunch and share the results of our labours. This group has helped each of us stretch and grow our creative abilities and solve problems. Along the way, one of us had the glimmer of an idea to take part in the local studio tour. As a result, we have banded together and added our venue to the tour, providing ourselves with a showcase for our work. This group has proven instrumental in creative growth for all of us. It can be hard to find congenial people in your area,but it is possible to search on-line for a cyber-tribe or start one.

Sometimes, problems get solved by happy accidents and messages from the Universe. Jung liked to call this happenchance "synchronicity."[5] When I was trying to decide what kind of computer and software would best support my photography, I needed a specific kind of assistance. My decision depended partly on cost, as I was also thinking about buying a house. Sitting down with a mortgage advisor helped me to understand my own finances well enough to see solutions. Together we developed a plan that granted me approval for a mortgage with enough money left over to buy a computer. From there it was a short step to calling a real-estate agent. Then a friend showed up who just happened to know something about photography and computers. The information these people provided arrived at the perfect time. All I had to do was pay attention and say, "Thank you!"

I never underestimate the power of strategic bribery to solve problems. When I was writing this book, especially at the beginning when the task seemed overwhelming, I used it to keep myself going (growing!). If I kept to my morning writing schedule, regardless of how easy or difficult the writing proved, I took myself somewhere pleasurable in the afternoon. I really enjoy going out for lunch, and when I was a teacher, I was rarely able to do this. Now that I work at home, it's something I enjoy. When I'm in need of some positive reinforcement, I take myself to one of the little restaurants I've been waiting to try, or I get my hair done.

When none of my strategies work, I know my energy or mood is off. This tells me I'm tired and need to take a longer break. Sometimes, sitting back and doing nothing for a while can be a good strategy.

It's important to acknowledge where we are in our process and recognize the achievement of our goals. When we've broken through a struggle, when we've created something we like, when we've achieved a dream, we deserve to celebrate it. Rituals matter. We need to create some—whatever is fun and appeals to us: breaking out the sparkling wine; inviting people for dinner. The importance of celebration was really brought home to me when I graduated with a Master's degree. I hadn't planned to go to Convocation because I didn't think I cared about receiving the actual diploma, a piece of paper. I'd done the work and that was all that mattered. At the last minute, I was talked into accompanying a friend and received one of the biggest surprises in my life. As I crossed the stage to accept my diploma, I experienced a stellar moment of pure joy in my achievement. Getting that degree took years of hard work and suddenly, I experienced my reward for it. Before crossing that stage, I had no idea how I would feel and nearly missed that profound moment of elation.

Exercise #1 New Approaches

Take a project you are currently working on and try a new approach. Sometimes we can find a solution to a problem by listing seemingly unrelated ideas, a form of brainstorming. See if the items in the list can be prioritized. Sometimes pairing two unlikely ideas can create interesting synergy. If you are writing a comedy or romance, what happens if you introduce a very dark character or event? Play with the ideas and see where they lead. In colour theory it's known that colours on opposite sides of the colour wheel (red and green, yellow and purple, blue and orange) can "pop" each other when placed together or side by side, even though it might seem at first that they don't really work together.

Don't censor any ideas at this stage; just get a flow of energy going. Editing can come later. You may well find more than one right choice or direction or answer to pursue. This brainstorming can lead to a series of pieces: variations on a theme. You can do it on your own or with another person.

Exercise #2 Clear Something

a) Identify an area in your life where you're stuck. Ease the anxiety of being stuck by doing a clearing exercise. What's one step you could take to initiate a clearing process? It can be something simple such as cleaning off your work surface.

b) If you need to deal with the critic at the same time, do so.

c) If you need support, ask for it. Call a friend or other creative person. Get a flow of energy working for you.

Exercise #3 Identifying Fear

a) Does procrastination ever interfere with your creative desires or keep you from your work? Why?

b) Do you have any fears about your creative work or your own capacity for it? If so, write about it in your journal.

c) What advice would you give yourself to handle these fears?

Exercise #4 Refocus and Take a Risk. Tackle a project with which you are unhappy.

a) Ask yourself what your goal is/was with this particular work.

b) Then apply the "What if . . . ?" question to it. (eg. "What if I changed the colour or size?")

c) If you can't bear to throw your work out, set it to one side and make a fresh start in a new direction. Be willing to change the game plan.

d) If you plan to cut up or otherwise alter the work, consider documenting what you've already done (a photocopy, a photograph, a digital snapshot, etc., something you can refer to later) so you don't lose the work altogether.

Exercise #5 Reward Yourself

a) Try this: in your journal or elsewhere, record what you'd like to get done in your project on a particular day.

b) Decide on a reward for doing this and then block out the time period on your calendar. If you do your creative work and then reward yourself, you'll accomplish two things at once in your life and feel great. This works especially well if you have an external deadline to meet.

Exercise #6 Give Yourself a Break.

Sometimes, just sitting still until you are calm is a good creative exercise.

a) Set a time in your day or take ten minutes now to catch up with yourself and all the things you do in your life. Work with the time you have available to you.

b) Sit still with your energy. Note whether you feel calmer afterwards.

Exercise #7 Celebrate This Day.

Carpe Diem. You only get each day once. Enjoy all it has to offer.

a) Pick something you feel good about and celebrate it today.

TEN

Habits of Spirit That Support Creativity

Albert Einstein, the German-born American physicist, who won the Nobel prize for Physics in 1921 for his theory of relativity, felt the most important thing to decide in life is whether we are optimists or pessimists. "There are two ways to live," he wrote, "You can live as if nothing is a miracle; you can live as if everything is a miracle."[1] Optimism, the "inclination to put the most favorable construction upon actions and events or to anticipate the best possible outcome,"[2] is a habit of spirit that supports creative work. It sustains our belief that what we do matters, and it supports our courage to experiment and take risks—to push the envelope and ourselves. It allows us to trust that the opportunities we desire are ever-present, that we will find them and rise to the challenges in our work.

Researcher Dr. Jill Ammon-Wexler[3] offers the following advice on optimism: "Intelligent optimists don't deny problems, they adjust to them while still seeking an opportunity for progress."[4] She goes on to say that optimists know there is at least the beginning of a solution for every problem, and that the search for that solution can be inspirational. According to her, optimists focus on things within their grasp that they can enjoy. They are not afraid of negative thoughts, which they realize offer some protection and help them stay realistic.

Brain research shows we are wired to be optimists. Two areas of the brain, the amygdala, and the rostral anterior cingulate, govern optimism. In a recent study done by American and British researchers, these areas of the brain showed increased activity when participants imagined positive future events. Test results showed subjects usually expected positive events to happen sooner than negative events, and imagined them with greater vividness. Dr. Phelps commented on the study, "Our behavioral results suggest that while the past is constrained, the future is open to interpretation, allowing people to distance themselves from possible negative events and move closer towards positive ones."[5]

This is important to creativity. It means we can influence the future by imagining what we would like to have happen and articulating it in a positive way. A recent Ohio State University study proved that even something as simple as nodding your head serves as "self-validation."[6] The researchers found that nodding your head up and down is, in effect, telling yourself that you have confidence in your own thoughts—whether those thoughts are positive or negative. Shaking your head does the opposite: it gives you less confidence.

It can be a useful creative exercise to check our beliefs. Do we feel optimistic about our creative work at the moment? Do we feel worthy of a healthy creative life? When I work through this exercise, using active reflection in my journal to find out, I usually discover I have more to gain than lose by choosing any given creative action. If there is a problem in a situation, something I need to be cautious about, the writing I do in pessimistic mode helps me to identify it. Writing as an optimist helps me find the solution. The process restores my positive energy.

Creative people have been using self-affirmation for centuries. Consider the following, recorded in Leonardo DaVinci's notebooks, "Obstacles do not bend me" and "I shall continue."[7] They tell us that DaVinci practiced optimism in the face of self-doubt, and that helped him create his legacy. When we decide to begin a creative project, we can affirm for ourselves our goal(s) and process. In the beginning, I needed help creating affirmations, and reminders to choose faith in my own creative abilities and the world at large. I still find the work of such writers as Julia Cameron, Shakti Gawain, Louise Hay, Susan Jeffers, Byron Katie, and Eric Maisel[8] particularly helpful. The first set of affirmations I wrote early in my art career was based on Julia Cameron's "Creative Affirmations" from *The Artist's Way*.[9] At that point I was still skeptical about the process and my own creative abilities, so I appreciated her guidance and incorporated some of her ideas. Like Cameron, I find it easier to remain optimistic when I acknowledge my belief in a higher power, a very creative One. Here is that first set:

- I am an artist.
- I create beautiful art.
- I surrender my old ideas.
- I welcome new and expansive ideas.
- I open myself to creativity in my life.
- My creativity blesses others.
- I believe in a Creator that values me and my creative work.
- My dreams come from that Creator, as does the power to achieve them.

Five years later, I added two more affirmations based on my reading of the works of Carolyn Myss,[10] particularly her idea of the personal honor code:

- I honor the Earth and recognize that all things are one.
- I honor myself.

These two additions remind me to affirm myself as having a place in the whole. I use them to deal with issues in my life and to honor my place in the grand design. The first affirmation reminds me to live simply when it comes to possessions and material things— quite a change from my earlier days as a consummate consumer. It also affirms my interest in creating images that comment on environmental issues. I am still uncovering the implications for an emerging ecological vision. I remain a bit of a mystery, even to myself, and there is always more of "me" to discover. I see that doing the work on myself to unearth my core beliefs is a process that connects me to the grand design.

As I spend time working with my creative process, I find my ability to write affirmations has improved. And they have changed in nature. At the end of each year, rather than compiling a list of New Year's resolutions, I have established a creative ritual of sitting down and revising my affirmations to reflect where I am and where I wish to be. Here is a list of my most recent ones:

- I keep myself centered.

- I respect, love and care for myself.

- I am gentle with myself. I take responsibility for myself.

- I recognize pain and emotion as cues to deal with my own issues.

- I protect myself from stress.

- I respect my body.

- I enjoy vegetables, fruit and grain and limit my sugar-fat-salt intake.

- I husband my resources, keeping my energy flowing in and through myself, using it wisely on the things that matter most to me.

- I do the daily work that keeps me healthy. This includes: exercising; meditating; eating properly; resting; writing and creating.

Through my work with affirmations, I have been surprised to discover how deeply rooted are my beliefs about failure and scarcity, and my impulse to inflict pain on myself. Two experiences in my teenage years shaped my beliefs about failure. The first happened when I was thirteen, and took the exam for the Bronze level Royal Life Saving. I was one of the youngest in that class, and though tall, I was slightly built. One of the tests involved life-saving holds and releases, done in the water with another person, whereby you had to free yourself from someone who acted as if they were drowning.

Sometimes, students in these classes were paired up to practice and demonstrate the skills, but on this day, the examiner told us we had to wrestle with him. He was a strong, heavily muscled man in his mid-20's and I didn't think I would be able to escape from his grasp, though that was required to pass. When it was my turn, we leapt into the water and he grabbed me, wrapping both arms around me tightly and pulling me under water. I struggled but couldn't shake him. When I gave the pre-arranged signal that I needed air, he was supposed to let go, but he didn't respond the first couple of times. When he finally let me up, and I was back on the dock, I was pretty shaken. I had a bloody nose and felt like I had been assaulted. I also failed.

The next lesson of that day came after the exam. My family had been waiting for me to be done, so we could go to the cottage. When I told my father I had failed, he simply commented, "Well, that was a waste of time!" He didn't ask why I failed, and I never told him. I went on to pass the exam the following year under better circumstances. I became a lifeguard and swimming instructor and that was my summer job for several years. Muriel's take on this: "Overcoming this failure was perhaps about saving your own life."

Another experience of failure came two years later when I failed Grade 11 math. The exam was in June and my allergies were bad that day. My mother, thinking to help, gave me an antihistamine to take before I wrote the exam. Unfortunately, most antihistamines put me to sleep, but we didn't know that at the time. Part way through the exam, I couldn't see the paper and I felt myself passing out. I got up, walked into the hall and sat down, leaning against the wall trying to stay upright. The nurse was called, and escorted me to her office. I tried to tell her I couldn't see the numbers on the page but she thought I meant I couldn't do the math (I had gone into this exam with a 70 per cent average.) She insisted I finish the exam. Needless to say, I failed.

I know from my experience as a teacher that these days, the family would produce a medical note and the exam results would be waived. But back then, a doctor's note simply got you admitted to summer school; otherwise I would have had to repeat the year. A summer in summer school certainly felt like punishment for my failure and my father was once again disappointed in me. Though I took math in Grades 12 and 13, I experienced severe test anxiety with every exam, and wanted nothing further to do with math after high school.

What we understand and communicate to each other about failure matters. I carried the sting of these failures with me for decades. I felt not simply that I had failed, but that I was a failure. In both situations, the emphasis was on results. In this mind-set, process becomes, at best, something to be endured; at worst, a form of punishment. There was no discussion or acknowledgment of the difficulties I had encountered, no sense that solutions could be found or that I had learned anything along the way.

I learned to see achievement as a high-pressure pass-fail event, where I was on my own, regardless of the circumstances— that I got one shot at success and I'd better make the most of it, or fail and be punished for failing. I internalized pressure to pass all forms of 'tests' the first time—that is at the root of my destructive perfectionism. Only success garnered approval and I felt I had to excel to feel valued. I derived confidence from being good at achievement and my drive to achieve gave me a sense of purpose and control over my life. I had learned to see life in terms of achievement, or "destination" only. I had lost my youthful optimism about life.

How we frame "success" for ourselves, and each other, also matters. Embedded in our culture is a belief that success is all that matters and the only thing that should be rewarded. It is the basis of the competitive model so deeply engrained in our culture. The shadow side of this belief is that "failure" is a waste of time that should be "punished," as is the idea that wasting time is a "sin." Venetia, a friend of mine who is a published author, tells this story about her struggle. She had written a non-fiction book about a popular, intriguing character in history. Once it was finished, she turned it over to her agent, who loved the book yet was unable to find a publisher for it.

Venetia says, "This failure, I think, incapacitated me. I lost faith in myself as a writer and felt like everything was over for me. What was the point of being a writer if no-one was going to publish my work? And I felt like that for quite a while." It took a couple of years, but her agent eventually found a publisher. Fortunately, Venetia was experienced enough to hang in through this difficult time and moved forward to new projects. Venetia adds she's also had time periods where she's had the urge to create, sat down to write and yet nothing has really come of it. She says, "You have to have faith in your work and find outlets for that creative urge when it happens."

The ritual of the juried show, a process used to create exhibitions of visual art at many galleries, has certainly tested my faith in my work and my view of success on more than one occasion. The juried show is a right-of-passage for visual artists, a way of putting one's work out in the public domain, gaining valuable experience, exposure and acceptance in the art world. I was introduced to it when I joined the Kitchener-Waterloo Society of Artists, which among other roles, acts as a kind of clearing house for juried shows in the region.

The jury process for a show works like this. Visual artists are invited to submit (new) art works to a juror or jury committee, and usually pay a fee per work for the privilege. The more prestigious the show, the higher the per-artwork fee. The money is often used to pay the jurors for their time and to help fund the gallery, money in the arts often being in short supply. Juror(s) usually hold positions in the art establishment of a region as artists with established reputations, or curators who manage galleries, and they hold the power to determine which works will be selected for display in an exhibition. Part of their mandate is to create what they feel is a cohesive show, and they can pick and choose as they see fit.

Artists drop off their work on a certain day and time and usually have to pick it up later that same day if it isn't accepted.

Since you can't know ahead of time whether your work will be accepted or not, you pretty much have to show up to find out. At that point the art-work has usually been assembled into two groups: accepted and rejected work. Collecting your work if it isn't accepted tends to be a very public experience, the equivalent of a creative walk of shame.

These days, because I am more careful where I submit my work, it is usually accepted into a juried show. However, in my early years that wasn't the case. One of the first shows I applied to specified an open call for all types of art-work. I paid fees for two of my multi-media artworks (contemporary canvases that had collage integrating fibre and metal bits). Neither was accepted. In fact, I noticed that all the pieces in the rejected pile were multi-media, and I was left feeling that multi-media work was somehow "less-than." Later, when I toured the show, I was shocked to discover that all the pieces were watercolour. And the juror was a watercolourist. Then I got angry: I felt I had been conned. This was no open-call show. If I'd known that ahead of time, I would have saved my money.

My second experience with rejection from a juried show was similar, though this time digital images had to be submitted on a CD, along with the fee. Again it was an open call, so I submitted an abstract piece that featured strong colour and texture to a prestigious show. I was disappointed to receive a rejection notice until I saw the show. The juror had chosen to go with black and white images. At least this time I was spared the walk of shame since notification was by e-mail.

The jury system, endemic to the world of the arts and a means by which reputations can be made or lost, is problematic. It's a competitive model that pits one artist against another for limited funding and showcase space. Though many of us recognize good work intuitively when we see it, the jury system asks that we compare the work of artists from diverse media backgrounds and make a judgment about what is "best." You may be an outstanding watercolourist and I a brilliant multimedia artist but neither of us is guaranteed entry to any given show. When we ask, "What are the criteria for decision-making?" we find there are no simple answers since, beyond the technical criteria of good work in any medium, the response to art (in any form) is often deeply personal. I imagine that is the reason so many jurors make a decision to go with a theme that ties many of the submitted pieces together. The difficulty for artists is that reputations are often built by being accepted into juried shows, especially the more prestigious ones.

When I was new to exhibiting my work, I thought rejection from a juried show was a reflection on my work . . . that it simply wasn't good enough, had been judged inferior by someone who should know. This was very discouraging. Many years and juried shows later, I see this is not necessarily so. Still I wonder how many young artists or those new to their work may have been discouraged from creating art altogether by similar experiences? It takes mental toughness to survive and thrive in such a system.

The accepted practice that artists fund juried shows from our own pockets whether or not we get accepted into them is also problematic. It can be expensive and a bit of a gamble to enter shows, and getting into a show does not mean your work will sell. There are a few galleries and venues that offer artists the opportunity to show their work at no cost, and some actually pay the artists a hanging fee. Competition for such spots is fierce. Even with lots of experience and some success, (I've been fortunate to land two such shows.) I find it an intimidating and discouraging process.

Some galleries have switched from a jury fee to a hanging fee, whereby only those accepted into a show pay a fee. As the pool of accepted artists is much smaller than the field of applicants, it costs the artist significantly more but at least there's a guarantee of space in the show. At some galleries, for a set fee, you can rent a hook for a specific period of time. However it's done, fair or not, artists usually pay to hang their work in shows. It's a flawed system to be sure and why, these days, some artists decide to skip it altogether, choosing instead to market their work directly on the internet.

Whether we choose to enter our work in competitions or not, there will be times when we feel we have "failed" because our work does not seem to live up to our own expectations, let alone anyone else's. It's easy to judge ourselves harshly, to think we are "wasting" our time and energy. It's a reality of creative work that not everything we produce will be brilliant. There will be false starts and dead ends.[11] We have to be careful to allow for the fits and starts of the creative process as we define for ourselves what constitutes success and a good use of our time. I've had to reframe my beliefs about success and failure, to understand that my "less successful" attempts are essential to my learning and understanding of life. Each attempt leads one step forward regardless of what it looks like, and success ultimately emerges from the sequence of attempts.

Fortunately for us, in creative work, there are often "do-overs" and this is important because so much of what we attempt is trial and error. Whether I like it or not, my best and happiest accomplishments often happen in the fullness of time and will not be rushed. It's okay for me to be who I am and learn as I go.

The sudden and unexpected death of my partner, Greg, shifted my understanding of life. I saw that time is finite for each of us and understood that the ultimate "test" of life is death. Death is where this journey of my life-time leads. Monique LaRue, winner of the Governor General's award for French fiction (2004) says in her 2010 Northrop Frye lecture:

> We could put it this way: everything that we have looked for, searched for, kept or accumulated for ourselves will be mercilessly taken away by death, and everything that we have taken from ourselves to give to others, everything we have wrenched out of our insides, all our lives, will stay behind in the lives of others.[12]

After Greg's death, I began to question how I wished to live and what I wished to leave behind. What was it I really wanted to do with my time and energy? I saw each day as a gift to be honoured, and I wished to live the gift. I shifted my attitude when I understood that to avoid or dismiss process (with all its inherent messiness) as a waste of time is to dismiss much of life. I realized I needed to see living as a cumulative process and appreciate it. Appreciating life means finding the gift in each experience and taking pleasure in the events of our days as we strive to use them as best we can. Exercising our creativity, inviting out of ourselves whatever is there, requires patience and persistence. Each time we take a step in our creative process, we affirm our courage and faith that what we have inside is worthy of expression, that there is value in what we are doing and who we are becoming.

I find I am always in need of re-inspiration as I seek to keep myself optimistic, centred and inspired. I often listen to or read inspirational messages when I am exercising, particularly Susan Jeffers[13], Wayne Dyer[14] and Marianne Williamson[15]. When I need a reminder that life is a gift, I Google Hubble galaxy images,[16] or go outside and look up at the moon and stars. Researchers at the Perimeter Institute for Theoretical Physics in Waterloo, Ontario, where I live, tell us that we are made of stars and we make up less than .03% of the matter of the so-far measured universe.[17] These are all reminders of the mystery and grandeur of the universe I belong to.

Whatever the unresolved or painful issues in our lives, a creative project can bring them to the surface. The process can and will test feelings of competence and confidence, and might leave us tempted to walk away. When we know we need to do something for ourselves, but are afraid to, that is when we have to take the leap of faith into the creative process. Hanging in and developing patience, problem-solving and conflict resolution skills help us to cope with the internal conflict and anxiety that are natural parts of the process. Learning to work with and through the struggle, affirming ourselves as we go, we develop confidence in our skills and abilities.

Over time, the creative process teaches us optimism. We learn there is an integrity and sense to the process that is affirming. We learn more about our path in life, and we begin to understand that uncovering its true shape is a lifetime journey. If we believe in ourselves, are willing to take risks and follow our dreams, we can achieve our goals and produce work that satisfies our soul.

Ellen's Story

Ellen clutches her painting gear to her chest as she walks towards the bus stop. She plans to attend a painting class at a nearby gallery, yet as the bus approaches, she finds herself assailed by doubt. Unable to take the next step forward, she watches as the bus passes by without stopping. She sits down on a nearby bench, angry with herself, and attempts to collect some courage. A second bus goes by. As the third bus approaches, she sends a little prayer skywards, gets up from the bench and walks to the stop. This time, she boards.

I am at my gallery that afternoon, preparing to teach an open-call acrylic class. The start time has passed and no-one has shown, so somewhat defeated, I begin packing up my gear. As I do, a slim, silver-haired woman suddenly appears. She asks if the class is still on.

"Of course!" I reply. "Welcome. Let's begin."

During the class, Ellen tells me about herself and the missed buses. Nervously, she shows me the collection of work she has brought. She tells me of her longing to create beautiful pieces. She fears that at 65, she is long past the age to do it. She is truly surprised when I tell her I think her work is beautiful and that she already has all the talent she needs to realize her dream. I explain that I am a creativity coach, and she asks if I would be willing to work with her. We set a date to meet in my studio the following week.

Within weeks of our meeting, Ellen's twin brother is admitted to hospital. He is terminally ill and dies shortly thereafter. Ellen completes a painting after his death… a dove and a Chinese woman dancing with magnolias… the dancing feet and skirt are very well-executed and the flowers are done primarily in pinks and yellow. Ellen takes this piece and makes it into a card, discovering the usefulness of the color photocopier for her work. The card is for her daughter, whom she hasn't seen for a year. She hopes it will help heal their relationship. She says the dove is about needing spiritual guidance. She feels depressed about her life and paints through her grief, dreaming of gardens.

In November, Ellen designs a Christmas card using one of her paintings. She is amazed to report that her church has purchased a print of this painting and is planning an open house where it will be unveiled. They wish to purchase a second print to give as a gift to the minister, who is leaving. She shows me samples of all the cards she has made of her paintings and they are beautiful. We discuss the different ways she can use her cards, and how to price her work. For the first time in her life, Ellen feels she is having success with her art. She develops a portfolio of her work, gets photos taken of it, prepares an artist's statement and biography, and enters five pieces in a juried show. She receives an invitation to sell cards at a downtown stationery store. She tells me, "A friend of mine has asked to use one of my paintings as a book cover and will pay me for my work!" She is thrilled her work will be published.

Ellen marvels at her "overnight" success, but the truth is she's been working for years to get here. "When we share our work with the public," I tell her, "we 'finish' the level we have been working at and allow ourselves to go forward to a new level."

In February, Ellen brings a self-portrait… her face is shades of black and grey against a multi-colored background… an Edvard Munch-like scream escapes her mouth as she regards her own hands. This piece spoke its title to her: Awakening. It is stark and somber compared to her usual pieces: a breakthrough. Ellen has painted her anger. She takes this drawing and has it made into a valentine for herself.

In April, Ellen arrives holding her copy of the book with her painting on the cover, and also a CD of her own work: concrete evidence of her creative achievement. She keeps two journals now to capture her ideas. Her daughter and her grandson help her plant her backyard garden. Ellen herself lays the flagstones in her garden and shows me the photos.

In June, two of Ellen's pieces are hanging in a juried show, a present for her 66th birthday. Ellen is delighted when I tell her that I am writing her story. She hopes it will inspire others. We both agree it's amazing what can result when we build confidence and provide a concrete plan in support of the creative spark.

Exercise #1 Optimism or Pessimism?

Complete the following exercise with a friend you trust, or in your journal.

a) Are you an optimist or a pessimist? How do you know? For the next week, listen to the comments you say out loud as well as those you say silently in your head. Record them if that is helpful. What beliefs do your thoughts and comments reflect?

b) Ask yourself: Is there something I'm afraid of in my creative work? Listen for and record the answer.

c) Working with what you have written use a "worst-case scenario" to exercise your pessimism imaginatively. What is the worst thing that could happen? And what would you do if that happened? Allow yourself to get dramatic, maybe even ridiculous. Use any creative medium you like to record the scenarios: drawing, painting, sculpting, writing …

d) Now take your work and reframe it optimistically into best-case scenarios.

Exercise #2 Affirmations

a) Create affirmations that support your belief in yourself and your creative work.

b) Generate some project-specific affirmations.

c) Write out your affirmations in your journal or on post-its or type them up on your computer and place them somewhere you will see them daily: your computer desk top, a bulletin board, a studio wall, in your journal, on your bathroom mirror...

d) The next time someone asks, "Is your glass half-full or half-empty?" nod at them, smile and affirm, "My glass is full and my creativity is overflowing. Life is good."

Exercise #3 Reframing Failure

a) Think about a time in your life when you experienced failure. Describe what happened. What resulted from this experience? How did you feel about it at the time? How do you feel about it now? How might your life have been different if you'd succeeded?

b) Looking back now, can you see what you might have learned from the experience? Has it served your creative work in any way?

Exercise #4 Staying Inspired

a) Compile a collection of audio and visual messages, whatever inspires you. Remember, you can also record your own.

b) Tune into them as often as you need to.

ELEVEN

Expanding Creative Capacity

What is important to us creatively and how do we make developing our creativity a priority in our lives? There are strategies we can use to expand our creative capacity. These include paying attention to our intuition, allowing it to guide us, and developing mindfulness practices. Becoming aware of and tapping into our emotions, monitoring what is going on within us and with our creative work and claiming emotional truth are helpful. So is paying attention to body messages. We can also facilitate the development of our creative capacity by studying our own work and learning from that of others. As we do so, we become aware of our creative limitations and push through them wherever possible.

Learning to recognize the voice of our intuition can help us to push our creative boundaries. This voice speaks constantly as impulses guiding us each step of the way in our lives and our creative work. This guidance is surprisingly accurate—like a GPS for our lives and creative paths. To be fully creative, we have to be able to hear the messages and act on them. We literally have to be able to "hear ourselves think" as intuitive messages can be softly spoken and fleeting—easy to confuse with other messages we send ourselves.

It can take detective work to understand intuitive messages. As with dreams, they are not always straightforward. Here is an example. I was driving to work very early one morning, feeling tired. I had not slept well. As I drove away from home, a little message went through my brain telling me to put my glasses on so I could see more clearly. It was tempting to ignore because I couldn't be bothered. But I had to stop for a red light anyway, so I opened my purse to get my glasses. They weren't there. I was stunned for a moment because I always keep them in my purse. For a moment, I couldn't think where they could be. Then I remembered I had taken them out to clean them the night before and realized I must not have put them back.

A day without my glasses when I'm tired is a recipe for a really bad day. I realized I had to return home and get them… a nuisance to be sure, and I grumbled as I was doing it. But that message saved me time, energy and pain: I was still close enough to go back home easily. Chances are good that if I hadn't discovered my glasses were missing until I got to work, I wouldn't have bothered going back to get them. It was just too far away. That little message to put my glasses on was actually an alert to a bigger problem of which I wasn't aware. It probably saved me from a migraine. One of the things I've learned in my creative work is that the universe likes efficiency; those deceptively simple intuitive messages are often designed to exert maximum impact with as little energy as possible.

It's surprising how often such messages can be prompted by other agents. People happen to appear "in time" to remind us of something we need to do. My sister called to say hello and suddenly I remembered both she and my brother had birthdays the following week. The series of red lights I had to stop for on the way to the store kept my speed down so I avoided being caught by the speed trap just ahead. And as I sat at a red light I suddenly remembered that I had forgotten to return some library books I had placed in the car earlier. As we pay attention, we may be surprised at what a communicative universe we inhabit.

Intuition thrives on truth. When I buy clothes that are too small or the wrong colour and style for me, that's a form of falsehood, an indication I have stopped listening to my authentic self and shut down my intuition. Chances are that piece of clothing will get donated to charity sooner rather than later. The more disconnects we have in our lives, the more difficult it is to hear and accept intuitive messages. We can foster truth by being honest with ourselves about who we are. Our intuition will tell us if we allow it to. Over the years, I've learned that though intuitive messages may not make logical sense, acting on them is in my best interest. They often seem less significant than they turn out to be; that's why they're easy to ignore.

According to Mona Lisa Schulz, author of *Awakening Intuition*, intuition is the language of the soul and we all have it.[1] She says intuitive messages can take many forms: mental visual images; auditory thoughts, sounds, or messages; body feelings about ourselves and others.[2] We can miss them altogether if we are in the habit of ignoring messages our minds and bodies send us. It takes some time and effort to learn how our intuition functions, particularly in the beginning if we have been in the habit of dismissing its messages as irrelevant, unnecessary and inconvenient.[3]

Another way we can expand our creative capacity is to improve our level of awareness, or consciousness of what is going on around us as we go about the business of our days. Consciousness, the hallmark of our humanity, incorporates our sense of identity, both personal and collective, our attitudes, beliefs and sensitivities, and internal awareness of the contents of our minds. There is evidence to suggest that there is a spectrum of consciousness and that it develops throughout our lives just as our brains do. Integration of the layers of human consciousness is a lifetime process[4] as is developing our creative capacity. Caroline Myss writes in *The Castle: An Inner Path to God and Your Soul*:

> *The management of one's personal power defines a conscious human being… It's work to get to know yourself and why you are the way you are, and why you love what you do and have the*

passions that you do. You require work. You are not a simple act of creation; you are complex and creative and conscious and unconscious.[5]

The degree of consciousness we experience, how closely we pay attention, changes throughout the day, as most of us are aware. Many things affect our level of consciousness. It's easier to focus when we are rested and interested in what's going on around us. It's more difficult when we are obsessing about time, money or an argument we had with someone earlier in the day. There are all kinds of expressions in our language to denote those moments when we "drift off," "check out," or "wool-gather." Most of us have been jolted back to the present by someone demanding to know if we're "paying attention."

There are many mindfulness practices that help develop greater consciousness. Meditation is one. I first read about meditation more than 20 years ago in a book called *Wherever You Go, There You Are* by Jon Kabat Zinn,[6] who pioneered the stress reduction program at the Massachusetts Institute of Health where he teaches meditation as a strategy. He categorizes meditation as time when we give up the constant doing of things and experience what it is to "be." He says over time this deepens our awareness of who we are. He lists some of his audio works at the end of the book and I ordered one of them. In it, he provides a complete set of instructions, making it clear that there isn't really a "wrong" way to meditate. As a beginner, I found that helpful.

Since then, I have discovered that many creative activities have a meditative aspect to them. The ladies of the medieval courts were practicing meditation while creating their fabulous tapestries. Many slow repetitive actions like knitting and needlework have the calming effect on the brain that is the hallmark of meditation. Madonna Gauding writes in the introduction to her "Meditation for Everyday" cards, "Meditation is simply making a choice to focus your mind on something. In fact, reading a book is a form of meditation, as is watching a movie… "[7]

There are many ways to practice meditation from sitting to standing to walking. For me, simple is best. Often in my practice, I will set a timer for 45 minutes, lie down on my yoga mat and just rest. Sometimes making it through 20 minutes is a challenge. Sometimes I fall asleep and am completely startled when the timer goes off. Personally, I no longer worry about emptying my mind. Most days it just happens on its own. For me, meditation time is as necessary as exercise. In fact, it is a form of exercise that helps me gain control over the activity of my mind.

My creativity loves this resting time: my creative work is always better afterwards. Even a short period of time can be effective. If my creative work is not going well, sometimes I will take a 10 minute time out. I lie down on my yoga mat, relax and let my mind calm down. When I return to my creative work, I find it much easier to focus. Creative ideas often spring spontaneously to mind after a meditation session. If I've pushed myself too hard and am feeling down on myself, meditation restores me, and the calming effect it has on my body and mind often lasts through the next day. As with physical exercise, sometimes I struggle to make myself take the time to do it, especially if my time is feeling squeezed. And sometimes it's tempting to turn on the television and park myself in front of it to relax instead of doing a meditation. But with TV, my mind continues to process input. In meditation, I turn off the stimulation and allow body and brain to rest.

As we improve our level of awareness, important things happen creatively. We achieve greater clarity in our work when we understand who we are and how we think. Literally, we can "see," or understand more clearly what we are trying to create and how to do it better. As we become conscious of what we are trying to accomplish, we develop a clearer sense of direction for our work. We recognize when we are impatient and struggling. We understand the value of the struggle and remind ourselves to stay with it. We apprehend solutions when they present themselves. The struggle is subsumed in the process and energizes our work.

It helps to let go of the rush of days and appreciate the moment, as Canadian singer-songwriter Dale Nikkel sings in his song, "*These Are the Glory Days*." In his introduction to the song, Nikkel tells the story of an epiphany he had one February day in Winnipeg when the temperature was minus 40 F. At the time, he, his wife and two small children were suffering cabin fever cooped up in their small apartment. He happened to glance out the window, saw the snow falling in all its beauty and realized every moment they were experiencing was perfect.[8] Those "glory" days are not back in the past or out there somewhere in the future as we might think. They are here and now, in all their messy, incomplete array. It's up to us to appreciate them and find inspiration in them.

It's a mindfulness practice to become less overwhelmed by everything that goes on in our lives. How important it is to give ourselves time, peace, space and solitude each day to notice what is here now and to hear ourselves think. Instead of cramming more stuff into our minds, we find out what's already there. Mindfulness can take conscious effort when we're caught up in a flurry of activity. Allowing dreaming and drifting time can also be a mindfulness practice.

Another way to foster creative capacity is to push through the gap between what we say and what we do. Any time we say we are going to do something and don't follow through, we are breaking a promise to ourselves, and leaking creative energy. It's easy to become overwhelmed by all the things we have to do in our lives, to become impatient and decide to skip something because there doesn't seem to be enough time. As creative people we need to develop conscious awareness of this tendency. Meditation, even a deep breath and a minute or two to refocus, help us see that we're ok, that keeping a promise to ourselves matters and we can take the time to do so. We can use a contract to close the gap and remind ourselves to honour our promises to ourselves.

We can expand creative capacity by becoming aware of and tapping in to our feelings and emotions. Both are part of consciousness and important to creativity. In creative work, how our work "feels" is critical. If something "feels" right, it may very well be, even if the mind (the critic!) judges it "odd" or "weird." Equally, if it doesn't "feel" right, it may not be, even if it looks like it could be. Either way, in order to develop creativity, we need to integrate feeling and thinking, to work consciously with our thoughts, feelings and emotions, our minds, bodies and brains.

Researchers like Dr. Candace Pert have discovered that what we think and feel is not just a product of our brains; it's also in our bodies. Her work with neuropeptides, neurotransmitters and neuroreceptors throughout the body has confirmed that the body has a "mind" of its own, a system separate from the brain which is capable of directing action and stimulating emotion. Pert refers to this system as the "bodymind"[9] and writes:

> *The new work suggests there are almost infinite pathways for the conscious mind to access—and modify—the unconscious mind and body...*[10]

Though we tend to use the terms "feelings" and "emotions" interchangeably and assume they somehow originate in our heads, the work of Pert and her colleagues suggests the two are different. They categorize emotions as the physical reactions of the body that occur automatically and unconsciously—for example, the pounding heart and sweaty palms when we are afraid. Feelings are what arise after our brains become aware of the physical changes we experience. In other words, they see emotions as physical response and feelings as mental effect.[11]

We may not be able to change our emotions, but we can change how we view and respond to them. So practicing our feeling skills is a legitimate activity. Imagine this scenario: "I'm feeling." becomes a complete sentence, just like "I'm thinking." When we say it, people wait respectfully, according us time to determine our feelings. Are we angry, happy, sad? What is the guidance we are being offered in this situation by our feelings? We learn to appreciate the wisdom residing in our feelings. As Pert writes:

We can no longer think of the emotions as having less validity
than physical, material substance, but instead see them as cellular
signals that are involved in the process of translating information
into physical reality, literally transforming mind into matter.
Emotions are at the nexus between matter and mind, going back
and forth between the two and influencing both.12

We can expand our creative capacity by continuing the journey to the centre of ourselves. As we explore our interests, we learn about and expand our truth. That truth feeds creative energy and manifests in our work. There are many ways to feed ourselves creatively. Realizing we can't take on any more this week and telling people so is a creative act when it makes room for ourselves and our work. Finishing tasks we've been putting off and feeling better when they're completed feeds creative energy. Making a date with ourselves and doing something fun will do it. (See exercise #6 in Chapter 4 for some suggestions.) Signing up for that class that appeals to us can as well. When we create the life that suits us best, we speak our lives in our own authentic voices. We feel "at home" with ourselves and our creative work improves.

We can improve our level of awareness and expand our creative capacity by paying attention to and learning from the work of others, maybe even subscribing to magazines outside our chosen field(s.) Poets might read *Ceramics*, photographers might like *Arts Canada*, designers might like *Art Dolls*. I enjoy *Canadian Gardening* and some of the surface design publications from both the US and Canada.

As we pay attention to the work of others, we may be prompted to see directions to pursue in our own. Certainly this has been helpful for me as I have sought to identify what kind of artist I am and where my particular orientation fits in the world of visual art. I don't paint realistic landscapes or portraits. My work is usually acrylic-based, featuring strong colours and textures, abstract shapes, layers of collage, and bits and pieces of ephemera. More recently, I have switched to hand-painted and sewn fabric mounted over stretchers. Surveying my work, I would say it best fits with contemporary North American abstract-expressionism.

Recently, I had a chance to view the work of some of the Abstract Expressionists in an exhibition on loan to the Art Gallery of Ontario from The Museum of Modern Art (MOMA) in New York City. When I walked into the rooms and saw the art on the walls I immediately felt an affinity with these works. I understood things about them: the challenges in the individual works, what the artists might have been trying to achieve and techniques they may have used to paint them. Further, I saw that sometimes, fields of colour are allowed to stand alone as the focus of the work and it is enough—an acceptance I've struggled with in my own work.

I loved Barnett Newman's comment, posted beside his work, "Abraham" (1949). This piece consists of a single central black vertical stripe against a black background. He wrote: "I thought the title "Abraham" would indicate that this was more than black on black... the terror of it was intense. It took me weeks to arrive at the point where I finally did it." Barnett Newman, in the process of creating a masterpiece, felt terror when confronting his creative work and had to push his own boundaries. How comforting it was for me to recognize that an artist I admire experienced anxiety similar to my own.

When it comes to creative capacity and expression, each of us is both teacher and student. There are things about our creative process only we can know. We discover those things by paying attention as we practice what we do. We learn to work with our intuition. We get better at discerning what we need to know and teaching ourselves the skills to take our work further. We do more with less energy. There is an ease and economy of thought that comes with attention and practice.

As we become more confident, our work improves and it speaks more clearly to other people. Clarity fosters a simplicity and efficiency that can be deceptive to the untrained eye. We take complex ideas and make them accessible and when we get it right, our struggle becomes invisible. We convey our message more efficiently. Others find our work inspiring without necessarily understanding the hard work that has gone into it. When we understand what we have accomplished, we are more able to teach others and help them on their own creative journey.

As our level of awareness increases, we foster connections in the brain and our imaginations have more to work with. We do not have to invent everything from scratch to be original. We find fresh approaches using tools and techniques with which we are already familiar. We produce original new work using in a new way something we already know how to do. Then we dream about what else is possible.

One of the joys of creative work for me has been discovering that my creative capacity is ever-expanding, self-integrating, self-renewing. Though I used to fear running out of creative ideas or not having any in the first place, I've learned that there is an ocean of them at our disposal, and the tide is always flowing. All we have to do is show up and be willing to do the work. Each experience adds to our store of knowledge and skill, and opens up new possibilities and directions to explore. Every experience adds to our creative capacity. There's easily enough to hold our interest for a lifetime.

Exercise #1 Tracking Your Intuition

a) For the next 24 hours, pay attention to "small" impulses and thoughts as they occur. Pick a safe one and act on it. Does anything interesting happen?

b) Notice what other people are telling you, sometimes just by walking into your space. Is there a message you need to pay attention to?

c) Pay attention to events that seem disruptive. What do they draw your attention to? Find the 'message' in the situation.

Exercise #2 Meditate

Find some time in your day to meditate, whether it's 5 minutes or 45 minutes. Try different types of meditation until you find the one(s) that work(s) for you. Sit at your desk, stare into space or at a candle flame. Lie on your back on a mat and empty your mind. Or see yourself in a place that is beautiful and peaceful. Try knitting or a walking meditation. Notice how you feel afterwards.

Exercise #3 Raise Your Level of Awareness

a) Time yourself for one minute and put your attention on your immediate environment. What do you observe in the space around you? Mentally list concrete details. What do you observe right in front of you?

b) Now, time yourself for one minute. During this minute, pay attention to what's on your mind. What do you notice?

c) Finally, time yourself for another minute and put your attention squarely on your own body. Monitor your breathing as you breathe in and out. Think of nothing else. What do you notice about your body? Does anything shift for you?

d) Keeping journal notes from these exercises can help you develop greater awareness of yourself and any patterns that exist.

Exercise #4 Mind the Gap

a) Identify any gaps in your life. Are there promises to yourself that you haven't kept? Why haven't you done so? What kind of gap has that created?

b) Choose a promise you'd like to keep and make a contract with yourself.

c) Post the contract somewhere you can review it daily.

Exercise #5 Have a "Feeling" Moment

a) Give yourself five minutes to pay attention to what you are feeling—the emotional state of your mind and body. Do not allow yourself to be confused by what you are thinking. The two are not the same.

b) For these five minutes, honor your feelings whatever they are and make them feel welcome, even if you are uncomfortable.

c) Write down what you felt.

Exercise #6 Learning From Others

Try having a really great conversation with someone to get an in-depth understanding of their creative work.

a) What are they attempting to create?

b) What methods do they use?

c) What challenges do they face along the way? If nothing else, you will find that you have company on the creative journey.

Exercise #7

Choose an artist whose work you admire.

a) Read a Bio of this person and search out critiques of his or her work.

b) Are you like him or her?

c) What do you learn from this acquaintance?

Exercise #8

a) Have you looked at a magazine new to you lately?

b) Did anything in it catch your attention?

c) Is there a message about an idea, something you might explore in your own work?

TWELVE

Creativity At Home

It's important to make a home for creativity in our lives. When we make space for creative activities in our homes and our communities, we honour this work as essential to our well-being. It's a way of treating our creativity with respect and acknowledging it as worthy of a secure and comfortable place to grow and develop. Doris McCarthy, member of the Order of Canada and the first woman president of the Ontario Society of Artists, had this to say about her home, Fool's Paradise, on the Bluffs in Toronto: "I'm a nest-builder by instinct and I built this nest which I have considered a joy, a sanctuary, a root, and all those things give you the emotion, security which helps you to create."[1]

This space where we store our projects, materials and tools makes them accessible. When we're ready to use them, they're ready for us. We keep the energy in our creative space positive. Doing these things gives our creativity permission to flower. The kind of space we need depends on the type of creative work we wish to accomplish. When I first began my creative journey, I was living in a two-bedroom apartment. My second bedroom functioned as home office, guest bedroom, storage for off-season clothing and equipment and creative space. I had to work around the computer on my desk when I wanted to work with my art supplies, potentially hazardous, as computers and water don't mix.

But I learned how to work neatly in a small space—a useful skill. I created the framed pieces for my first exhibitions there. Perhaps not surprisingly, the pieces I created were relatively small. Though I didn't find it ideal, I made this space work for me.

Eventually, as my creative activities expanded, I found a three-bedroom apartment, and dedicated one of the bedrooms to creative work. Not surprisingly, I began to work on larger pieces. We grow to fill our spaces. It's wonderful to have a room to ourselves, because then we don't have to put everything away when we're in the middle of a project. We have the freedom to come back and work without set-up and take-down time. If a dedicated room is not an option, utilize whatever space there is. For some types of creative work, the basics will suffice: a desk or table for workspace and storage containers for tools and materials. Art supplies can be kept in portable storage bins, baskets or rolling carts and stored out of sight when they aren't needed. Closets, shelves and cupboards all work well.

Working with something like welding or stained glass might require a basement or garage workspace with room for storage of tools and unfinished projects. Cooking or baking will require kitchen space. That could be a shelf for cookbooks and magazines, a cupboard for storage pans, and hooks for aprons. When there's no possibility of space at home, renting or sharing a studio space with other creative people may be an option. Some studios even rent by the hour. These days, my creativity seems to require a surprising amount of empty, uncluttered space, both in my physical surroundings and in my mind. I find ideas surface more easily when I allow that space. Literally. Clutter, whether physical or psychic, holds energy and runs interference, like static, coming between who I am and what I wish to create. I have noticed the same correlation between creativity and minimalism elsewhere. For example, art galleries contain much open space and little furniture. This starkness allows the artists' work to fill the space as dramatically as possible, and the viewer can absorb the work free from distraction.

Initially, I found it challenging to give clutter the boot—to get rid of "stuff"—and claim space for my creativity. I grew up in a household where items only got disposed of when worn out. My parents grew up in the Great Depression of the 1930s and lived in England after the Second World War when rationing was still in place, so they couldn't count on going out and buying things the way we do now. Once, when I asked why we had so many balls of string and piles of elastics in the kitchen, my Mom replied, "You never know when we might need them." So I learned that getting rid of stuff was a risky business and became a bit of a pack-rat myself, a habit I found I needed to change as I became more engaged in my creative work.

"Have nothing in your house that you do not know to be useful or believe to be beautiful,"[2] William Morris, the famous artist and designer advised. Good advice I've taken to heart. Gone are the worn thirty-year-old couch and loveseat that no longer suit my living room. I donated them to charity. Sounds simple, but even knowing I needed to make these changes, my apprehension surfaced that I was making a mistake I would live to regret. Recognizing the voice of my infernal critic, I put it on "hold." Happily, once these items were removed, I felt lighter, no longer held back by things that weren't useful. That old furniture held a lot of energy tied up in memories and events from the past and I'm happy to be free of it. I now own a beautiful new sofa that gives me pleasure and suits my space.

The next step in moving forward was to remove the single bed from my third bedroom (I now have a blow-up bed in the cupboard for emergencies!) and convert that room to a second studio for fiber arts. I gave my materials a home, and it's easier to work with them. I have more space to assemble pieces and I'm better able to visualize the work I'm trying to create. That little bit of empty space leaves room for the arrival of new ideas, things, people and energy.

As we grow and develop creatively, we need to update our spaces to reflect who we have become. When I began my creative activities many years ago, everything was crammed together into one part of a spare bedroom. Now I have the equivalent of two studios in my home where I "go to work" each day. My painting, art activities and creativity mentoring practice are housed in one of the rooms and the second holds my computer, my photographic equipment and my fiber arts materials. Sorting each of my activities into their own spaces has helped me to clarify my vision, to see particular needs and directions and to move forward personally and professionally in my creative development. It's amazing to me how much stuff I have purged over the past few years as I've assigned space for my creative life to grow.

Getting organized and keeping space clutter-free are important steps to develop the free-flow energy of creativity. As without, so within: it's difficult to shape our lives to suit us when we feel alienated by the environment we live in. When clutter distracts us, it's more difficult to hear ourselves and claim our passions. Once I have a clutter-free zone, I (try to!) keep it that way. It's easier to keep clutter from building up than it is to remove piles of it after the fact. This exercise in self-discipline helps sustain creativity.

Sometimes, we need to clear the air, creatively speaking. As adults, it's our job to maintain an environment that's healthy for our creative growth as well as for those in our care. We need to pay attention to the energy that surrounds us. The atmosphere in our homes can be affected by things such as physical pollutants (that can include chemical smells and contamination from our creative materials), improper lighting, distracting noise and emotional fall out.

My father was a chain smoker, so I grew up in a home filled with cigarette smoke back in the days before there was great awareness of the health risks. The air I breathed was further contaminated by the arrival of family pets. When I was 13, my brother brought home a kitten. Within days, I developed breathing problems. None of the adults in my life made the connection between my health, smoke and an allergy to cats. Instead, our family doctor prescribed an inhaler and a narcotic to help me breathe. In the absence of information, it was difficult to make a better choice. My brother loved his kitten, as did everyone else, including me, and that cat was part of our family for the next twenty years.

In a family, maintaining everyone's good health must be a top priority. It's a prerequisite to fostering creativity. We need to pay attention to those we love and listen to what they are saying. When they offer us perceptions that don't fit with what we think, we need to take the time to work out what that might mean. Problem-solving is part of the creative process, and becoming familiar with it nurtures creative development. I have to remember to ask questions, do research and get input from others. I work towards possible solutions, then prioritize them. I try to keep emotions from interfering. Staying calm can be difficult if a solution seems to favour one person's needs over another, or means giving up something we love, such as the family pet. In my family, keeping the family cat taught me to put the needs of others before my own health, and I've had to work hard to change this habit.

Having good lighting is also important to creativity; it helps us to see what we are creating. I like a lot of windows wherever I live, especially in my studios. As well as helping me to see nuances of colour, lighting affects my mood, and a lack of it can interfere with my willingness to do creative work. For me, not much dispels the gloom of the long Canadian winter as well as electric lights. I turn lights on all over the place when the sun sets. Fortunately, the home I grew up in had lots of natural light, but I remember an on-going battle with my parents every winter, about turning lights off to save electricity.

Light is so important to us that there's a syndrome associated with the lack of it: Seasonal Affective Disorder or SAD.[3] One of the treatments is exposure to energy in the form of the full colour spectrum of light. Sunshine and the production of Vitamin D in the human body have also been linked. Studies suggest that a number of chronic diseases like osteoporosis are linked to insufficient quantities of vitamin D[4], though the link is not yet clear. In November in Canada, where I live, as the days shorten and the nights grow longer, I feel an urge to hibernate—to crawl off and curl up in my bed until the light returns. Taking extra vitamin D has helped my winter energy levels.

I can sometimes counter the effects of low light with colour. My mood improves when I paint with great splashes of intense colour. I "drink" in colour the same way I eat carbohydrates for light. I crave them, as my body tries to "eat" the light stored in fruits and vegetables. Exercise outdoors also helps. In my younger years, at the end of a day of skiing or skating in the winter sunshine, I felt exhilarated. Now, I go for walks at noon in the winter months, when the light is brightest. I use a full-spectrum light in my studio to ensure the light is good even on the gloomiest of days.

Light, sound, colour, shape and texture, the building blocks of art, interior design and many other creative activities, are so important they are used by therapists to effect healing. When children who survived the devastating Sri Lankan tsunami in 2004 were given the opportunity to play with crayons and paper, they drew the waves and their experiences with it. They were given the opportunity to talk about what had happened and to share their experiences for some collective healing. Unfortunately, in Sri Lanka attending to mental health has not really been part of the culture so this kind of opportunity was limited.[5]

I know from my own experience that there is a connection between creative activities and good mental health. I have done some volunteer work for Spark of Brilliance[6] a community-based mental health initiative that promotes healing and transformation by providing arts-based recovery programming and services to people of all ages and all abilities living with mental health issues and other life challenges. Judith Rosenberg, the initiative's founder, and director, identified the need to empower people with mental health concerns to discover their particular Spark of Brilliance when her son, an aspiring artist, lost all artistic memory through acute psychosis.

Judith, whose work led to a provincial award for Good Citizenship, has this to say about the link between creativity and mental health:

> *When people are engaged in creative expression there is a deep sense of 'self' brought to the surface and given a voice. Historically, those who live with mental health issues and illnesses have experienced poverty, isolation and have been shunned from society. By shining light on the gifts and talents of all citizens we are recognizing that such contributions are valued and held in high esteem. Through honouring all citizens equally and creating space in society to celebrate the arts, communities become more compassionate and enriched!*

In my family, where there is a susceptibility to mental health issues, everyone has benefitted from creative activities. My sister, who is clinically depressed, gets treatment. She loves quilting and finds that creative activity lifts her mood. My dad was diagnosed with depression before he died and never found a medication that worked for him. He used to carve wood though he never had time to do much of it. He made a few pieces in his lifetime: a couple of coffee tables, some carved boxes and a lamp. My brother treasures the pieces my dad carved, and was inspired to take up carving also, creating wooden horses for merry-go-rounds. Pre-Alzheimer's, my Mom used to sew and enjoyed Chinese brush painting.

I do not suffer from clinical depression, but I feel depressed when my creativity gets thwarted for periods of time, as has happened when I am living an over-packed schedule. Setting up my studios and making a home for my creativity means I always have a place to go to restore myself. Exercising my creativity regularly maintains my own mental health, keeping my mood and energy positive—creativity is that powerful.

My first forays into art and the healing world of colour were simple. I would spread a pack of coloured markers in front of me and choose whichever one appealed to me at that moment. I did a scribble drawing on a page in a blank journal. I didn't attempt to draw anything recognizable. I just reflected my mood of the moment using colour. Colour-dabbling proved a satisfying exercise, which emptied out some tangled thoughts and emotions onto the page. When I was done, I would date the result and write down whatever events had happened in my life, along with what I had been feeling. By the time I completed one drawing, my colours usually became clear and bold. I could literally alter my mood—lighten up—using colour.

Over the course of a year, I discovered certain colours reflected certain states of mind. I traced my use of various colours and found when I was tired or depressed, I used grey and pastel colours. Red meant blood or anger. Orange was connected to education, yellow to courage or grace. Green was usually a plant—my physical self. Pale blue and deep blue were self-expression, wisdom and connection. Purple reflected my creativity.

Shortly thereafter, I came across an exhibit of paintings using the colours of the Chakras. Chakra is a Sanskrit word, meaning wheel or disc. Historically, the idea can be traced to the Upanishads. In this system, seven energy "wheels" align with the spine beginning at the base, with the Muladhara or root chakra, and ending with the Sahasrara, or crown chakra, at the top of the head. Interestingly, Western neurological research has confirmed the existence of corresponding nerve centers at each of the seven designated sites. In various Chakra traditions, the seven centers are associated with a colour, and personal, interpersonal, psychological and spiritual issues.[8] I hadn't heard of this energy system before, and was surprised to discover the colours, which had emerged naturally in my work, corresponded with the colours associated with the seven chakras.

It's not just in our homes that we need to make a place for our creative activities. As Judith Rosenberg indicated earlier, we need to ensure that space for creativity also exists in our communities. One of my best exhibition experiences happened in the small community of Harriston, Ontario, where a friend and I were invited to show our work for a six-week run at the community gallery.[9] Located on the top floor of the beautiful historic Public Library building, the gallery is run by a volunteer Board of Directors. Some of them are artists themselves and are dedicated to ensuring the arts hold a vibrant place in their community.

Together they maintain the gallery space, solicit work from artists in the region and publicize exhibitions through the Gallery website, posters and news releases. They go out of their way to support guest artists by assisting with the set up of the exhibitions, inviting the townspeople including the editor of the newspaper to the opening, and showing up themselves en masse. After the opening, they take the initiative to provide copies of the review from the paper and other publicity materials to the artists. It is a wonderful experience to feel so valued by a community.

When a community bands together this way, and creates a space to honour a creative enterprise, everyone benefits. Polished works are made accessible to the community. The work of the creator is validated, as is the experience of the viewer. Everyone is offered a connection to the creative journey and reminded of its importance. For the time it takes to view the work, the creative spark is relevant to each of us. We see things from a new perspective and have a view into another world, one that differs from our own. Sometimes, that's all it takes to inspire us to find our own creative path if we are not already on it, and to continue the journey if we are. We are all reminded of the importance of supporting each other in our creative ventures.

Note: It's important to claim the space in which you wish to create. Get a sense of what you would like your space to look like, then think, act and behave it into shape, one step at a time, one routine at a time. Identify this space as the symbolic home for your creative materials. If other people share the living space, they need to know this creative refuge is off limits. Whatever your space, designate it a "no-fail" zone, where playing and experimenting rule the day, and free rein can be given to the all-important questions: "Who am I now?" "What do I dream of creating?" and "What if...?"

Exercise #1 Inventory Your Space

Before you assign space for your activities in your home and your life, it's good to check what's already there.

a) Take a tour of your house. Carry a pad and pen with you if it's helpful, but you can also investigate by standing in the doorway and observing each of the rooms and spaces in your home.

b) Take inventory. What's in each room that's useful? What are you finished with? What do you need in the space now for it to function efficiently?

c) Analyze your list room by room. What do you need immediately that you can afford? What do you need to work towards accomplishing? How will you do that?

d) Prioritize, then take action to improve the efficiency of one of your spaces. Find homes for the things you want to keep and get rid of stuff that is not useful. Reduce to simplest terms. Tidy up those piles of paper on your desk, the clothes in your closet. Better still, sort through them and get rid of what you don't need.

e) If this process seems painful and overwhelming, remember that there are professionals who can give you a hand. Find someone who knows how to work with creative people.

Exercise #2 Check the Energy Quality In Your Home.

a) Walk through your home with pad and paper in hand checking the physical environment. How is the air quality? What are the noise levels? Do you notice anything affecting your physical environment?

b) Then do an inventory of the emotional energy in your home. How safe and nurturing is your space for everyone living under your roof?

c) Is there anything you need to do to "clear the air" in your home?

Exercise #3 Check Light Levels and the Use of Colour In Your Home.

a) Are you satisfied with the light in your home? If there are specific locations that need improvement, how might they be improved?

b) Check the use of colour throughout your home, and from room to room. Does the use of colour in your home affect your mood?

c) Does anything need to be changed or updated? Make a list.

Exercise #4 Quick Colour Therapy

Do this whenever you're in the mood. On a sheet of blank paper, create a scribble that reflects your emotions. Work quickly without over-thinking.

a) Empty a pack of coloured markers, crayons or coloured pencils in front of you.

b) Pick whatever colour(s) appeal to you.

c) Using the first colour, scribble as much or as little as you like.

d) Then select a second colour and do the same. Repeat until you feel you are done. You can also draw a circle first and then scribble inside it, creating a mandala.

e) You can do the same kind of exercise using torn paper.

f) On the back of your work record the date, your mood, the circumstances of your day and any other appropriate observations.

g) Collect your papers in a folder or notebook. When you have a good collection go through them and see what information they have to offer.

Exercise #5 Community Involvement

Have you considered contributing your creative interest and expertise to the community? Many organizations need volunteers. Volunteering can be a great way to meet others, find out what's going on and give back to those who often have no voice while expanding your own creative capacity. One caution only: let it support your own creative work, not take its place or take time away from it.

a) What kind of activity would you like to take part in?

b) How much time do you have available for this kind of activity?

c) What setting would you like to work in?

d) What age group would you like to work with?

e) If you joined this venture, what would your purpose be?

THIRTEEN

Building Creative Energy

As creative people we need to understand that caring for ourselves is part of what keeps our creativity healthy and builds energy. It takes energy to create and we need to feed that energy in important and specific ways from eating and drinking to exercising, relaxing and recharging. There are steps we need to take to keep ourselves grounded and optimize the flow of creative energy. I can be a bit obsessive once I get going on a project. I'll work for hours ignoring or forgetting to do the things that sustain my creative energy and I've had to develop strategies to keep myself on track. Early on in my creative work I'd set a timer or alarm clock to remind me to get up and walk or eat. By doing so, I've trained my brain and body to know when I've done a good morning's work and it's lunchtime. Even though I sometimes feel it's a nuisance to stop working, especially when I'm in the middle of a project, feeding my body renews my energy. Taking that break also gives my mind a chance to rest and refocus. Ultimately these steps improve the quality of my work.

The creative activities I do, especially writing, require a lot of sitting, and my body doesn't like that. If I sit too long, my lower back muscles protest and I feel drained by the time I quit. Getting up, walking away, and stretching regularly prevent muscle stiffness and fatigue, and my body serves me better in my creative work.

This, in turn, affects my mental well-being. When I sit too long or push myself too hard, I experience doubts about whatever work I've just completed and then about myself. I have to remember NOT to hit the delete button under any circumstances when I am in this frame of mind.

Creativity needs to be well fed. Literally. When we eat the wrong foods, we can expect our creative energy levels to slump. There are so many issues around food these days, so many choices and so much advice about what to eat, the average person has difficulty sorting through it all. Grocery stores are laden with temptation for the unwary and it takes self-discipline to shop wisely. Aisles are filled with processed and packaged foods, which make their way into many a grocery cart because they are convenient and we feel pressed for time. Unfortunately, many of them are high in salt, sugar and fat content, not to mention additives. There is ample evidence linking high salt levels and hypertension, and studies have shown that keeping blood sugar levels balanced throughout the day maintains steady energy and assists with cognitive function.[1]

Emotion and early conditioning complicate our food choices. As a society we use food as comfort, reward and even punishment. Family issues of power and control often manifest around food. In my family, trips to restaurants for lunch and dinner were a family treat, as were trips to the Dairy Queen on those long hot summer nights before air-conditioning was common. When we were children and had done something wrong, dessert was withheld as punishment. From early on, I associated sweet stuff with pleasure and being deprived as punishment. To avoid the temptation to load up my cart with sweets, I affirm "My life is sweet," and "I'm already sweet enough." I keep a running grocery list of things to shop for as I run out of things and I've learned not to buy chocolate and other foods I can't eat, because invariably they cost me energy in the form of food drama: wasted cash and migraines.

For the most part, I can live migraine free by avoiding the foods that trigger them. Doing so is worthwhile. Once a migraine is underway the pain can last anywhere up to four days. And once it clears, I'm left with a migraine "hangover." Needless to say, my creative energy and focus are off during those days. A couple of migraines a month can seriously cut in to my creative time, not to mention my enjoyment of life. I get irritated with myself for making poor choices and end up giving away or throwing the offending food out. It's better and healthier to keep my energy for my creative work of choice. As the late Betty Ford, former First Lady of the United States advises: "Don't compromise yourself. You're all you've got."[2]

Most studies agree that eating a balanced diet including protein, fruit, vegetables and fiber helps to maximize energy, so this is what I buy. Study after study confirms the importance of the vitamins, minerals and anti-oxidants contained in fresh fruit and vegetables in maintaining health. Yet as a nation, we are buying and eating too few. Cooking is a creative outlet and as creative people, we can establish a palette to satisfy our palate by working our way across the colour spectrum of fruits and vegetables,[3] choosing every colour from the red of sweet peppers to the purple of beets and eggplant. It can be creatively satisfying to include them if we shop carefully and cook simply.

To keep the flow of energy going, we need to master healthy eating and the time crunch. When I'm keeping to my creative schedule to work from 9 am to 12 noon, I'm pretty hungry when lunchtime arrives. I don't want to spend a lot of time cooking, but I am not one who can skip meals and function effectively. If I skip meals I get fierce cravings and become cranky: not a good creative state. I prepare meals ahead of time, often using a slow-cooker on weekends and storing meals in the freezer so they're ready to go during the week. If I cook chicken for dinner, I prepare extra to have on hand for sandwiches the next day.

In the afternoon, 4 p.m. is my down time, and I get cravings. If I'm smart, I remember to take mid-morning and mid-afternoon snack breaks and eat some protein, tuna fish or a hard-boiled egg, to tide me over to the next meal. Though it took me some time to train myself, not buying junk food in the first place is one of my strategies for good eating. Being lazy, I'll eat what I have on hand. If it's not there, I can't eat it. I keep fruit, vegetables, melba toast, flat breads and graham crackers on hand to crunch. I've kept charts and post-its on the refrigerator, when I need reminders about what to eat.

Here's a simple meal plan for a non-vegetarian healthy eating day:

Breakfast:
oatmeal, a soft-boiled egg, a glass of water, some fruit or calcium-enriched orange juice and a piece of whole wheat toast for breakfast. (I cook with rice milk and I use it on my cereal.)

Lunch:
chicken with steamed vegetables, a potato or brown rice or a whole wheat roll. Fruit salad from fresh fruit for dessert. I often have my main meal at noon because I sleep better at night if I eat light in the evening.

Dinner:
some form of protein (fish or meat) and vegetables. I use the water they have been cooked in for mashing potatoes. I might have salad with a dressing I make myself. To avoid additives, I use a combination of oil, vinegar, garlic, fresh herbs and Dijon mustard. I take vitamin supplements daily along with calcium since, for me, dairy products cause migraines.

Mid-morning and afternoon snacks:
protein, veggies, fruit, crackers.

I find this kind of meal plan easy to follow, shop for and cook. It doesn't cost a lot of money and it keeps my energy levels in good shape for creative work. Fast food is rarely part of my diet. Taking the time to plan, shop and cook good meals, is another way of exercising creative muscle.

We need to guard against dehydration. Our bodies are 70% water[4] and we need to immerse ourselves in the flow. When we hit a creative "dry spell," we drink a glass of water to refresh ourselves and think about fluidity in our creative process. Two experiences with sunstroke and a struggle with caffeine taught me the importance of water for the body. On a canoe trip in Algonquin Park when I was 13, I got badly sunburned, but didn't know the problem was serious until I passed out and woke up in the camp's infirmary. The second time, when I was a young teacher working in the Caribbean, I attended a day-long snorkeling picnic excursion to a tiny island. There was little shade and the amount of drinking water was limited. By the end of the day, I was so disoriented I couldn't get my balance and was walking into walls. I had to drink salt water to restore my balance—not a pleasant experience.

My struggle to quit caffeine also taught me respect for my body's need for water. At first, I substituted fruit juice for coffee and tea as it supplied the taste and sweetness I was craving. When it wasn't available I drank cups of hot water. Then nutritionists recommended limiting our intake of fruit juice because of its high levels of sugar and low levels of fibre. I gave up the fruit juice and got into the habit of drinking water, a habit I have kept ever since. These days, it seems, everyone carries water bottles, and there's better awareness of the need to keep hydrated.

Strange but true: I have observed that what feels like a hunger pang can actually be my body's signal for water. I experienced these pangs even when I had eaten fairly recently, so I knew I wasn't really hungry. Then I discovered that if I drank some water, they went away.

Physical exercise is another way to build and restore our energy. The creative 'muscle' benefits from physical exercise because creativity lives in the body and is expressed through it. Our creativity is mind and body at play as well as at work. The body withers and creativity grows stale when not exercised. Getting our bodies moving helps keep our creativity moving; integrating the two helps keep the momentum.

Exercise also offers us the chance to practice body awareness. Paying attention to body messages is a way to tune in to our energy levels. Creatively speaking, when it comes to the body, "never mind" is a way of tuning out important information. Bodies let us know when we need to get moving, when our energy is in full creative mode and when we need to take a break. Subtle messages, such as an unexpected reluctance to put yellow on the paint brush, or a desire to use sweeping physical movements, offer useful guidance in our creative practice. Paying attention to such body messages and acting on them expands our creative capacity.

How important is physical exercise for the body? For years, I had an administrative job that kept me sitting in a chair at my desk for much of the day. The diagnosis of osteopenia a couple of years ago galvanized me into realizing all this sitting was affecting my health. The gift of a pedometer from my sister helped me do something about it. After a week of clocking the number of steps I took in an average workday, I discovered I barely made it to 5000 steps if I didn't get to the Y. My body was telling me to try a different approach. I accepted the challenge to take 10,000 steps a day.[5] To build my bones, I also signed up for a women's weight training class at the Y and I added additional aerobic training to my weekly routine. I vowed to take a half-hour walk each working day, rain or shine.

At the time, I was working in an environment with an unwritten rule that administrators didn't take lunch breaks. We were supposed to be available to students, parents and staff throughout the day. I felt uncomfortable going against the culture, but I needed to eat and I needed to walk. Each day, I put my cell phone in my pocket so I could be reached in case of emergency, told the office staff where I was going, and headed out the door. I was amazed how much better I felt in the afternoons after walking. It cost nothing, relieved stress, energized me and provided fresh air all at the same time. I felt more alive for my administrative tasks in the afternoons and I had energy left over to do some quality creative work in the evenings.

I walk or go to the Y most days. I have been able to follow this fitness plan because I enjoy it. No matter what kind of mood I'm in beforehand, I always feel better afterwards. No exceptions. When I don't exercise regularly, I have trouble sleeping. And that always affects the quality of my creative work. Even a short walk clears my mind and re-energizes me so I can make better use of the rest of my day. Knowing my body's needs keeps me motivated on those days when I'm pressed for time and tempted to abandon the plan.

Mind and body function better when they are tended with exercise.[6] Some forms of exercise such as Tai Chi, martial arts and Yoga are designed to foster the connection between body and mind. I enjoy Yoga, a form of exercise I find good for developing balance, both physical and metaphorical. I have found it especially helpful in developing my awareness of breathing and relaxation. The rhythmical repetition of the various postures has taught me to move more deliberately when I'm in my studio: to slow down and be patient, to take one step at a time with confidence. I like working this way. Yoga is also excellent for stretching those cramped muscles in the lower back, hips and legs, after a day in the studio. Over time, I've learned to work into those stretches my body initially found difficult: to find my limitations, breathe into them and then gently push past them, as I do in my creative work. I have found that when it comes to body messages, sometimes, the universe demonstrates a sense of humor. Occasionally, when I haven't done much creative work in a while, my sciatic nerve will act up. I literally get a pain in my butt. Or perhaps more accurately, I'm giving myself a pain in the butt by not getting off my butt and working creatively. More than once I've had the experience of this pain going away when I've done some creative work!

My creative energy levels are helped by what I call "puttering" time. I wander aimlessly around the house or simply sit staring out a window. My creative energy doesn't respond well if I'm constantly multi-tasking or over-thinking. I have learned that ideas are percolating somewhere deep in my unconscious mind even when I think nothing is happening. Not doing much of anything allows those ideas to come to consciousness. Walking is good, too.

It's taken me a few years to adjust my pace and allow that "empty time" without feeling guilty. Over the course of 30 years in a fast-paced corporate environment, I trained myself to make use of every available moment just to get everything done, and I learned to move fast. For the first few years working on my own in my own home, I found the habits of multi-tasking and always doing "useful" things difficult to give up. Yet I knew my body and my mind needed down time to conduct their conversation.

Both my body and my mind need time to rest and I have learned to create that space. One way I do this is to sit in the hot tub at the Y after exercising. I also treat myself to an hour's massage every couple of weeks. Both strategies help release the tension I carry in my shoulders and back when nothing else does. Spending time with friends relaxes me. I love to travel when my finances allow and the opportunity arises. There's something about getting away from home and being unreachable by electronic devices that gives my brain a rest and helps me see with fresh eyes when I return. When I can't afford to travel, when I have lots of creative work to do, or when I'm feeling overwhelmed, I've been known to place a weekend moratorium on e-mail and all electronic devices to "create" a "holiday." It's really good not to feel guilty about this.

Sometimes, my creative energy is improved by breaking away from my schedule and switching gears altogether. If I've been writing, I go to my art studio and splash some colour around. Working with colour gives me a lift. I keep an art journal just for this purpose. Getting out of the house helps. I enjoy taking my camera out for a walk, either on my own or with another photographer.

Although scans of brain waves show differences for meditation and sleep, taking a nap also has a beneficial effect on creativity by resting body and mind. This is supported by research. A National Institute of Mental Health study showed that a midday snooze reverses information overload. Reporting that, in some cases, napping could even boost performance to an individual's top levels, the NIMH team wrote: "The bottom line is: we should stop feeling guilty about taking that 'power-nap' at work…"[7]

Exercise #1 Check Your Kitchen

a) We starve our creative energy when we don't feed ourselves properly. Take pen in hand and a pad of paper, or use an electronic device and inventory the food in your kitchen. Make headings including meat/protein, vegetable, fruits, grain products, desserts and junk foods. Take into account any specific dietary requirements you may have (diabetes, celiac etc.) Now go through all cupboards, drawers, the refrigerator and freezer and any other stashes of food you have squirreled away.

b) What do you notice about your buying and eating habits? Which food groups are under-represented and which are over-represented?

c) Are there stale-dated items? Throw them out.

d) Are there items you dislike or really shouldn't eat? Can you donate them to a food bank?

e) Re-organize your cupboards to serve your needs more efficiently.

Exercise #2 What's the Cost?

a) Notice how much money you spend on food groups. Money is a form of energy just as food is.

b) Does your purchasing reflect healthy energy choices and foods that work for your body? What about for others in your household?

c) Are you living within your budget?

d) Are you leaking creative energy in the form of overspending and under-nourishment?

e) Now try a journal exercise on your food and energy habits. Are there any habits you need to change?

Exercise #3 Create a Healthy Eating Day

a) Plan a day's worth of interesting meals that work

across the colour spectrum. Make sure they are meals you would enjoy cooking and eating.

b) Flip through your favourite recipe books and allow something new, or a recipe you haven't made in a while to catch your eye. These days there are so many resources available on the Internet, it's relatively easy to find good recipes that take specific dietary requirements into account. Make healthy food choices to maximize your energy. Remember you can get help from other family members and if time is really at a premium, then just focus on one meal for this particular day.

Exercise #4 Add Colour

a) Next time you go grocery shopping, check your cart for the colour of fresh fruits and vegetables. Check out the produce department for interesting fruits and vegetable to try.

b) Find recipes that call for them. Next time you go shopping, buy and try them. If you're not in the habit of doing so, incorporate colourful fruits and vegetables into your meals at least once a week and build from there. You will be exercising your creativity, building your energy and nurturing your body.

Exercise #5 Immerse Yourself In The Flow

a) Take a time out and drink a glass of water. Refresh, rebalance and restore creative flow.

b) Immerse your hands in water and wash something. Never underestimate the power of a little soap and water to clean up your creative space and get the flow going again.

c) Water something: the grass, plants...

d) Try some creative work using water-based media.

Exercise #6 Body Awareness

Pay attention to your body for the next 24 hours. Make notes if you wish to track patterns. Is there anything your body is trying to tell you?

Exercise #7 Get Some Exercise

a) Walk or jog; join a fitness program, a recreational or competitive sports team. Find the type of exercise that suits you best and make it a habit.

b) Create an exercise plan for one healthy day. Get creative about your exercise program. Allow for fun and spontaneity.

Exercise #8 Give Yourself a Hug.

Here's a fun exercise to try if you don't have any physical restrictions. Start your day with a hug.

a) Lying on your back, bring your knees up to your chest and loop your arms under them.

b) Gently press your thighs to your chest and hold this position for three minutes. You should feel your back muscles relax.

c) If you prefer, wrap your arms around your body and give yourself a hug.

Exercise #9 Lighten Your Load

a) Find or create some "empty" space in your day and make a "plan" to do nothing. Sit in a rocking chair, or on a bench in a public space. Close your eyes or stare into space. Breathe and be peaceful.

b) Find or create some "empty" space in your week.

c) Give yourself a "holiday" and mark it on your calendar or planner.

d) Do something that you find enjoyable and relaxing. Wander downtown or sit in a café. Enjoy!

FOURTEEN

Body at Work; Body of Work

Since Rene Descartes' famous pronouncement in the 17th century, "I think; therefore, I am," western thought has separated mind from body[1] and given the logical processes of the left brain priority over those of the right. This has given rise to one of the more destructive misconceptions about creativity: that the truly creative mind will transcend any and all suffering because the logic of the brain is superior to the so-called 'softer' processes that originate in the body—symptoms, gut feelings, intuitions and emotions. This chapter is about turning up the volume to hear body messages more clearly. The pay-off is better creative health.

There are many examples of creative people who have overcome severe physical handicaps. Prudence Heward was one. She suffered from asthma all her life, and her ability to paint was further curtailed by an automobile accident in 1939. Still she went on to paint some of her most famous portraits after that.[2] Mexican artist Frida Kahlo, best known for her self-portraits, also had life-long struggles with her health. She contracted polio at the age of 6 and was severely injured in a bus accident as a teenager.[3] Theoretical physicist and cosmologist Stephen Hawking suffers from a neurological disease related to ALS that has left him paralyzed, yet he has written books and made significant contributions to quantum physics including research into black holes.[4]

Such stories are inspiring, but they also help preserve the belief that creativity and suffering are somehow linked: that we have to suffer to make anything worthwhile. They also foster the notion that we must overcome the symptoms of the body rather than recognize and harness body wisdom for our creative development. Many of us have physical challenges to overcome every day of our lives, but suffering and creativity do not have to go hand in hand. Those "softer" body processes hold valuable information. The better we understand and act on them, the better we can nurture our creativity. If we do, we and our work will thrive.

Our bodies are both "bodies at work" and channels for our "body of work." Because creativity lives in the body and is expressed through it, caring for our selves in all ways helps to nurture creativity, by keeping it the self-renewing well-spring of pleasure and enjoyment that it is meant to be. It's simple: the better we treat ourselves, the more creative energy we will have. To be fully creative, to maximize our available energy, we have to be able to distinguish the body's messages from all the others we pick up moment by moment from the world.

Each body expresses itself in a unique way in symptoms, feelings and urges, rather than words. Since we don't come with owner's manuals, we are the only ones who can work out what our bodies are trying to tell us.[5] We have to learn our way around our own bodies so we recognize when we feel good and when we are losing energy. Pain and fatigue drain us, leaving us less able to do the things we love. Sometimes, we have to play detective in our own lives, working by trial and error to decipher the messages and how best to act on them.

The symptoms the body develops form the built-in "diagnostic" system meant to guide us through life. Sometimes we fail to notice and acknowledge symptoms when they present themselves because we are distracted by the events of our lives. We need to learn to track signs of distress.

Like so many of us these days, I'm pretty self-disciplined and efficient when I'm in good shape physically. But the stresses of everyday life work against my creativity when they deplete my energy. When my body experiences fatigue, pain and dis-ease, I require more energy to accomplish ordinary tasks, and I don't get to the creative ones. Here's how my body speaks her mind. The further down my list, the stronger and more insistent the message is that my body is running low on energy to the point where it can't function without help.

- I experience pain or tightness in my solar plexus. This is "stress central" for my body.

- I feel overwhelmed by the constant onslaught of demands and unable to deal with them. I feel this in my head and it makes me want to wring my hands. I close the door to keep others away.

- I feel there is more work than I can do. My "To Do" list seems impossible.

- I bite my nails.

- I feel tired. I get clumsy. I miss my home and have a desire to retreat to my bed.

- I feel a need to solve my own problems rather than everyone else's.

- I am unable to spend time doing any of the things I love.

- I feel unhappy and depressed and at the same time send myself a message that I'm not allowed to take a time out. I am not a good companion to anyone, let alone myself.

- Food becomes problematic… there are no groceries in the house; I don't want to cook or eat. I crave sugar, caffeine, chocolate and other foods to which I'm allergic.

- I have an urge to cry for no apparent reason.

These body messages alert me that I need to give myself some kind of break, so my body can recover. If I don't, my creative work suffers and I risk becoming ill or injuring myself. For me, these signs are often indicators of physical fatigue and one of the best remedies for me is to get some sleep.

Often, we ignore the messages, even when we understand them, especially if it means making changes in our lives. When we don't honour our body messages—to get sleep, for example— we become vulnerable to those habits, substances and experiences that distract us from our distress by giving us a hit of temporary energy. Chocolate, caffeine, sugar, alcohol, various types of tranquilizers, retail therapy. . . there's a long list of the things we reach for. Unfortunately, some become addictions, few rejuvenate the body, and many interfere with true creative energy. Clarissa Pinkola Estes, author of *Women Who Run With the Wolves*, writes:

> ...*when a woman is starved (of wild worth), she will take any substitutes offered, including those that... do absolutely nothing for her as well as life threatening ones that hideously waste her time and talents or expose her life to physical danger... The way to hold on to what we have...is to see what mistakes a woman trapped can make. Then we can backtrack and repair.*6

When we are starved for our creative work and worth, the same things hold true. The substitutes we reach for interfere with our creativity, wasting our time and talents. The solution is to acknowledge the problem, make repairs and get back on track.

Most of us have bodies that are pretty resilient, and there aren't always immediate consequences for ignoring or self-medicating a problem. Gaining some understanding of how our bodies work can help us to understand why we respond to certain substances and experiences the way we do. For me caffeine was a challenging addiction. It took years to figure out that my body can't handle the stuff.

My response to caffeine goes something like this. First, I get a lift; my mood improves. I get happy and become energized, "wired" in fact. I can multi-task like nobody's business and get tons accomplished. Then I start exhibiting signs of nervousness. Within half an hour of ingesting caffeine, I start biting my nails and tapping my fingers or feet. My level of irritation with other people rises, and I am very quick to experience and express anger. I have difficulty sleeping for the next 24 hours. I have violent dreams and wake up feeling groggy and irritable. I have trouble concentrating. I feel depressed as my body crashes into withdrawal. At this point, the temptation to ingest more caffeine is very strong. If I give in to the temptation, the next shot of caffeine will irritate my sciatic nerve. In short, my body's response to caffeine is pain.

The coffee ritual was deeply embedded in my family life. Whoever got up first at our house put on the coffee. Freshly-brewed, it was synonymous with family time and a day full of promise and possibility. I loved the smell of it wafting through the house first thing in the morning and the taste of that first cup with cream and sugar. I was allowed my first small taste of it when I was a child and began drinking it with breakfast somewhere in my early teens. I looked forward to it each morning. My father, who drank eight cups a day without a problem, would sometimes tease me about how I just couldn't get started without my morning coffee.

In those years, I had trouble getting to sleep at night and would stay up late reading. I also had trouble getting up in the morning but attributed this to being a "night" person as there are a lot of these in my family also. Since no-one else in my family seemed to have a problem with caffeine, there was no reason for me to think I did. I didn't make the connection between caffeine and my inability to sleep until much later in my life and when I did, it was because of tea, not coffee. My grandfather used to mix his own blend: two parts loose black tea to one part of a smoky Chinese tea called Lapsang Souchong. He brewed it in a silver teapot. I loved the elegance and the exquisite smoky taste and brewed it for myself on Sunday afternoons in the early years of my career.

Perceiving the connection between the actions we take and the symptoms the body expresses can be challenging. I experienced severe headaches on Monday afternoons, in those same years and was puzzled about the cause. One day I came across an article linking caffeine and headaches. I wondered if this could be true for me, so I started tracking my headaches. Sure enough, those headaches showed up like clock-work almost 24 hours to the minute after I drank a cup of tea. My body's delayed response had fooled me into thinking tea had no effect on me when in reality I was experiencing caffeine withdrawal a day later without knowing it. Studies have since shown that caffeine can stay in the body much longer than was originally thought, and women's bodies process it at a slower rate than men's do.[7]

I enjoyed the taste of tea and coffee and they were integrated so completely into my life, that it took me a long time to realize and acknowledge they are toxic for me. For years, I found it easier to take a pain killer (a clue if ever there was one!) than to give up caffeine. But the side-effects of various painkillers made me uneasy as well. I was using one drug to combat the effect of another. My body wanted off the roller-coaster.

Since I first began my struggle with caffeine, research into genetics, addictions and the pleasure centres of the brain has provided clues about why addictions are so hard to conquer. Caffeine and sugar are two substances known to stimulate the pleasure centres of the brain. When pathways to the pleasure centres in the brain get stimulated over and over, a habitual pathway develops and an addiction can begin to form. If the pathway is well-enough developed, we will experience a craving when the substance fails to appear.

Some studies suggest that the body's caffeine-tolerance is linked to genetics. One study suggests that the general population is spilt 50-50 when it comes to caffeine. There is a genetic marker that determines how quickly the body metabolizes it and there is a link between slow metabolizing and the risk of heart attack.[8] Half of us might be wise to eliminate it from our diet, whereas the other half can drink it without much effect. Paying attention to the body's responses helps work out which half of the population we belong to.

Research suggests that cravings can have any number of interactive origins. Scientists have identified digestive tract bacteria that play a role in various food preferences including chocolate. Research has shown that our tongues have unique configurations of taste receptors, linked to genetics. Some of us receive more of a flavor "hit" from food than others, which can make us desire certain types of foods, such as the sweet-tasting ones. And cravings can reflect mood. Deciphering the causes of a struggle with addiction can take time, energy and attention. Some addictions require medical intervention. Body chemistry is complex. If we need help, we must get it. Our creative energy is at stake.

It is possible to work creatively through pain and sleeplessness but it's better if we don't have to. To overcome an addiction, we have to develop new habits and pathways to pleasure. In other words, we have to reprogram our brains. To stop popping headache remedies, I had to overcome my early conditioning, change some deeply engrained habits and pleasures and find some replacements for coffee and tea. I had to make a conscious decision to stop inflicting pain on myself and I have to keep making that decision every day.

It's difficult to stay caffeine-free when coffee, tea, colas and chocolate are so much a part of our culture that there are coffee bars on every street corner. Still today, the scent of freshly-brewed coffee and tea triggers those receptors in my brain and makes me crave a cup. But I know drinking the stuff will cause me pain and be a betrayal of both body and self. In this culture, we overlook the fact that caffeine is a drug because we believe it's unlikely to do the kind of physical damage other controlled substances will.

One of the benefits of creative work is that it offers a healthy pathway to pleasure. But it's difficult to attain optimal performance—to hear our inner voice, to hold the camera steady, to draw a smooth straight line—when our nerves are feeling jangled. If there's a habit to change, finding and substituting something safe can make quitting easier than going "cold turkey." The substitution has to be repeated until it becomes the new habit.

Giving up coffee and tea took persistence. I had to retrain my coffee-loving taste buds to accept something else. Unfortunately, decaf also wires me (all decaf contains some caffeine). So in the beginning, out of desperation and for the comfort of something warm to hold, I took to drinking cups of hot water. But I kept giving in to the urge for caffeine, and then had to come back to the strategy of accepting a substitution. My family made puzzled comments about my new habits, which in turn made me self-conscious, so it was hard work. Through repetition, I became comfortable with the change to the point where I could accept herbal tea as an alternative and my family now offers it to me automatically.

But the story doesn't end there. As the years went by, I discovered chocolate, alcohol and all forms of milk products also gave me headaches that aspirin couldn't touch. Further research led me to discover that these substances are all classic causes of migraines. Frustrated by the number of substances causing problems, I got a referral to an allergist for testing and was stunned by the results. My list of foods to avoid included all milk and soy products as well as the foods associated with the birch tree allergy. According to my allergist, all immunological determinants in apple, celery and carrot are present in birch pollen. Food sensitivities are a secondary consequence via immunologic cross reactivity.[9] What a nuisance! Whether I like it or not, they are toxic to my body and I have had to give up all of them. I was truly shocked to discover that I could be anaphylactic for hazelnuts, another item on the Birch tree list, and took to reading the ingredient labels on food very carefully.

I've had to change my shopping, cooking and eating habits to gain more control over what I put in my body. I do a lot of my own cooking, and that takes time, effort and energy, but removing the foods from my diet that I'm allergic to has eliminated my headaches. My energy level is more stable and I sleep better at night. Sleep keeps my energy and focus available for my creative endeavors. I have found it challenging to stop desiring the foods I am allergic to, especially chocolate. I've adopted the slogan, "Just say No," to keep myself on track but it's taken me a long time to learn that the short-term pleasure is not worth the longer-term pain. I feel guilty when I disrespect my body and guilt can tie up psychic energy. I know what I need to do to live peacefully with my body; choosing to do so daily is my challenge.

Learning about our bodies is always worthwhile. Yet there is much in the culture to keep us from paying attention to them. Workaholism is encouraged. Just look at the number of people who don't take the holidays they are entitled to each year.[10] And how many times do we put off a medical appointment to avoid a little discomfort? Should we wonder why so many people develop life-threatening illnesses? The statistics for heart attacks, stroke and other serious illnesses are based on the deaths of real people; each one represents a partner lost, a love mourned. What we don't know or don't pay attention to is killing us.

My partner, Greg, suffered a life-ending stroke very suddenly at age 55, while driving home from work one Friday afternoon. He drove through a red light into the plate glass window of a main-street store. No-one else was injured but Greg died the next morning. He had every risk-factor for stroke... smoked heavily from the time he was in his early twenties, had a high-stress job, loved high-fat foods, didn't exercise and didn't visit doctors. Those of us left behind to grieve can't help but wonder if his death could have been prevented. And the hard truth is we'll never know. Death is non-negotiable.

It's one of life's lessons that we can't change another person's behaviour. We can only change our own. Early detection of problems is still our best strategy for remaining healthy. So much can be measured now and so much information is available to us, but keeping medical appointments and pursuing the results take time and effort. Our bodies are pretty resilient, and there aren't always immediate consequences for ignoring a problem. Bodies can and often do heal themselves. But not always. Chronic disease can take years to manifest, and may not have any symptoms. That's one of the reasons we can go on thinking everything's OK, even when it's not.

Each new thing we learn about our bodies can require us to revise our personal plan of care. When I was struggling with caffeine, I learned I was at risk for Osteoporosis, a chronic disease characterized by gaps in the structure of the bone. I added calcium and vitamin D supplements to my diet and a weight training program to my fitness routine. I wondered what message my body was trying to send me through this symptom, so I did quite a bit of journal work using circle shapes in different colours to represent the osteoclasts (bone destroyers) and the osteoblasts (bone builders). I created pages to represent what I thought osteoporosis looked like and what bone-building looked like. Then I wrote whatever came into my mind as I was working with these images and ideas.

My experience suggests that illness can have metaphorical as well as physical meaning, if we are open to exploring it. Osteoporosis is a disease of erosion over time. I looked at the ways I was outstripping my own internal resources faster than I could replace them, and realized the way I was living was too demanding for the internal resources of my body. Trying to be an artist, a photographer and a writer while managing a demanding, stressful corporate career and juggling it all with a home and social life was leaving me drained and ill. My body was not designed to live at this kind of multi-tasking speed. The price was being paid by my bones. I felt "bone-weary" and even completed an art page showing what that looks like.

Since osteoporosis particularly affects the spine and hips, the central supporting structures of the body, I inventoried what structural supports I had in my life. I got orthotics for my feet to give myself a firmer foundation to stand on. Mortgage rates had fallen to the point where it was cheaper to buy than to rent. So I bought my house and gave myself my own home for the first time in many years. Then I looked around for the people who could help me design and create the life I needed to live: one that didn't drain the life from my bones. I needed time to dream and do nothing—time to replenish soul and body, and it didn't exist in the schedule I was living.

I needed a guide who could help me explore my images and the messages they represented—someone who could help me sort out the decisions I needed to make for the sake of my health. I couldn't find an art therapist, so I chose to work with a Jungian analyst as they are trained to work with intuition, dreams and images. During the course of this work, I was very surprised to receive a strong message from myself that I needed to "go back and fill in the gaps in my life" to be healthier.

As I surveyed my life, I realized I had started many projects but never seemed to find the time to finish them. All this unfinished work was draining my energy in critical ways. At the same time, I seemed to be floundering a bit when it came to having a sense of direction for my life. It seemed to me that one of the meanings of the message was that my way forward would be found by going back and finishing up some of these projects… filling in the gaps in my work.

I have since realized that this particular message is a foundational guideline for me creatively. In my work, I can always find a way forward by going back to the work I have already begun or completed. There's always more to learn from what I've already done. This is also a message about going back and keeping the promises I have made to myself. I need to develop the "backbone" to keep my internal integrity in the face of demands from the world. I need to stay true to myself. As a result of this work, I eventually made the decision to take early retirement and shift into the career that allowed me to work full-time with my creative energy and abilities.

What might life be like if we treated our bodies and ourselves with the respect we deserve? We can give ourselves back what the world takes out of us or we can ignore our bodies and fill the emptiness with one of the host of addictions offered to us by our abundant world, risking serious injury and illness later. When we treat our bodies with respect, we feel better mentally and physically. We can concentrate better, we are more interested in what we are doing and in life generally, we're able to do more and our creative output is better. Our quality of life is at stake. How do we want to use our life energy and time on Earth? What would we like to be remembered for? These are some questions to think about as we engage the challenge of caring for our selves.

Exercise #1 Monitor Stress and Get Creative With It

a) For the next week, pay attention to the stressors in your life. Identify and list them. Track your body's responses to each one.

b) At the end of the week, rank these signs of stress in order of severity.

c) List three simple changes you could make this week that would benefit your body. Choose one and act on it.

Exercise #2 Track Your Distractions

a) What experiences, habits and substances do you use to relieve stress?

b) What do you turn to when you need a break and your energy flags?

c) List as many things as you can. Put a star beside the healthy ones.

d) Choose one of the stress-relievers you did not star. During the coming week, notice what circumstances cause you to choose it. Track your body's response to this substance, experience or habit. What do you notice? Is it helping you or causing new problems?

Exercise #3. Health Check

Make any health-related appointments you've been putting off and keep them. These include visits to doctors, dentists, optometrists and alternative practitioners such as physiotherapists, chiropractors, therapists and naturopaths for wellness care.

Exercise #4 Deal With the Incompletes

a) Survey your own life. Do you have unfinished projects or assignments that drain your energy when you think about them? List them.

b) Is it time to acknowledge that some of them will never be completed and need to be discarded or passed on to others?

c) Might some of them take a new and/or different direction?

d) What's one step you could take this week to improve the situation?

FIFTEEN

Heart Matters

In an ideal world, we would all know how to live interdependently. We would have (and be) supportive, understanding partners and friends who are comfortable with the demands of creative work. Our families would know without being told when we need space and solitude, and give them freely, opting to pursue their own needs and interests. In reality, pursuing our creative interests while living with others can be challenging. We have family members and friends who require our company and attention. We have children, adults with disabilities, or aging parents and relatives who may not receive the care they need if we don't provide it. While attending to their needs is a way we exercise love, compassion and generosity, we have to be careful to balance their care with our own needs. To do our creative work, we have to know and understand what's in our hearts and use that knowledge as a compass to guide us.

When I was thinking about my health and trying to decide whether I could afford to take early retirement, I created an art journal and worked through the Chakras using colour and writing to explore issues associated with each one. Particularly helpful was my work with the fourth, or Heart Chakra, associated with issues of love, compassion, and emotional response. I hand-carved an eraser alphabet and stamped the words of a "Heart Manifesto" for myself, stating the changes I needed to make in my life, knowing I would make them and that they would alter the direction of my life. It took me four pages to create my Heart Manifesto, which reads:

> On retiring early: I am not the person I thought I would become, so I am leaving the corporate world behind and choosing to create my own life. In my heart, I know I am a deeply creative person, and I work best with lots of freedom, time, space, solitude, silence and spontaneity to bring forth that which is within me. I am not sure where this new path will take me but I'm willing to find out. I am willing to follow my heart. Heart whole and fancy free. Shakespeare said it best: "This above all, to thine own self be true and it must follow as the night the day, thou canst not then be false to any man."[1] It's important to honor one's self. People say 'Follow your heart' as if this is an easy thing to do. The reality is that doing so means overcoming fears, taking leaps of faith and making major changes in one's life—always challenging things to do, making choices.

While creating my chakra pages, I discovered that colour and energy are more than just metaphor for the body. Working with colour and my emotions grounded and energized me. This experience, perhaps more than any other, confirmed for me that we are bodies of energy, and it's good to remember that at some level everything we do is an expression of energy. Our energy, perhaps the most precious thing we have, can be blocked or interrupted by so many things: stress, illness and injury, whether physical, emotional or psychic. But we are also fully capable of experiencing and working with our energy to feel healthier and more creative.

Various alternative health care providers have discussed energy and balance at length for years but it took an appointment with an osteopath for me to experience the power of such a practice. Osteopaths work with energy, and I was intrigued enough by my experiences with the Chakra colours to visit a practitioner. During my first appointment, I was astounded to see in my mind an image of my own energy flowing through my body. Until that point, I had never dreamed such a thing was possible—yet working with this practitioner, I could literally feel my energy shift.

Each time I have gone back, I have felt and visualized my own energy, to the point where I can now detect in what area of my body it is concentrated before the osteopath begins her work. Whatever route we choose, allowing ourselves space and time to work through our issues is a way to restore and nurture our creative energy. Listening to our bodies and working with our energy offers another way we can heal ourselves.[2]

Another way we can learn what's in our heart is by giving ourselves the gift of solitude. Creative work can be "sole work" as well as soul work. Solitude helps us to protect our creative time and energy. It frees us to hear ourselves without interference. We can relax, daydream and visualize ideas when we know our concentration will not be interrupted. Solitude is not to be confused with loneliness. Solitude allows us to determine and articulate our needs whereas loneliness is that sense of isolation we experience when we are not in touch with ourselves. If we require solitude and never give ourselves this gift, we will be lonely for ourselves, no matter how many people are around.

I grew up in a family of extroverts. For a long time, I didn't understand that constant company exhausts me. Our house was not large, or set up to accommodate separate space for anyone. Until I was 13, I shared a bedroom with my sister. In my family, being removed from company and sent to one's room was a form of discipline. As a result, I grew up confusing solitude with loneliness and punishment. It took me a long time to understand that solitude is a choice. It means that, for this period of time, I am choosing to be with myself and only myself. I will be tuning into my own needs and desires, and this is essential for me to know who I am.

Through my analysis and my reading of work by Swiss psychotherapist, Carl Jung, I have come to understand that solitude is sometimes essential. It's not merely a selfish indulgence, or wrong, as I somehow learned, but one of the ways I recharge. Claiming solitude has given me the peace and space to find out what's important to me, to work out solutions to problems in my life, to discover what gives me pleasure and what causes me pain. It has allowed me to create bodies of work in my chosen media.

I need solitude for writing. It's hard work for me to turn my thoughts into words. Writing is not much fun as a spectator sport and I'm not much fun when my train of thought gets interrupted. So I turn off my phones, and if my family is around, I close the door to my study. It helps me to stay organized and frees me to create. Keeping the words and ideas flowing requires me to dispense with all psychic debris I accumulate in the normal course of life, however painful. Somehow, working at creative expression brings the debris to the surface, and clearing it away encourages further creative expression. For me, the two processes are reciprocal. I require hours of solitude to sift through the psychic debris that surfaces, figuring out what it means and what to do with it. I have had to learn to sit with uncertainty and wait for clarity. This internal work takes time and energy, sometimes limiting what I have to offer others. It's a fine balance, a tightrope I've been walking to keep myself tuned into the world, yet anchored and sometimes suspended in myself.

Solitude is not a concept we find easy in our culture. Most of us can visualize ourselves sitting peacefully alone in a rocker on a porch, on a bench in a garden, or enjoying a beverage of choice in pleasant surroundings. However, we are constantly directed by advertising and the media, among other things, to give our energy to others and to put it into activities outside ourselves: to conform to the tenets of an extroverted life. There's an expectation that we should want to be with people and others may be perplexed when we choose solitude. This can cause some tension when it comes to creative work.

In the early days, when I was writing my journal pages every morning before breakfast, this was such an unusual thing for someone in my family to do that it caused considerable consternation. For the first several weeks, one after another my family members would come into the room where I was working, (even when I had closed the door!) and start talking to me, asking what I was doing and what I wanted for breakfast or making comments to one another about what I was doing, trying to get me to give up my writing and join them. Perhaps they were just being sociable or maybe they were genuinely confused. Maybe, because they didn't understand my need to write, they saw it as rejection—a message that I'd rather not be with them. It took resolve and good communication skills to help them understand that this was about my needs, not my feelings for them. I had to be firm and consistent that this was something I was going to be doing from now on. I assured them I would join them when I was done.

Some of us are afraid to choose solitude for fear of what we might discover when we are alone with our thoughts, feelings and emotions. What will we do if we discover the life we are living bears little resemblance to the one we long for? It takes courage to allow ourselves to feel pain. Solitude can help us work out what to do about it. It has been said that when we don't deal with our own pain, we give it away to others: "Hurt people hurt people." What many of us think of as loneliness is really a fear of being rejected. We are afraid we will be alone, not through choice, but because no one wants us. That confusion of solitude with loneliness and rejection is often about self-esteem. Working out the answers— letting them emerge—is living the creative process.

There is no substitute for time alone, and there's no point in feeling guilty about requiring it. There are creative ways to fill this need. Maybe we can work out a reciprocal arrangement with a friend or neighbour that frees up time for each of us. One writer I know trades households one day a week to get time for writing. She babysits a friend's children with her own, then the next day, her friend takes the children, leaving her free to write for the day. Alternatively, maybe we can house-sit short term for a friend. Possibly we can pay for the services of another person to provide help to free us for a couple of hours a week.

If we know we need solitude and are afraid of being lonely, there are creative solutions. We can ease into it. We can bundle up a journal, sketch-pad or portable computer and take ourselves to a coffee shop, the library or the seating area of a mall. We can have the best of both worlds: company of others without the distraction of having to talk to them while we engage in our own work.

It can be challenging to nurture and protect our creative selves while living in relationship with others. I have had to learn to articulate my need for time, space and energy to the people I live with and love. I entered marriage unaware that I was out of touch with the creative part of myself. It is fair to say that I was never wholly present to myself, or to the relationship. In addition, I had romantic expectations and preconceived ideas of marriage. I believed that my husband and I would be everything to each other—that he would fulfill my emotional needs and take care of me and I would do the same for him. Our marriage was about what I had been brought up to believe one should be: partnership, nice home in suburbia, two cars, holidays away. We spent most of our time with each other, to the point where I gradually let my contact with friends go and believed that was fine with me. Throughout my marriage, I directed my creative energy into this intimate relationship and put the needs of others before my own.

In the early years of our marriage things went well. When I wasn't at work, my energy went into cooking great meals, furnishing the house, creating a home. With a full time job, a husband and a home, the list of things to do kept me permanently busy if I let it, and I did. But as happens in life, eventually a crisis arose that tested my resolve and the structure of the marriage. For us as a couple, this was the issue of children and our inability to conceive. Though we attempted counseling, when I began to understand my needs, I didn't have the communication skills or confidence to articulate them clearly to my husband, and I was afraid to try. The marriage unraveled rapidly. I felt a failure and it took time to understand how things had gone so wrong.

The breakup of the marriage began the process that finally connected me to myself. To cope with my grief, I kept a journal and wrote my way through the breakup. Having an outlet for my thoughts and feelings gave me clarity. Because that was the year I took the leave from my job, I was free during the day for the first time in my life, and had time to fill. I became introspective and did a lot of writing to explore my inner terrain. I unearthed old scripts and childhood patterns. Prompted by a discussion with a friend, I thought and wrote about expectations. There is nothing simple about expectations: they can be pervasive, insidious and restricting. I was surprised to see how constrained I had been. I realized I had spent a lot of time trying to understand others in my life when the person I really needed to understand was myself. I had to free myself from patterns of thinking and behaviour that originated much earlier in my life if I wanted to find contentment, fulfillment and happiness. I created a set of affirmations to help me keep my energy where I wanted it to be creatively:

- My gifts are mine. I nurture them, appreciate them, enjoy them, use them in the best way possible, and share as I choose.

- Anything I share with or give to anyone else is a gift.

- Anything anyone gives me is a gift.

- I am responsible for taking care of my own needs.

- It is not reasonable to expect others to meet my needs.

- I am not responsible for another capable adult's needs.

- My problems are mine to solve.

- I am the best person to solve my problems and fully capable.

- What looks like someone else's issues may be a projection of my own.

- I can choose how I respond.

I found that identifying and eliminating some of the more limiting expectations governing me led to a greater sense of freedom in my creative work. I was more willing to explore directions without knowing where I was going… to colour outside the lines.

There are creative ways to include family members in our activities and doing so can provide unexpected benefits. My sister is dyslexic and has ADHD. Many years ago, when I was learning my way around art tools and materials, I would register the two of us for classes and workshops and we would go together. She was interested in doing creative work, but didn't know what forms or media to pursue. She also had difficulty learning in a standard classroom setting. When we partnered, she could watch me, and I could give her some assistance if she needed it. I knew her well enough that I could often tell what she needed, and she didn't have to be embarrassed to ask a stranger for help. The workshops, including one we took on painting fabric, introduced her to quilting as an art form, and suddenly she felt at home. She loved working with strong colour and designing her own patterns, so she joined the quilt guild in her city, and now makes beautiful art quilts.

Here's what my sister has to say about her creative journey. "It's my seventh year of learning from my friend, Betty, who owns a quilting store. I belong to the quilting group she runs in her store every Thursday morning. Betty is good at working with students like me who have learning disabilities, and I have learned lots of techniques from her. I love working with fabric and making quilts.

"Right now, I am making a quilt that expresses my wild side, the animal in me! I'm using beige, green and gold fabrics in the middle and I will be adding wild animals to the border. Then I am moving on to quilts for two three-year olds. The first quilt will be lime green, orange, dark blue and then a panel with the solar system on it. I am going to add aliens to the plain material in bright multi-colours. The aliens are going to be embroidered on the plain material in wild colours: lime green with bright orange and with as many wild colours that match the material. This is for a little girl who is about three and she is into bright colours. The next quilt will be a hockey quilt for a three year old boy. I will need to buy the material first.

"A trip to a new quilt store is the best thing. I like the colours and the unique materials there are in this world. I have an eye for the most outrageous bunch of colours. The more outrageous, the better I like it. I so enjoy picking out material for people; the material-picking is the most fun part of the trip. It gives a whole new meaning to shopping for me because there are so many possibilities. I don't like clothes shopping but searching for that perfect fabric for a quilt is an experience that I truly enjoy. I like the fact that material shopping can be an all-day affair with another quilter. I enjoy getting feedback from friends who comment on my colour choices. 'Oh my goodness, that's awful!' they'll say, or 'That's really cool.' And sometimes 'That is really you, Jen.' The comments have been really funny at times and we break down and laugh so hard it's infectious and the store-owner laughs too."

It's good to teach and share with others what we know. We don't have to be perfect at something to share. They will take what they need from us and filter out the rest. My Mom has Alzheimer's, but still loves to go on outings with my sister and me. She has no interest in quilting, and can't remember what it is I do, but she goes along happily with us as we check out quilt and art stores, when she knows we will have lunch or tea together afterwards. It takes more energy than going on our own, but we accomplish a number of valuable things including quality time together.

Families can prove challenging. All that drama and conflict they are capable of generating can drain creative energy. My brother and sister do not get along. Their conflict distresses me and, though I'd like the situation to be different, I've had to accept that how they deal with each other is their choice. Most of the time I visit them separately. When we are all together, which happens infrequently, they make an effort to get along for my sake. I find the situation stressful and for my own well-being, I limit the time I spend in this situation.

In my adult life, I have lived single, married, separated, divorced, widowed, childless, in a family with my partner's children, and on my own. What I have learned is that no way of living is perfect. Each brings its own set of challenges and rewards. Since my partner Greg died, I live alone, and though that can mean solitude, it helps that I have made friends with it. I make myself my own first choice. For a while after his death, I had to challenge myself to overcome my fears about going out alone, but I gradually got used to it and now I don't really think about it any more. I go places, do interesting things and live deeply in my own life. I visit with friends and people who make it a point to live in positive, caring energy.

Is there a loneliness of the soul? It seems to me that true loneliness of the soul occurs when we are not able to express the deepest parts of ourselves. Working with our creativity offers us a way to access and express those deep and sometimes hidden parts of ourselves. Giving free rein to creative expression offers us the chance to love ourselves and to offer love to others. I am willing to experience the full range of my emotions: to laugh with others and at myself, and to cry; to share my thoughts and feelings; to be vulnerable; to open myself to psychic and creative work.

Though it can be challenging when I don't see immediate rewards for my effort, I am willing to experience my humanity. I know that the stuff of every day—love and joy, loss and grief—can be a catalyst for creative work and healing. Keeping trust and faith in ourselves, and staying centered in positive practice, we reap the rewards of better relationships, health and creativity and follow the path with heart. We heal ourselves, and those around us. We make space for the possibility of joy.

Exercise #1 Create Your Own Heart or Dream Manifesto.

a) Choose an issue that attracts or drains your energy. It could be something to do with your health, your life, or a dream you have. Write about it first if that is helpful.

b) Draw, paint or colour a full page exploring what it looks and feels like to you. Use colour, stick figures, objects, shape or scrapbook punches, fibres, representational scribbles, words. Whatever works. Don't worry what your page looks like. Just draw what it feels like… how it feels in your body.

c) When done, use journal-style writing to explore in words what the picture and creating it mean to you, and any messages you discovered in the process. Remember:

- There is no wrong way of doing it.
- You are the only one who knows what your drawings mean.
- Stay out of your mind… get into your body.
- Trust your instincts.
- If you sense resistance to explore a particular issue, there are two options. The issue might need more gestation before it is ready to be explored, in which case you can just note it and come back to it later. Alternatively, you might want to explore the resistance as the "issue." What is the message in the resistance?
- Honour your process.

Exercise #2 Claim Solitude

One way or another, designate a time one day this week to be with yourself. Free yourself from all tasks and electronic devices.

a) If getting time on your own is an issue for you, list the challenges you face.

b) For each, work out the requirement(s).

c) Then create a list of ways these requirements could be met. The point of this exercise is to figure out how to create some solitude for yourself and to be comfortable with it. What you do with the time is up to you. You can sit and do nothing; go for a walk; visit the park; do something enjoyable on your own.

d) Take a journal if you wish and record thoughts as they arise or you can do this later. How does it feel to be on your own?

Exercise #3 Expectations and Old Scripts

Think about your expectations with regards to your own life.

a) What are they?

b) How might they be limiting you?

c) Are you following any old scripts that are limiting your creative expression?

d) Explore your expectations in writing.

e) Then create your own affirmations for the life you wish to live.

Exercise #4 Family Matters

a) Think about your own family. Are there unresolved conflicts and injuries draining your energy? List them.

b) Pay careful attention to what you tell yourself as you are compiling your lists. Can you see a way to resolve the issues or ease the conflict?

c) Is it possible to make peace with your family for your own good? Are there family members you can ask for support and co-operation?

d) If not, are there steps you can take that allow you to restore and maintain your own peace of mind and creative energy?

SIXTEEN

Living in the Labyrinth

Many of us dream of being paid well for jobs that allow us to do what we love. Those of us who work at a job spend up to 40 percent or more of our waking hours at or travelling to work.[1] That's a lot of hours in a year, and a lot of years in a life. It's important to feel that what we do with those years matters and to derive satisfaction from them. How do we go about choosing a job or career that will be satisfying for such a length of time? And what do we do if the job we end up with isn't our dream job? Where does our creativity fit in?

Most of us have a sense of what draws our interest and know intuitively what fields might hold rewarding work for us. Thomas Moore in *A Life At Work* calls what draws us and makes us willing to struggle to achieve a dream our "daimon." He writes:

> *For the ancient Greeks, a daimon is an unnamed urge that pushes you in a certain direction. It is the force behind the passion and tenacity of your yearning… The daimon is a primal creative urge. It doesn't inspire a single well-defined career… it can also wake you up with a startle… offering you a kernel of vision for your future. This is one of the functions of the daimon.*[2]

To recognize the *daimon*, we have to ask ourselves what mysterious power keeps us looking in a particular direction.

Chances are good we will be able to exercise our creativity through work if it's in a field that draws our interest.

Early in my life, I was attracted to teaching. When I was in Grade 6, I was sent to junior classes to read to them when their teachers needed a few minutes to do other tasks. Though I was interested in other things through my years in high school and university, I retained the desire to teach, and moreover decided I'd like to teach English at the high school level. I enjoyed working with teenagers, and I was confident I could do a good job. Though I was invited by the faculty at university to enroll in the Master's English program—and might have enjoyed that—I felt the need to earn a living. Consequently, I put myself through teacher's college.

I enjoyed my career as a teacher. I had a strong purpose, focus and role in life—felt that what I did mattered and served a larger purpose. I was educating young people and helping them to realize their capabilities, so they could move forward in their lives and eventually take their place in society as responsible citizens. I always had company in the venture. I was part of a community, working with people I liked and respected. I enjoyed working with my students and designing my classes. For the first 10 years or so, my work was my creative outlet and I found it satisfying. I could be as innovative as I liked providing what I did fit the Ministry of Education Guidelines. I enjoyed that freedom.

I was fortunate to find a career that allowed me to exercise my creativity freely and completely, but there are other possibilities. It is possible to hold a job that pays the bills while creative work, either paid or volunteer, is done in a second job later in the day or on weekends. Actors, models, make-up artists, and stylists often take classes and work in shows at night or on the weekends. I took art classes and took part in art shows while I was teaching.

Some people prefer the unrestricted freedom to explore their creativity outside a job. A female friend of mine who is a writer works shifts on the assembly line at a car manufacturing plant. It's not for everyone, but it supports her lifestyle and suits her writing habit. The money's good, the shift work provides a schedule where both days and nights are free on an alternating basis, and at the end of her work day, she can walk away free to focus her attention on the novel she is writing.

Identifying and following the urgings of our *daimon*(s) does not guarantee a perfect creative outlet, job or career. For most of us there will be drawbacks and setbacks in our work, and that was certainly true for me. The teaching workload can be heavy if done properly. In the public school system, a teacher's hours are tightly scheduled. In addition to the daily preparation, delivery, and follow-up, when I was not in my classroom teaching, I was marking and preparing units for later in the year, attending staff meetings, holding interviews with parents, and coaching extracurricular activities.

Often, I found it all-consuming and didn't have much energy left by the end of the day. In my first year, an assistant department head of English, a woman whom I respected, cautioned me, "Corporations are like giant vacuum cleaners. They suck out all you have to give and then move on to the next person." Despite this warning, I was shocked later that year to learn the job I had poured so much of myself into had become redundant as a result of falling enrollment.

The principal called me out of class one Monday morning in March to tell me my job no longer existed. He then expected me to go back to my class and finish teaching. Being new to the profession, I was unaware there was a protocol for redundancy and that I would be transferred to another school. No one informed me of this, so within 24 hours, I had resumes mailed out around the province, and within two days, I had a job offer I was prepared to accept. It was a full week before anyone in my home board told me three other high schools in the area had jobs I was qualified for, and interviews had been lined up for me. In the end, I chose to stay because I was tired of moving.

That was a traumatic experience, and pivotal in shaping the direction my career would take. I was angry about how events had been allowed to unfold. I saw that good communication and people skills were sadly lacking at the administrative level. I learned that I could put my heart and soul into my work, give it my best, and still be cut at the end of the day—or in the middle of the day. I was the only one who really seemed to care.

I was also introduced to the teachers' federation and the role it played in job protection. Though they were slow off the mark with me, I was very grateful for the clauses in the contract that protected my job. In the end, the transfer turned out to be a good thing. I liked my new principal, my colleagues and the students. Life improved. Even the architecture of the building was better—I had my own classroom with a full bank of windows. I had spent my first year teaching in a room with no windows. Because I arrived before 8 a.m. and left in the dark after coaching, I hadn't seen daylight during the week for two months of that first winter.

I stayed at my second school for 10 years. In that decade, I found new ways to exercise my creativity at work. I became involved in the federation and began applying for positions of added responsibility within the board, a journey that would occupy much of my time and energy for the next 20 years. I became an English Department Head, enrolled in a Master's degree program and took the principal's qualifications. I hadn't initially set out to become a principal; I had no role models and had difficulty finding female mentors.

When I started teaching in the mid-seventies, the population of public high school teachers in Ontario had a 70-30 male-female ratio. In the board I worked for, at that time all 16 high school principals were men. For much of my career, as I sought positions within the secondary structure, I was interviewed by panels of men, from three to seven at a time. I had to look to the elementary panel to find women principals willing to mentor me. My *daimon* surfaced again: I held a conviction that it was time for women to be high school administrators, and I was in a position to take on that challenge.

Concurrently, I had a second "career" in the federation. I was elected and appointed to various committees including the regional executive and collective bargaining team, and the provincial Status of Women committee. I even had the audacity to start a women's committee locally. By necessity, most of the work of the federation is carried out after school hours, so I often found myself working evenings and weekends. Though it was tiring, there were rewards. I found the work of establishing a committee and formulating clauses for collective bargaining to be stimulating and creative. I enjoyed the camaraderie of working closely with others to improve working conditions for everyone in education. Holding a leadership position in the federation was also recognized as a route to a leadership position within the board, provided I performed well. I affixed my signature to years worth of collective agreements for the board, and won provincial awards for excellence in my work.

It used to be that one would settle into a job or career in one's 20's and stay there for life. These days, it's more likely that we will hold down a succession of jobs, each offering us the chance to hone our skills and discover the kind of work we enjoy, so it's important to reflect on where we've been. It's how we keep ourselves on track, headed in our preferred direction. It also allows us to inventory our skills as they develop. This is just as true for creative work as it is for our day jobs. Many excellent creative opportunities require us to submit applications showcasing our skills, abilities and accomplishments. Each updated resume opens new opportunities we can apply for.

As it turned out, I had to apply three times over the course of four years to be short-listed for a position as a vice principal even though my work was good, as were my interviews. I never got a definitive reason why my application was turned down. Twice I was told, "Next time you'll make it." I suspected that my work on behalf of women had a negative impact on my advancement to an administrative career but had no concrete evidence.

I found those years discouraging and developed a mantra for dealing with corporations: persistence is everything. Eventually they would run out of excuses to keep me from where I wanted to go. And they did. Years afterward, a couple of the men who had been on the teams interviewing me told me that my work on behalf of women had been unfairly held against me. I had been labelled a female willing to challenge the status quo. Looking back, it seems to me this was actually a strength. In a high school, the administrative team consists of the principal, the vice principals and various support staff. For years, I was the only woman administrator in the high school where I was assigned.

I enjoyed the challenge of the job, and as an administrator, was finally in a position to assist others, both male and female. I worked with good people, but there were no other women at my level within the school to talk to about the problems and daily challenges, and I found I was often lonely. I had to learn to speak up often and early, to have confidence, to be my own best advocate. Things are different now. The gender balance of the teaching population has shifted, as has the make up of administration.

How do we balance the need to earn a living with the need to make a life? Looking back, I see that during those years, I had three outlets for my creative energy: my job, my marriage and my home. I put too much of it into my job and didn't cultivate my personal creative self-expression outside of these three spheres. I was an introvert living an extroverted life. I directed most of my energy outward to the world around me, unaware that by constantly doing so, I was eroding my sense of self.

When I was on the cusp of achieving my position as vice principal, I often felt physically drained. My marriage ended and we had to sell our house. In the shifting tides of my personal life, my job was the constant that kept me anchored but even there, circumstances changed. The board introduced an early morning start time for high school students, which meant I had to be at work by 7:30 a.m. or earlier, always working against my circadian rhythm. I was commuting weekly to Toronto to complete my master's degree. My "To Do" list of household tasks and errands never seemed to get done.

There is one more thing worth mentioning about these years. Whatever the work we do, our jobs exist in a particular historical context, and mine was no different. Education is a provincial government jurisdiction and teachers are at the mercy of the party in power, especially if it has a majority government. These were the 1990's in Ontario when the Conservatives, led by Mike Harris, had their sights firmly fixed on restructuring education in a way that didn't sit well with many teachers. Though often in my career, I have felt powerless as I learned about changes to my job from reading the front page of a newspaper, I found these years particularly depressing. I felt attacked by my own government— my employer—and that attack played itself out daily in the public eye. I found the climate toxic.

As it happened, in the years when I was applying to be a vice-principal, I became eligible for a year-long, self-funded leave of absence, the result of a leave plan I had discovered in the contract during my years in collective bargaining. Essentially, if an employee was approved for a deferred salary leave, the board established a trust fund into which was deposited a pre-determined percent of the employee's yearly salary. In my case, I chose to defer 20 per cent of my salary for four years. In the fifth year of the plan, I was eligible for a year off with 80 per cent of my salary. In addition to providing a year off, this exercise taught me to live on less than I earned, a life skill that has proven useful.

Taking that year off was not without risk. I was on the short list for a vice-principal position. A male superintendent had once counselled me that if I ever had to choose between time and money, to opt for time as that is a finite resource in life. Now, that same superintendent asked me if I'd rather have my vice-principal position or the year off. When I said I wanted both, he replied: "You know the board doesn't work that way." In fact, one of my short-listed male colleagues had taken a leave the previous year and had been promoted into a vice-principal position on his return.

At any rate, I was in need of a break, decided to take a chance, and by doing so, changed my life.

My creativity was energized and released. I discovered a world outside the workplace. I had the chance to travel the world with a group of friends. I had time to think about my life and realized I had missed a lot. I took photographs, and that was the beginning of my personal creative odyssey. I met Greg, lived with him for part of the year, and thought about moving to be with him permanently, even though there were no jobs for me in his area. As I contemplated resigning from the board, I got "the call" and was offered a vice-principal position in my home board. Greg felt I should take the job because I had worked so long and hard to achieve it. Though it was a tough choice, I did. My *daimon* was still calling.

When I returned to work in my new position as vice-principal after my year off, I found the political climate further deteriorated under the Mike Harris government. That fall, there was a province-wide strike in education. For the first and only time in my life, I walked a picket line, as did my colleagues from teacher to vice-principal to principal. And at the end of it, the government retaliated by legislating principals and vice principals out of the federation, ending decades of collegial co-operation within the school environment, permanently and irrevocably altering the state of the union.

I am one who prefers to work in an atmosphere where I feel supported by the community and the system as a whole. Needless to say, it didn't take me long to sign up for another self-funded leave. In fact, I decided that I was going to keep taking advantage of them for the rest of my career until I could retire. My *daimon* and I had lost interest in much of the venture of education, something that would have been inconceivable to me earlier in my career. And the *daimon* governing my need for creative expression was calling. My friend, the Jungian analyst comments, "The *daimon* morphs into a demon when denied by the ego. We see this in the nightmares that haunt us."

How do we cultivate, incorporate and express our creativity in both our work and whatever time remains to us outside of work? In the early decades of my teaching career, I was not conscious of my personal creative needs. I thought I could get all the challenge I needed from my job. At that point I didn't really understand the difference between extrinsic and intrinsic motivation and reward. Though the work I was doing required careful thinking and reflection, it did not tap the deepest reaches of my soul and never would.

This didn't necessarily mean I was in the wrong job. It meant I needed to cultivate other aspects of myself outside of work, especially my creativity, if I wished to live a happy, balanced life, and I wasn't doing that. I had given up things that gave me energy, like movies and concerts. I did a tiny bit of professional writing but found that marking papers used up the quality of attention I needed for more than that. I had begun to keep a journal but I had not yet learned to restore myself by tapping into and giving expression to the deep well of my own creative energy and abilities for their own sake (and mine). I had yet to discover and access the rich resources of my own internal creative world.

Though I continued to work hard at my job, and had new experiences that kept me growing, I was beginning to turn my focus away from my career and work that I no longer found completely satisfying. It was past time to bring my life into the balance that had eluded me for so long. I wished to spend my time exploring my own life, and enjoying Greg's company. I set up an art studio and began working in it. I began the search for my own voice and preferred media of expression. I joined professional groups that supported my activities of choice: art-making, photography and writing.

Unfortunately, most of these groups met at night and I didn't have the time or energy to attend. I did enter some of the open competitions sponsored by these groups and found the deadlines helped me to focus my creative work. I found myself becoming intrinsically motivated: this was work that sparked my creative imagination and tapped into my heart and soul. The world opened up for me as I followed the call of my internal desires. In these domains, I was answerable only to myself. I had concrete results to show for my time and energy, and I owned what I produced.

But the true brilliance of spreading my creative wings was the antidote it provided to all that was so draining in my daily working life. A few minutes alone with a tube of brightly-colored paint was powerful enough to shift my mood and restore my energy. When I was unable to sleep at 3 a.m., I discovered that if I got up and spent a few minutes painting or writing in one of my journals, I could then go back to bed and sleep soundly for the rest of the night. I had the surprise of discovering that even with the little bits of time and attention I was able to give, both my skill level and the quality of my work improved. And what was so unexpected, I had the joy of creating beautiful work. Over time, I recognized the importance of this work to the state of my well-being, and my creative work emerged as a vocation.

From my experiences, particularly in education, I learned that the dream of the ideal career may be more romantic than pragmatic. Even when one chooses what one wishes to do and is paid well for it, it's still a lot of work. Since exiting education, I have had moments when I've experienced disappointment about how that career ended. For so long, I thought I would become a principal, if not a superintendent, and I invested a lot of time and energy pursuing that path. Instead, I walked away.

Coming to terms with my decision to leave education helped me to distinguish between a job, a career, and a life's work. A job, whether perfect or not, is the particular work one does each day. If paid, it is a means to an end, usually supporting our daily life. We also do various unpaid jobs throughout our lives, and these can be just as important to the overall shape of our lives. Jobs tend to change over time, as mine did, whether by design, restructuring, accident or serendipity. A career is built from the jobs one does over time in any particular field or related fields, and a career, too, will evolve. A career may or may not end with retirement, and it is possible to have more than one at a time. Every working parent knows of what I speak.

One's life work, however, is more complex; it has profound value as an expression of who we are. It encompasses all the work of any kind that we do over the years of our lifetime, whether we choose it, fall into it accidentally, or are conscripted; whether it is paid or unpaid. A life's work incorporates all the choices, all the contributions we make to the larger society through our jobs or our careers, our volunteer efforts, our social connections at work, in partnerships and with family and our creativity. A life's work also includes the development and expression of the self as we take on myriad tasks and mature through the years. This development only ends when we die. When we think of our lives this way, then a job or even a career is a piece of the puzzle. However fulfilling, they are unlikely to be enough by themselves, as I discovered throughout my career in education.

Life presents us with challenges and opportunities that we never expected, and these will be part of our life's work. As I mentioned earlier, when Greg died, I spent a couple of years working with a Jungian analyst to come to terms with my grief and to work out where to go from there in my life. I found the analytical work deeply satisfying and wondered if I should become an analyst myself.

At the time, Muriel was completing her analytical training at the Jung Institute in Zurich, Switzerland. At her invitation, I travelled to Switzerland and attended some of the lectures at the Institute. Sitting in the lecture hall listening to the various speakers, I realized that I didn't want to become an analyst; what I really wanted to work with was creativity, mine and others', in all its many guises. Since that time, I have found that working with creativity sometimes benefits from analytical work. That Jungian grounding, rather than being a wrong path, has proven useful.

It takes considerable creativity to balance and blend all the aspects of our lives into a meaningful, coherent whole. It can also take considerable time to sift through all of it consciously, taking to heart our successes, resolving our problems, forgiving and repairing our "mistakes," altering directions. It can take years for some of our ideas to germinate, and still more years to build the skills, connections, independence and interdependence that make for a life that is fulfilling, deeply-lived and creatively expressed.

There are rhythms and cycles to our work as there are to our creativity. Sometimes both can seem to be "sleeping," even though ideas are percolating under the surface. This is a time that requires patience. Other times we are in the full rush of creative ideas. The ebb and flow are natural parts of the process. As we work with them, we will discover when we need to be stimulated and when we need to rest. We are truly rich if at any given point, we have made peace with ourselves, our work and the circumstances of our lives. We can move forward doing what we do best, then relax and sleep well at night.

Exercise #1 Fields of Interest, Satisfaction and Creativity

a) What, if any, fields of interest/work most draw your attention? Are you currently working in one of these fields?

b) Can you exercise your creativity in your job? If not, why not? Do you have the power to change the parameters of your job?

c) If you do not enjoy your job, are there organizations, ideas or activities you could explore that might help you find new work or make your current work more creative and satisfying?

Exercise #2 Career History

To understand where you are now in your creative life, sometimes it can be helpful to trace how you got where you are in your life now.

a) Have there been events in your job or career that have been instrumental in shaping where you are now? If so, what are they?

b) Have these events impacted your creativity in any way?

c) Can you identify any patterns in your career history?

d) Do they tell you something about your creative abilities, interests and accomplishments?

Exercise #3 Inventory Your Conditions of Work

a) What are the benefits and drawbacks to your work? Make this list.

b) Is there anything you'd like to change? If so, what steps can you take?

c) If there are things you dislike and can't change, are they costing you energy?

d) What strategies do you use to cope?

e) Is there scope to exercise your creativity within these challenges?

Exercise #4 Creativity, Workplace Hours and Flexibility

a) Have you ever considered taking a time-out from work or working fewer hours? What would make this opportunity possible for you? What might you do with the time if you had it?

b) Though not all employers offer the kind of leave I was able to take advantage of, sometimes it's possible to make your own "leave plan," even if it's short or part-time. Review your current financial priorities including savings habits. Are there changes you could make that would give you more flexibility than you currently have?

Exercise #5 Seeking Balance

a) Do you have balance in your life? If not, what changes might you need to make in order to create it?

b) When you find your work draining, what gives you back energy? Do you do these things? If not, why not?

c) Make dates with yourself to restore your energy. Write them on your calendar and keep them.

Exercise #6 Review: the Big Questions

Keeping in mind that the number of years we have to live is finite, it's good to reflect regularly on where we are, and ask ourselves the following questions:

a) Do I have a sense of my life's work? Where am I in life at the moment?

b) How do I wish to use my energy? Am I directing it where I wish it to go?

c) What do I wish to accomplish?

d) Am I on track, or do I need to alter course?

e) Where am I in my creative life? Are ideas flowing or do I need to rest?

f) Am I happy?

SEVENTEEN

In the end is my beginning

When I first embarked on this journey five years ago, I wondered if I could make a career for myself as a photographer, artist, and writer. I had a vision of walking away from my job in education one day, and into my new fully-fledged creative career the next. That's not exactly what happened. Turned out, there was a bit of a gap between my vision and my lived experience. Even though I had good plans and had laid the ground work for years beforehand, moving from a life where every hour of the day is scheduled, programmed and accounted for, to one where each day is a blank slate, left me feeling anxious and confused. This was unexpected.

It's only in looking back that I realize making the transition from working in the corporate world, to working on my own was more difficult than I had anticipated. The day I walked away from my career, I lost the bulwark of my routines, and then discovered there is nothing trivial about them. Though I had struggled within their confines, they had also provided me with a secure comfortable base. I had confidence in myself, and a safe place to return. Suddenly just living through each unstructured day felt risky. Furthermore, though I had extricated myself from my education career physically, the routines etched in my brain by 30-plus years of repetition took more than two years to purge. I was way out of my comfort zone and not confident of what I was attempting. I had to give myself permission to be who I am, a person with a great desire for both written and visual creative self-expression. I had to commit to living that life by developing the habits to support it.

Even though I was motivated to create and practice new patterns of behaviour, this proved challenging and at times, downright frustrating. I wasn't used to so much freedom and unplanned time and found myself overwhelmed at the thought of all the hours in the day that had to be filled. There was nothing I had to do and no-one around to talk to. Most of the people I knew were still at work. Without an official job to validate me, I felt like I'd suddenly lost my purpose and role in life, that I was unimportant. I felt guilty getting paid (my early retirement pension) for being at home doing "nothing" when I wasn't sick. I was not used to the emptiness, and didn't yet see it as full of possibility. I found myself not quite knowing where to start. It took effort and self-discipline to create and practice new routines. I suppose that is what makes change so difficult.[1]

I was also tired and physically drained. I spent the first couple of weeks as a couch potato watching the Winter Olympics. I was lucky to have something so inspiring to fill those first empty days; it restored some of my energy and optimism. TV can serve as a comfort structure, as can anything capable of stopping our unoccupied mind from drifting into the past or jumping ahead into the future, conjuring destructive scenarios and anxiety.[2] The seduction of TV is that it's easy to get hooked on the mindless freedom from anxiety it offers, so that we spend increasing amounts of our free time watching it, instead of becoming actively engaged in creative work. Perhaps that is why creative people such as Madonna banish it from their lives. I have not been quite that brave.

The rhythm of my days shifted completely over this period. I was waking up on my own about 7:30 a.m., late by workday standards, but natural to my body. That extra sleep allowed me to take back the night. I had a social life at night for the first time in decades. It gave me pleasure and creative energy to attend movies and concerts during the week, and I found friends with whom to share those events. I could eat meals and exercise later in the day and my body was happy with that. I had time to sit on my deck during the day with no neighbours around, to reflect on where I was in my life, to enjoy my home and the peace of the outdoors.

Since my days were free, I began to work through my list of household tasks (another comfort structure!). My home was now my workspace and I wanted it to be comfortable and inviting: I had it painted and bought new furniture. Getting these things done reminded me that this kind of creative work also takes time, energy and effort: six weeks for delivery of a pair of chairs; two weeks for the painter to arrive and another two weeks for the painting to be done, though the estimate had been for one week.

I joined professional and interest groups in art-making, photography and writing. I had the time and energy to attend evening meetings and there I found groups of people to network with, along with opportunities to take part in workshops, competitions and exhibitions. Entry deadlines gave me motivation to focus on my creative work. My days began to fill with creative activities and I was working in my studio again. As I constructed routines based on these interests, my new life began to take shape. As I gained comfort with them, I began spending hours at home doing my creative work and writing my book.

I learned my best creative hours are in the morning and that if I do my creative work in the mornings, I use my time well, and my days work out the way I want them to. I feel good about myself for doing my work and am rarely plagued by guilt about procrastinating. Though I had to grit my teeth and face the fear of the blank page the first several months until I got used to my writing routine, I've been disciplined enough to sit at my computer most mornings and write.

This, too, has been more difficult than I expected. I often struggled with confusion and uncertainty, in the effort to articulate my thoughts clearly and to get them typed into the computer.

Though it might not show on the outside, retrieving ideas from the depths is demanding physical, mental and emotional labour. It takes patience, concentration, attentiveness and much, much longer than I imagined. The hardest part of my creative work is to create something new—something I haven't seen before, for which I have no blueprint. I have to take a leap of faith, plunge into myself, and trust that something will come of my time and effort. The process is uncompromising in that it will settle for nothing less than honesty. I am finding that if I want to write my truth, I have to live it, eliminating as much as I can the gap between what I think in my head, what I feel in my heart, what I experience with my body and what I say to the world.

I thought I would make art in the afternoons, but by the time I am done a morning of writing, I'm hungry and my body is tired of sitting. I often experience a form of creative angst that signals fatigue. In short, I'm drained of focused attention and creative energy, and I have to take a break. Three routines help me at this point in my day: meditation, walking and lunch. However, by the time I've completed them, it's usually somewhere around 2:30 p.m. and I no longer have the same quality of concentration that I have when I start my day. Establishing art as an afternoon routine is happening gradually as I gain comfort with the shape of my day. When I have an art exhibition deadline approaching, I flip my activities and do art in the morning.

It's important that we bring ourselves to our creative work with good reserves of energy and clear minds whenever possible. If we know when we do our best creative work, we can design our schedules with that in mind, protecting our best creative time. Whether we are best early in the morning, late at night or sometime in between, the quality of our work will be better for it.

Despite my struggles with my writing in the past years, I finished this manuscript. I have also created artwork for more than twenty group and solo exhibitions. This past year, I took part in two studio tours for the first time, and they proved very successful. Along the way, one of my art works won the curator's choice award at a juried show in a respected gallery and resulted in a prestigious solo show. That experience is recounted at the beginning of this book.

I joined an artists' cooperative gallery and that has been an extraordinary experience. There are 20 of us artists, all local, who belong to the co-op. Our gallery is a storefront space in a downtown mall, donated to us free of charge by the corporation that owns the mall. Our understanding with the corporation is that we will fix up the space, staff it on our own and provide art experiences to the public as a community service. We can be moved or let go at any time if someone wishes to rent our space. So far, we've been granted a new space elsewhere within the mall each time someone's wanted our space, and this has happened several times.

As a co-operative, we've become a hybrid enterprise, in the business and management of art as well as the creation of it. We devised a non-profit system to fund and staff the venture, whereby each artist pays a fee (currently $20.00 a month) for things like creating a website and promoting our work. In addition, each artist agrees to take three four-hour gallery-sitting shifts per month. No commission is applied to our work if it sells, so the money goes directly to the artist. The volume of sales is certainly greater than any one of us could generate on our own, though perhaps not as high as we would like. It's still more difficult to convince people to spend their money on art than it is to get them to buy groceries, fast cars and other luxuries.

An in-house gallery committee mounts a new show of our work every six weeks. That alone has motivated me and kept me growing as an artist. Over the five-year time-span of the gallery, I am pleased to see greater visual interest, increased skill, depth and complexity in my work and that is perhaps the chief benefit for me. There are many other benefits as well. This gallery has provided terrific exposure for us as artists. Our website and advertising flyers keep the community informed of our events and that information reaches a lot of people. We see a broad cross-section of the public come through our doors to browse, interact with the artists and sometimes purchase work. The corporation benefits by having otherwise unrented space full and active, contributing to the overall vibrancy of the mall. What a boon to the community, the arts and artists if more corporations could follow this model. We always have a waiting list of artists wishing to join the gallery. That says to me there is a community need for the development of more spaces like ours.

In these years, I've had success in photography as well, all the more surprising as I put it on the back burner while my energy has gone into writing and art. But I still love beautiful photographs because they capture and hold perfect moments of time. I bought a good digital camera and have begun to learn my way around it and Photoshop. I have experimented with lenses and new techniques. I entered a photo in the digital category of a juried competition at a university and received an honorable mention. Step by step, my skill level is increasing.

Have I made enough money through these efforts to survive? The short answer is no. In fact, everything to do with money made me nervous for the first couple of years after I left education. It's taken me a while to adjust to my new financial circumstances. My pension, though less than I was earning through teaching, frees me to do the work I love and I am deeply grateful for that. Though I've made more than I expected from the sale of my artwork, materials, matting and framing remain one of my biggest expenses, only covered if I sell the work. I have done some supply teaching to help pay the bills.

It has been interesting to discover that I could probably have a new career teaching art and creativity at college and university, extending to the graduate level. I have received unsolicited invitations to teach at two universities and a college, in addition to a special art school in Elora, where I taught for a couple of summers. In these classes, I teach interested, motivated adults and that has been an exhilarating, gratifying experience. I can see that if I wished to pursue opportunities at other colleges and universities, the door is open, and I could probably earn a good salary.

So once again, I have found myself wrestling with the question about whether to teach. It takes me weeks to write the manuals of original exercises and put together the materials I use for a week-long class. It tires me physically, and it takes time away from my other creative work. I'm no longer willing to work the kind of hours I used to. That might be a function of age, of having already put in more than 30 years in a career, of having pushed myself hard over the course of those years, of having the cushion of a pension, of wanting better balance at this stage of my life. If I were younger, I might take up the challenge. At this point, I'm not sure I want to and the joy is I don't have to.

After five years on this creative path, my life feels as full as it did before I left education, so much so that recently I've actually had to cut back on the number of commitments I accept. I'm finally in a position to choose the ones that most appeal to me. And that is a great place to be. If I were younger I would probably work more hours, and accomplish more. Not putting in the hours means there are projects in my head that might never get done, things I'm capable of that I might never achieve. But I'm beginning to make peace with doing less. These days I prefer to respect the well-being of my body, integrating time with friends and relaxing. Doing so makes for a happier more fulfilling life, and my creative vision is more focused as a result.

As I write this chapter, I am discovering that the process I have used to make this major transition in my life follows the same pattern I use in my creative work. Like every other creative project I've attempted, changing careers began with an emptying out in preparation for an energy shift. "Do-er" that I am, I find this a lonely, difficult stage. I used to confuse it with depression. Though intellectually I know better, it feels like there is nothing left for me in life. I have nothing left to give, no energy of any kind and there is nothing for me to receive. I've learned that I have to be with it for however long it takes. I sleep, lie on the couch and stare into space a lot at this stage. I prefer hibernating at home to being with people. I often find myself cleaning up the clutter around my house at this stage. I throw out or give away stuff that is no longer useful: a metaphorical expression and reflection of my physical and spiritual state. In the energy wave that propels my life, though it feels like I am at the bottom of the trough, this is the stage where I grapple both consciously and unconsciously with the need to move forward. I begin storing up the energy to do so.

Then gradually my energy shifts. I know I am in the next stage of the process when I suddenly find myself going to the library and checking out non-fiction works on topics that are newly interesting. This is the quest for inspiration. I buy magazines, go to movies, seek out interesting experiences, meet new people, gather resources that appeal to me. I become interested in ideas and enduring values. I wonder about the best way to live this short span of time I am allotted. I am like a sponge, absorbing what is around me and I become passionately engaged in thinking about how to incorporate what I see into my life and work. I carry a little notebook with me so when inspiration strikes, I can capture it for future reference. The wave of energy is moving me upwards from the trough.

When I start to create new routines, and have a desire to go to my studio to see what I can create with these new ideas, I am in the third stage of my process. Those first tentative steps usually have good energy to them, though I'm sometimes disappointed with the results. Where is my instant gratification? I have to remember that experimentation is necessary, and a valuable part of the process. I have to stay with it and have faith that it will take me where I need to go. I use a lot of positive self-talk at this stage, and I journal through everything, so I'm always reaching to articulate my vision clearly.

Then comes the serious and most challenging work of the new quest as I struggle to reshape my life, to give rise to something new. When I am deeply engaged in the struggle, I tend to hibernate so as to focus my energy where I need it most: in the dialogue between my body, brain, heart and soul as I search for the truest means I am capable of to give shape to whatever wishes to find expression. I usually recognize it intuitively when I find it.

At this stage, energy is carrying me up the slope of the wave to a higher level than I've been before. I don't know this territory and I have lots of moments of uncertainty, anxiety, struggle as I seek to fine tune how I do things, the quality, visual interest and aesthetic appeal of my work, whether it's for myself or a broader audience.

The fifth step is trying it out in the world… the peak of the wave and the beginning of the trip down the backside of the slope to the emptying out where the cycle will begin again. As I finished the first draft of my manuscript, I realized I needed to take it for a test drive. I gave copies to trusted friends asking them to read it and write comments on the pages they felt needed revision. Laying myself bare on the page for others to see caused me some apprehension, but taking the risk proved worth-while. They drew my attention to passages where greater clarity was needed and helped me to find and eliminate ones that didn't work. Their feedback was invaluable and guided me in re-shaping the manuscript before I sent it to an editor.

Seeking inspiration, gathering resources, taking first tentative steps, experimenting, reviewing, polishing results, finishing and sending out to the world, emptying out…. The process of creating something new is the same, whether in life or creative projects and it is this rhythm of life that can make us feel we are riding a roller coaster. The issues I've written about in this book are issues I've had to face many times, and the strategies I've written about are the ones I've used to re-engineer my life. And why not? Building one's life is the most creative of acts.

Five years ago, I feared it was too late to start my new career—that I was kidding myself to think I could suddenly set out to do this six decades into life. So I'm pleased to discover that all those years of living count for something. My life experience has given me the gift of focused attention, helping me to make quick progress. I have been able use the skills and knowledge I acquired over those decades in education and elsewhere effectively in my new activities.

I am finally able to create the life that suits me. Freed from the need to earn a living, I can express whatever I wish in my creative work. That is a privileged and profound freedom. I have established the creative career I dreamed of, and I feel I am where I wish to be. My life has an underlying happiness to it now that was missing in my earlier years.

Ideally, we would know and follow our passions early in life, but starting later in life works too. All my years of experience as an employee, within a union, as a "boss" in a corporation, working collegially and independently, taking time out from work, and working on my own at home prepared me for the challenges of shifting into a new career and starting my own business. Seen from this perspective, leaving education was a graduation, something to celebrate, a joyful step taken to advance the work I now feel called to complete. Sometimes we only learn the rightness of a decision by living it. That, too, is the leap of faith and the creative process.

These days I find I am quite content to stay home and do my own work, and that tells me more than anything how far I've travelled in the past five years. I no longer need or seek so many distractions from the external world. I'm more focused on the activities prompted by my internal one. In these years, I have made the transition to being a writer. I write to make sense of my life and to find my truth, and this book has helped me to do that.

Already, I find the germ of an idea for a new book floating in my head. This is unexpected, a place I never thought to arrive. Yet I know deep within, it is part of who I am. And I see it is not an especially easy place to live, as it demands much. But then the best things often do. They stretch and grow us in ways we never thought possible, never anticipated and would not necessarily go into on our own. Sometimes images come into my brain like waking dreams to inform me about where I am in my life, and one emerged for me as I was writing this chapter.[3] I saw a butterfly emerging from a cocoon, wings still damp, fully-fledged but vulnerable.

I feel I have come full circle in my life. In my earliest years, I had a rich creative life that was supported by my family, the school system, and the community. Now, I have this life again. Somewhere along the way, in the course of living, I lost track of part of myself or got knocked off balance. It seems that giving up something at the core of myself was the cost of growing up. Those high school and university years gave me a solid knowledge base which I'm grateful for, broadened my horizons and made my career possible, yet didn't teach me what I needed to know about creative work or how to sustain the self-expression I enjoyed early on.

Missing something, I turned to external distractions and addictions, ingesting and creating painful negative scripts which I then spent much of my life trying to free myself from. The struggle has taught me that it takes a great deal of comfort and safety to be willing to risk feeling that internal chaos, anxiety, and emptiness, which may be the shadow side of creativity, a legacy of our brain power, and part of being human. It took me a lot of work to identify, understand and solve the problems and decades to develop the consciousness to recognize that creative self-expression is a valid purpose in life, as is living the process. Somehow returning to my creative work has helped me regain my footing in life and restored my sense of internal balance. I feel whole again.

If creativity is natural to all of us, and I, with all my advantages in life, could still lose touch with it—there are implications for how we sustain it over the course of a life-time. There is a whole industry devoted to helping athletes reach top levels in their fields, yet much of creative development is simply left to chance. We can do better, for our children and for ourselves.

When it comes to our children, we need to support and nurture the development of their mental, emotional, spiritual and creative fitness and well-being, just as we support the development of their bodies through physical fitness. We do this by observing their interests, listening to what they have to say, and sometimes hearing what they are not saying. We can introduce them to activities they might enjoy, and participate with them in the things that matter to them, always being careful to refrain from imposing our dreams. When they show interest and promise, we can nurture them with whatever means are at our disposal, time and attention being the most important resources. Additional teaching and coaching may also be valuable and available through school and community programs. There are no substitutes for hands on experience and good teaching.[4]

And it's important for us to continue our own development as we reach adulthood. We need to seek out opportunities, to encourage and support each other in pursuing what we are passionate about—whatever gives us joy and makes meaning in our lives. Nurturing creative interest is meant to be a life-long adventure.

Earlier in my life, I understood joy to be a form of euphoria, an exuberant, exhilarating kind of happiness. More recently, I see that for me, joy is the profound essence of the human experience. In fact, I think the questions I really explore in my art and writing are, "What is my truth?" and "What does joyful expression look and feel like?"

For much of my life, expression of my joy has been mitigated by struggle. In fact, I would say much of my early work is a pale imitation of joy… or perhaps more accurately, a pale intimation of joy. Deep joy for me is brilliantly-coloured, multi-layered, nuanced and textured—a thing of great beauty and clarity. When I feel it, the whole of me dances inside and so does my work. It's taken me time and effort to reach that place consistently and that, if anything, is the argument for beginning one's creative journey early in life. Ultimately, I believe my work will prove optimistic and life-affirming, incorporating pleasure, pain, rapture and despair. I feel close to capturing and reflecting this; I still have more to learn and express. Muriel reminds me, "The twin of joy is grief. The grief years make true joy years possible."

By living the creative process, I've learned more about my path in life. I've learned uncovering its true shape is a lifetime journey, as it is for all of us. Expressing creatively what is in me is integral to who I am. I'm not sure where the gift of creative expression came from, but when I try to bottle up that energy, I get into trouble emotionally. I have been given the means to express it, and despite how much work and struggle it might take, doing so is deeply satisfying to me… is in fact my bliss.

Sometimes I wonder if I will stay fit and live long enough physically, mentally and emotionally to accomplish this work. I am confident the challenges of the work I see in my head will be enough for a lifetime. Other times, I think about retiring from my new career—of freeing myself from the expectation that creative expression must be translated into a career. What would happen if I just played and allowed myself to explore? I look around and see artists and creative people of all types still working well into their eighties and beyond: my grandmother, the artist Doris McCarthy, writers Leo Tolstoy and Maya Angelou, and so many others. I take them as my role models. That is how I hope the years ahead will play out for me. Since I can't know what my future holds, I also try for balance in my life. I am choosing to live so that I experience happiness now, and so that I use the sum of who I am in the best, most creative way I know. This journey of creativity is what I wish to show the world and to leave as my legacy.

> The art gallery is filled to capacity for the opening this September evening. I survey the room. This is an artist's co-operative gallery and I am one of 20 artists who collectively run this space in an urban mall in my hometown. Three of us are featured in this particular exhibition and these canvases vibrate with soul-satisfying colour that lives up to the show's title, "Blaze of Colour." For years, it has been my dream to create work using intense fields of colour that stand alone as the focal point. Finally I have done so and I'm excited to be sharing this new work.

I stand in the middle of the crowd soaking up energy from the artwork and the buzz of conversation in the gallery as viewers engage with the art and each other. I feel fully-fledged as an artist. In these works, my voice is clear and fully expressed. My creativity has taken concrete form and stands front and centre for all to see. I am in the world and part of it as I wish to be.

Though this concludes the events of this book, it begins my journey into a new phase of creativity, one that is as yet unknown to me. I will travel further on this, my path. And I invite you, dear reader, to join me. Take up the adventure and navigate your own creative odyssey. Together we will make the world a richer, more beautiful and soul-satisfying place.

Exercise #1 Review: Free Time

a) How much free time do you have in a week?

b) Make an inventory of the activities that absorb your free time.

c) Is your creative work on the list?

Exercise #2 Rhythms of the Day

a) What are the best times of day for your creative energy?

b) Do your routines support your creative work?

Exercise #3 Addressing Challenges

a) What are the questions you wrestle with about your creative work?

b) Do you have any answers for your questions?

Exercise #4 Stages of Creative Work

a) Do you recognize the stages of your own creative process?

b) Most of us find some stages easier than others. Which stages are easiest for you? Most difficult?

c) Can you consciously identify where you are in a particular project?

Exercise #5 Taking Leaps of Faith

a) Have you taken any leaps of faith recently?

b) Are there any you'd like to take? If so, what are they and how might you go about them?

c) What are the activities that challenge you the most in life... the ones that you find almost too difficult to do?

d) What makes them difficult? What are the rewards if you make the effort?

Exercise #6 Visualization

Do you have any images for yourself and where you are in your (creative) life?

Exercise #7 Reflection

a) What are the big questions you wonder about in life?

b) How do you hope the years will play out for you?

c) What would you like to show the world and leave as your legacy?

d) What does joy look and feel like for you? What gives you joy?

Notes

Introduction

1. Reprinted with permission from Muriel E. McMahon, Jungian Analyst Dipl. Analyt.Psych.(Zurich)

2. Marion Woodman. *Addiction to Perfection: The Still Unravished Bride*. Inner City Books: Toronto: 1982, p. 99.

Chapter 1 Losing My Voice

1. Adam Sherrif Scott, Library and Archives Canada (2008-03-19) June 20, 2011 <http://collectionscanada.gc.ca>.

2. Prudence Heward, National Gallery of Canada, Canadian Painting in the 30's <http://cybermuse.gallery.ca/cybermuse/enthusiast/thirties/artist_e. jsp?iartistid=2 (Nov. 5, 2012) Wikipedia The Free Encyclopedia, Wikipedia. org (June 20, 2011) <http://en.wikipedia.org/wiki/Prudence_Heward>.

3. Samuel Beckett. *Waiting for Godot*. New York: Grove Press Inc. 1982.

4. T.S. Eliot. *Prufrock and Other Observations* London: The Egoist Ltd. 1917; Bartleby.com (1996) March, 2011 <http://www.bartleby.com/198/1.html>.

5. *The Gospel of Thomas*, translated by Stephen Patterson and Marvin Meyer; selection from Robert J. Miller, ed., *The Complete Gospels: Annotated Scholars Version* (Polebridge Press,1994) The Gnostic Society Library: The Nag Hammadi Library. (March 14, 2011) <http://www.gnosis.org/naghamm/ gosthom.html>.

6. Hardin Craig. (ed.) *The Complete Works of Shakespeare*. Illinois: Scott, Foresman and Co.1961. *Hamlet* (Act 1 sc.3 ll 78-80).

7. Claudia Bepko and Jo-ann Krestan. *Singing at the Top of Our Lungs*. New York: HarperCollins, 1993, p. 9.

8. St. John of the Cross. *Dark Night of the Soul* 16th century poem. Wikipedia The Free Encyclopedia, Wikipedia.org (March 28, 2011) <http:// en.wikipedia.org/wiki/Dark_Night_of_the_Soul>.

9. Richard Florida, *The Rise of the Creative Class*. New York: Basic Books, 2003, p. 44.

Chapter 2 Eleven Creative Truths

1. Answers.com *Britannica Concise Encyclopedia.* (1994-2011) Encyclopædia Britannica, Inc. Mar. 15, 2011 <http://www.answers.com/topic/creativity>.

2. Geoff Colvin. *Talent is Overrated: What Really Separates World Class Performers From Everybody Else.* New York: Penguin, 2008, pp.63-67.

3. Malcolm Gladwell. *The Outliers: The Story of Success.* New York: Little, Brown 2008, p. 56. The paragraph continues: "In fact researchers have settled on what they believe is the magic number for true expertise: ten thousand hours."

Chapter 3 Nurturing Creativity

1. Thomas Alva Edison. Thinkexist.com Quotations (1999-2010) March 20, 2011. <http://thinkexist.com/quotes/thomas_alva_edison/>.

2. Richard Florida. *The Rise of the Creative Class.* New York: Basic Books, 2003, p. 33.

3. Eleanor Roosevelt. The Quotations Page: Michael Moncur, (1994-2010) March 20, 2011 <http://www.quotationspage.com/quote/35592.html>.

4. In addition to my years of Jungian work, I found Julia Cameron's books very helpful and wonderfully affirming of the creative journey. (See reference list)

Chapter 4 Inspiration and Vision

1. Inspiration, The Free Dictionary.com The American Heritage Dictionary of the English Language, 4th Ed. (Houghton Mifflin Co. 2000) March 20, 2011 <http://www.thefreedictionary.com/inspiration>.

2. Tom Thomson. *Tom Thompson Art Gallery* (2011)March 20, 2011 <http://www.tomthomson.org/>.

3. William Blake. *The Alchemy Website, Levity.com* Adam McLean (Glasgow, UK; 1999) Mar 20, 2011 <http://www.levity.com/alchemy/blake_ma.html>.

4. Frank Lloyd Wright. About.com Architecture (The New York Times Co. 2011) March 20, 2011 <http://architecture.about.com/od/periodsstyles/g/organic.htm>.

5. John C. Maxwell. Thinkexist.com Quotations (1999-2010) March 20, 2011 <http://thinkexist.com/quotes/john_c._maxwell/>.

6. C.G. Jung. *Memories, Dreams, Reflections.* New York: Vintage Books, 1989, Prologue.

7. Terry Fallis. *The Best Laid Plans.* Toronto: McClelland and Stewart, 2007 as told to the audience for One book One Community, Fall 2010,Waterloo.

Chapter 5 Dreams and Creative Vision

1. Carolyn Myss. *The Castle: An Inner Path to God and Your Soul.* New York: Simon and Schuster, 2007, p. 23

2. Marion Woodman. *Addiction to Perfection: The Still Unravished Bride.* Toronto: Inner City Books, 1982, p.137. The passage continues: "We begin to recognize our individual identity in what was once confusion. Gradually we set up a dialogue between our ego and the Being who is weaving the pattern.

In that dialogue is soul-making. The dialogue between the ego and the self creates the Soul… changes life from a meaningless puzzle into an awesome journey." I found Jung's book, *Man and His Symbols* (New York: 1964) and *Awakening Intuition* by Mona Lisa Schulz (New York: Harmony Books 1998) useful dream resources also.

3. ibid. p. 87.

4. Gail Blanke's book, *In My Wildest Dreams*. New York: Fireside Books, 1998 is an excellent resource on this topic.

Chapter 6 Articulating Voice

1. Voice: Merriam-Webster.com (2011) March 20, 2011 <www.merriam-webster.com/dictionary/voice>.

2. John M. Grohol, PSYD. *Cognitive Dissonance and the Lies We Tell Ourselves.* Founder and editor in chief: World of Psychology blog on PsychCentral <http://psychcentral.com/blog/archives/2008/10/19/fighting-cognitive-dissonance-the-lies-we-tell-ourselves/ (Oct. 2012).

3. Caroline Myss. *The Castle: An Inner Path to God and Your Soul.* New York: Simon and Schuster, 2007, p. 66.

4. There are many good resources for identifying and changing internal scripts. Ones I found useful include Gail Blanke. *In My Wildest Dreams*. New York: Fireside, 1999. Martha Beck. *Finding Your Own North Star* New York: Three Rivers Press, 2002. Dr.Phil McGraw. *Self Matters* New York: Free Press, 2001 as well as the works of Dr.Carolyn Myss, Louise Hay, Byron Katie and Julia Cameron listed in the references section at the end of this book.

5. Dr. Donald Hebb: University of Alberta (2005 2008) March 5, 2012 <http://www.psych.ualberta.ca/GCPWS/Hebb/Hebb.html>.

6. Dr. Wilder Penfield: Library and Archives Canada (2008) <http://www.collectionscanada.gc.ca/physicians/030002-2400-e.html>.

7. *Neuroplasticity and the Changing Brain* Bridget Colla, June 2009, suite101. comMedia.Inc. Mar. 5 2012 <http://bridget-coila.suite101.com/neuroplasticity-and-the-changing-brain-a122831>.

Chapter 7 Cultivating The Spirit of Creativity

1. Oliver Wendell Holmes, Sr. Wikipedia The Free Encyclopedia, Wikipedia. org (March 2011) March 28, 2011 <http://en.wikipedia.org/wiki/Oliver_Wendell_Holmes,_Sr.>.

2. Clarissa Pinkola Estes. *Women Who Run with the Wolves*. New York: Random House, 1992, p. 336 "Animus can best be understood as a force that assists women in acting in their own behalf in the outer world. Animus helps a woman put forth her specific and feminine inner thoughts and feelings in concrete ways—emotionally,sexually,financially,creatively, and otherwise—rather than in a construct that patterns itself after a culturally imposed standard of masculine development in any given culture."

3. This was a suggestion that emerged from a discussion in one of my art journaling classes by a student whose critical voice always sounded like her husband's.

4. Two movies I recommend that portray these ideas are *Pollock*, (released September 2000) about Jackson Pollock, the American abstract impressionist painter, and *Finding Forrester*, (released Dec. 2000) about the writing process.

5. Alexander Graham Bell. CKA Famous Canadian Quotes Canadaka. net (2011) March 28, 2011 <http://www.canadaka.net/modules. php?name=Quotes_List&page=1>.

6. The myth of Orpheus and Eurydice: *Women in Greek Myths*, Ailia Athena (2008) <http://www.paleothea.com/Myths/Orpheus.html>.

7. Michelangelo. Wikipedia The Free Encyclopedia, Wikipedia.org (March 2011) March 28, 2011 <http://en.wikipedia.org/wiki/Michelangelo>.

Chapter 8 From Dreams to Priorities to Plans

1. Frank Rose. *The Creation of Avatar*. wired.co.uk <http://www.wired.co.uk/ magazine/archive/2010/01/features/the-creation-of-avatar?page=all October 20, 2012. It took James Cameron more than ten years to create his groundbreaking 3D film, *Avatar*.

2. There are legions of books on the planning process. Through my job in education, I was fortunate to attend leadership and planning process workshops based on Stephen R. Covey's work *The Seven Habits of Highly Effective People* (New York: 1989) and *The Four Roles of Leadership for Educators* (Premier: 2001). The Board I worked for, like many corporations, did its own form of multi-year planning. While these and other works have influenced my planning, I found I had to develop my own strategies for my creative work.

3. You can find more information about this on my website at <diaeeastham. com>.

4. Clarissa Pinkola Estes has an excellent chapter, "*Nourishing the Creative Life*" in her book, *Women Who Run with the Wolves* (New York: Random House, 1992) In it she writes: "Begin; this is how to clear the polluted river. If you're scared, scared to fail, I say begin already, fail if you must, pick yourself up, start again. If you fail again, you fail. So what? Begin again. It is not the failure that holds us back but the reluctance to begin over again that causes us to stagnate." *Women Who Run with the Wolves*. New York: Random House, 1992, p. 343.

5. Julia Cameron provides sample contracts for creative work in *The Artist's Way*, New York: Putnam,1992, pp 23, 202.

Chapter 9 Ascending the Curve

1. Clarissa Pinkola Estes. *Women Who Run with the Wolves*. New York: Random House, 1992, p. 157.

2. Von Goethe: Famous Quotes.com Interlution (2011)March 28, 2011 <http://www.famousquotes.com/show/1026309/.

3. Stephen King. *A Memoir of the Craft On Writing*. New York: Scribner, 2000, p.196-197.

4. Leonardo DaVinci. Thinkexist.com Quotations (1999-2010) March 20, 2011 <http://thinkexist.com/quotation/art_is_never_finished-only_ abandoned/11376.html>.

5. Synchronicity. Wikipedia The Free Encyclopedia, Wikipedia.org (March 2011) March 28, 2011 <http://en.wikipedia.org/wiki/Synchronicity.

Chapter 10 Points on the Compass

1. Albert Einstein. Thinkexist.com Quotations (1999-2010) March 20, 2011 <http://thinkexist.com/quotes/albert_einstein/>.

2. Optimism. Merriam-Webster.com (2011) March 20,2011 <http://www.merriam-webster.com/dictionary/optimism> .

3. Dr. Jill Ammon-Wexler. CanadaOne.Com Biz-Zone Internet Group Inc. (1998-2010) March 28, 2011 <http://www.canadaone.com/bio/jammon_wexler.html>.

4. Dr. Jill Ammon–Wexler, *Intelligent Optimism*, (2005) March 28, 2011 <http://personal-development.com/blog/28/intelligent-optimism/>.

5. The Phelps Lab, New York University. Phelps study was reported on the CBC television news 24/10/2007. Phelps and colleagues reported their findings in the October 24, 2007 issue of Nature <http://psych.nyu.edu/phelpslab/pages/home.htm>.

6. Jeff Grabmeier. *Nodding or Shaking Your Head May Even Influence Your Own Thoughts* Ohio State University Research study by Richard Petty (2003) March 28, 2011 <http://researchnews.osu.edu/archive/headmvmt.htm>.

7. Michael J. Gelb. *How to Think Like Leonardo DaVinci*. New York: Delacorte Press, 1998, p. 88.

8. These resources are listed at the end of the book under References.

9. Julia Cameron. *The Artist's Way*. New York: Tarcher/Putnam, 1992 pp. 36-37.

10. Carolyn Myss. *Sacred Contracts: Awakening Your Divine Potential*. New York: Random House, 2001 "The third chakra is… the place where you define your sense of integrity and your personal code of honor… An honor code is essential for you to maintain a healthy spirit and body. Compromising your values or lacking a spiritual backbone puts you at physical and spiritual risk." p. 184.

11. David Bayles and Ted Orland write in *Art and Fear*. California: Capra Press, 1993. "Virtually all artists encounter such moments. Fear that your next work will fail is a normal, recurring and generally healthy part of the artmaking cycle. It happens all the time: you focus on some new idea in your work, you try it out, run with it for awhile, reach a point of diminishing returns, and eventually decide it's not worth pursuing further… all media have their equivalents. In the normal artistic cycle this just tells you that you've come full circle, back to that point where you need to begin cultivating the next new idea." p. 10.

12. Monique LaRue. *Between Books* (The Writer's Time). The Antonine Maillet-Northrop Frye Lecture. New Brunswick: Goose Lane Edition,2010, p. 40.

13. I use two audio cassettes from the *Fear-Less* series by Susan Jeffers (Hay House: 1990): *Inner Talk For Peace of Mind and Inner Talk for a Confident Day*

14. I like the 8 CD set by Dr. Wayne Dyer, *Your Ultimate Calling; Change Your Thoughts—Change Your Life Living the Wisdom of the Tao* (Hay House: 2007)

15. I listen to *On Intimacy* and *On Dealing with Anger* by Marianne Williamson. New York: HarperCollins, Harper Audio, 1993.

16. Hubble galaxy images: http://hubblesite.org/gallery/album/galaxy/.

17. I often attend the free public lectures offered once a month at The Perimeter Institute for Theoretical Physics <http://www.perimeterinstitute. ca/> The idea that we are made of stars has surfaced through a number of the lectures.

Chapter 11 Expanding Creative Capacity

1. Dr. Mona Lisa Schulz. *Awakening Intuition: Using Your Mind-Body Network for Insight and Healing.* New York: Harmony Books, 1998, p. 25.

2. ibid. p. 340.

3. Clarissa Pinkola Estes offers the following advice: "Another way to strengthen connection to intuition is to refuse to allow anyone to repress your vivid energies . . . that means your opinions, your thoughts, your ideas, your values, your morals, your ideals." *Women Who Run with the Wolves.* New York: Random House, 1992, p. 118.

4. Ken Wilber, *The Spectrum of Consciousness* (Wheaton, Il: Quest Books, 1993) Preface to the second edition. March 20, 2011 <http://www.amazon.com/ Spectrum-Consciousness-Quest-Books/dp/0835606953>.

5. Carolyn Myss. *The Castle: An Inner Path to God and Your Soul.* New York: Simon and Schuster, 2007, p. 45-66.

6. Jon Kabat Zinn. *Wherever You Go There You Are.* New York: Hyperion Books, 1994.

7. Madonna Gauding. *Meditations for every day.* London: Octopus Publishing, 2007, Introduction.

8. As told to the audience at Centre in the Square, Kitchener, Ontario (Nov. 2010) <http://www.dalenikkel.com/>.

9. Candace B. Pert writes: "Recent technological innovations have allowed us to examine the molecular basis of the emotions and to begin to understand how the molecules of our emotions share intimate connections with, and are indeed inseparable from, our physiology. It is the emotions, I have come to see, that link mind and body. *Molecules of Emotion: Why You Feel The Way You Do.* New York: Scribner, 1997, p.18.

10. ibid p. 141.

11. ibid. p. 189.

12. ibid p 189.

Chapter 12 Creativity at Home

1. Doris McCarthy from her obituary, "Artist Doris McCarthy Dies at 100," (CBC News Thurs. Nov 25, 2010) April 12, 2011 <http://www.cbc.ca/ news/arts/artdesign/story/2010/11/25/doris-mccarthy-obit.html>.

2. Morris. BrainyQuote.Com, BookRags Media Network Inc. (2001-2011) April 1, 2011 <http://www.brainyquote.com/quotes/authors/w/william_ morris.html>.

3. Canadian Mental Health Association. Lam, Dr. R.W. Seasonal Affective Disorder FAQs (2001) March 18, 2011 <http://www.cmha.ca/bins/content_page.asp?cid=3-86-93-291>.

4. The Osteoporosis Society of Canada. Quick links, VitaminD (2011) April 1, 2011 <http://www.osteoporosis.ca/>.

5. Global Television News report by Anne Marie Medawake. Special follow-up story about the children who survived the tsunami. (Feb. 23, 2005) <http://www.globaltv.com/>.

6. Spark of Brilliance (2009) March 3, 2011 <http://www.sparkofbrilliance.org>.

7. Personal correspondence with Judith Rosenberg.

8. Chakras: Wikipedia The Free Encyclopedia, Wikipedia.org (March 2011) March 28,2011 <http://en.wikipedia.org/wiki/Chakra>.

9.The Harriston-Minto Heritage Gallery (2011) March 23,2011 <http://guelpharts.ca/mintoarts/section.php?sid=402>.

Chapter 13 Building Creative Energy

1. "Maintaining blood sugar levels, even in the absence of disease, may be an important strategy for preserving cognitive health, suggests a study published by researchers at Columbia University Medical Center (CUMC)." Cognitive Aging. *Science Daily*. Retrieved April 1, 2011, from <http://www.sciencedaily.com/releases/2008/12/081230072238.htm>.

2. Betty Ford: JustQuotes.com (2006-2011) March 20, 2011 <http://www.just-quotes.com/compromise_quotes.html>.

3. This idea is suggested in Canada's Food Guide: NMS.on.ca (2009) March 23, 2011 <http://www.nms.on.ca/Elementary/canada.htm.

4. Howard Perlman, *The Water In You* (2011) April 1, 2011 <http://ga.water.usgs.gov/edu/propertyyou.html>.

5. 10,000 steps a day: The Walking Site.com (1998-2005) April 1, 2011 <http://www.thewalkingsite.com/10000steps.html>.

6. see the Public Health Agency of Canada guidelines: <http://www.phac-aspc.gc.ca> and click on physical activity. (2011) April 1, 2011.

7. Power Nap Prevents Burnout; Morning Sleep perfects a Skill, Jules Asher: NIH News release (July 2, 2002)"Evidence is mounting that sleep—even a nap—appears to enhance information processing and learning. New experiments by NIMH grantee Alan Hobson, M.D., Robert Stickgold, Ph.D., and colleagues at Harvard University show that a midday snooze reverses information overload and that a 20 percent overnight improvement in learning a motor skill is largely traceable to a late stage of sleep that some early risers might be missing…" April 1, 2011 <http://www.nih.gov/news/pr/jul2002/nimh-02.htm>.

Chapter 14 Body at Work; Body of Work

1. Candace B. Pert. Molecules of Emotion: *Why You Feel The Way You Do*. New York: Scribner, 1997. Dr. Pert Has this to say about the mind-body split: "…since the seventeenth century… Rene Descartes, the philosopher

and founding father of modern medicine, was forced to make a turf deal with the Pope in order to get the bodies he needed for dissection. Descartes agreed he wouldn't have anything to do with the soul, the mind or emotions—those aspects of human experience under the virtually exclusive jurisdiction of the church at the time—if he could claim the physical realm as his own. Alas, the bargain set the tone and direction for Western science over the next two centuries dividing human experience into two distinct and separate spheres that could never overlap, creating the unbalanced situation that is mainstream science as we know it today." p18.

2. Prudence Heward. Wikipedia The Free Encyclopedia, Wikipedia.org (June 20, 2011) <http://en.wikipedia.org/wiki/Prudence_Heward>.

3. Frida Kahlo, Wikipedia The Free Encyclopedia, Wikipedia.org (June 20, 2011) <http://en.wikipedia.org/wiki/Frida_Kahlo>.

4. Stephen Hawking. Wikipedia The Free Encyclopedia, Wikipedia.org (June 20, 2011) <http://en.wikipedia.org/wiki/Stephen_Hawking>.

5. Dr. Mona Lisa Schulz. *Awakening Intuition: Using Your Mind-Body Network for Insight and Healing.* New York: Harmony Books, 1998. "Our bodies speak to us every day in every way through their own vocabulary of symptoms tied to emotions and memories from the past and the present. We can learn to read those symptoms in the same way we learn to read signals in relationships or other areas of our lives." p. 116.

6. Clarissa Pinkola Estes. *Women Who Run with the Wolves.* New York, 1992, p. 220.

7. Caffeine Metabolism: Women have a greater sensitivity to caffeine than men and their bodies may take much longer to detoxify caffeine and recover from its stimulating effects (Mathias, et al, 1985) source: Mathias, S., Garland,C., Barrett-Connor, E. and Wingard, D.L. 1985. Coffee, plasma cholesterol, and lipoproteins. A population study in an adult community. *American Journal of Epidemiology.* 121(6):896-905 March 28,2011. <http://teeccino.com/building_optimal_health/81/Caffeine-Metabolism.html>.

8. Caffeine and heart attacks: Cornelis MC et al. (2006) JAMA 295(10): 1135-41. April 1, 2011 <http://www.ncbi.nlm.nih.gov/pubmed/16522833>.

9. This information is contained in a brochure on birch tree allergies provided by my doctor who is an allergy specialist.

10. *Canadians Are Vacation Deprived: Study.* "Canadians are taking less vacation time, making workers here amongst the most holiday-deprived in the world, according to a study by the travel site Expedia.ca and Ipsos Reid. This puts Canada third on a list of holiday-deprived nations. Workers in the U.S. take the fewest holidays, an average of 14 days, followed by Australia at an average of 17 days." (May 18, 2006) CBC.ca (2011) Mar. 23, 2011 <http://www.cbc.ca/canada/story/2006/05/18/canadian-vacation-days.html#ixzz1BmNexYN7>.

Chapter 15 Heart Matters

1. William Shakespeare. *Hamlet* (Act 1 sc.3 ll. 78-80).

2. Caroline Myss. *The Energetics of Healing.* 2 videotape set; USA: Sounds True, 1997.

Chapter 16 Living in the Labyrinth

1. Robert Kubey, and Mihaly Csikszentmihalyi. *Television and the Quality of Life How Viewing Shapes Everyday Experience.* New Jersey: Lawrence Erlbaum Associates Inc., 1990. "People who have jobs spend roughly 1/3 of their waking hours at work or traveling to work; about 40% of their time is spent in maintenance activities such as shopping cooking, eating and child care, and approximately 30% is devoted to leisure activities (Szalai, 1972) Of this… the single activity that clearly absorbs the most time in modern societies is watching television.

2. Thomas Moore. *A Life At Work: The Joy of Discovering What You Were Born To Do.* New York: Broadway Books, 2008, p121. The passage continues: "The Romans believed that a child is born with his daimon, or in their language, genius.." It's a fertile idea: that the deep passion and drivenness that stays with us all our lives is there from the beginning. It becomes more defined as we grow older, or perhaps we simply learn more about what it is and where it can take us."

Chapter 17 In the End is My Beginning

1. And possibly why so many newly-retired people, up to 25%, desire to return to the work-force. Immen, Wallace. *Getting back in the game.* Globe & Mail [Toronto, Canada] 19 Feb. 2011: B18. Canadian Periodicals Index Quarterly. Web. 6 Mar. 2012.

2. Mihaly Csikszentmihalyi. *Flow: the Psychology of Optimal Experience.* New York: Harper and Row, 1990. "Contrary to what we assume, the normal state of the mind is chaos. Without training, and without an object in the external world that demands attention, people are unable to focus their thoughts for more than a few minutes at a time. It is relatively easy to concentrate when attention is structured by outside stimuli, such as when a movie is playing on the screen or when, while driving, heavy traffic is encountered on the road." p. 119.

3. When I was completing my Master's degree at University of Toronto I took a course instructed by David E. Hunt that taught visualization techniques and discovered I had some facility with the process. [David E. Hunt. The Renewal of Personal Energy. Canada: OISE Press, 1992.

4. Geoff Colvin. *Talent is Overrated: What Really Separates World Class Performers From Everybody Else.* New York: Penguin Books, 2008, pp. 172-173.

REFERENCES

Ackerman, Diane. *An Alchemy of Mind: the Marvel and Mystery of the Brain.* New York: Scribner, 2004.

Allison, Henry E. *Benedict de Spinosa: An Introduction.* New York: Vail-Balloul Press, 1987.

Aurelius, Marcus. *Meditations.* New York: Penguin Classics 2002.

Bayles, David and Orland, Ted. *Art & Fear.* California: Capra Press, 1993.

Beck, Martha. *Finding Your Own North Star.* New York: Three Rivers Press, 2002. [good for identifying the stages of change; internal scripts]

Benzel, Rick. ed. *Inspiring Creativity: An Anthology of Powerful Insights and Practical Ideas to Guide You to Successful Creating.* California: Creativity Coaching Association Press, 2005.

Bepko, Claudia and Krestan, Jo-ann. *Singing at the Top of Our Lungs: Women, Love and Creativity.* New York: HarperCollins, 1993.

Benson, Herbert and Proctor, William M.D. *The Breakout Principle: How to Activate the Natural Trigger That Maximizes Creativity, Athletic Performance and Personal Well Being.* New York: Scribner, 2003.

Blanke, Gail. *In My Wildest Dreams: Simple Steps to a Fabulous Life.* New York: Simon and Schuster, 1998.

Boden, Margaret. *The Creative Mind: Myths and Mechanisms.* UK: W&N, 1991.

Brooks, Robert and Goldstein Sam. *The Power of Resilience: Achieving Balance, Confidence and Personal Strength in Your Life.* New York: McGraw Hill, 2004. [Excellent for rewriting those negative scripts, developing empathy, self-awareness and communication skills]

Bruyere, Rosalyn L. *Wheels of Light.* New York: Fireside, 1989.

Cameron, Julia. *The Artist's Way.* New York: Putnam, 1992.

Cameron, Julia. *The Vein of Gold*. New York: Putnam, 1996.

Cameron, Julia. *Walking In This World*. New York: Putnam, 2002.

Cohen, Herb. *You Can Negotiate Anything*. New York: Bantam,1982.

Colvin, Geoff. *Talent is Overrated: What Really Separates World Class Performers From Everybody Else*. New York: Penguin Books, 2008.

Covey, Stephen R. *The Seven Habits of Highly Effective People*. New York, 1989.

Covey, Stephen R. *The Four Roles of Leadership for Educators*. Premier: 2001.

Csikszentmihalyi, Mihaly. *Flow: the Psychology of Optimal Experience*. New York: Harper and Row, 1990.

Csikszentmihalyi, Mihaly. *Creativity: Flow and the Psychology of Discovery and Invention*. New York: HarperCollins, 1996.

De bono, Edward. *Serious Creativity: Using the Power of Lateral Thinking to Create New Ideas*. New York: Harper Collins, 1992.

Dorner, Dietrich. *The Logic Of Failure: Recognizing and Avoiding Error in Complex Situations*. New York: Basic Books, 1996.

Durling, Sharon. *A Girl and Her Money*. Tennessee: W Publishing Group, 2003.

Dyer, Dr. Wayne. *Excuses Begone!* California: Hay House, 2009.

Dyer, Dr. Wayne. *The Shift*. California: Hay House, 2010.

Estes, Clarissa Pinkola. *Women Who Run with the Wolves*. New York: Random House, 1992. Florida, Richard. The Rise of the Creative Class. New York: Basic Books, 2002.

Ford, Debbie, *The Dark Side of the Light Chasers*. New York: Riverhead Books,1998.

Friel, John and Linda Friel. *The 7 Best Things (happy) Couples Do*. Florida: Deerfield Beach, 2002.

Gawain, Shakti. *Meditations: Creative Visualization and Meditation Exercises to Enrich Your Life*. Novato, California 1991.

Gelb, Michael J. *How to Think Like Leonardo DaVinci*. New York: Delacorte Press, 1998.

Gilligan, Carol. *In a Different Voice*. Cambridge: Harvard University Press,1982.

Gladwell, Malcolm. *The Tipping Point*. New York: Little, Brown and Co., 2002.

Gladwell, Malcolm. *Outliers: The Story of Success*. New York: Penguin books, 2008.

Hay, Louise. *You Can Heal Your Life*. California: Hay House, 1984.

His Holiness the Dalai Lama, *The Art of Living: a Guide to Contentment, Joy and Fulfillment*. London: Thorsons, 2001.

Hunt, David. E. *The Renewal of Personal Energy*. Toronto: OISE press 1992.

Jeffers, Susan. *Feel the Fear and Do It Anyway*. New York: Fawcett Columbine, 1987.

Jung, Carl. *Man and His Symbols*. New York, Dell Publishing, 1964.

Jung, Carl. *Memories, Dreams and Reflections*. New York: Vintage books, 1961.

Katie, Byron. *Loving What Is: 4 Questions That Can Change Your Life*. New York, Three Rivers Press, 2002.

Kent, Corita and Steward, Jan. *Learning by Heart*. New York, Bantam Books, 2008.

King, Stephen. *A Memoir of the Craft On Writing*. New York: Scribner 2000.

Kraft, Ulrich. *Unleashing Creativity* .Scientific American Mind, (Vol. 16 #1).

Kubey, Robert and Csikszentmihalyi, Mihaly. *Television and the Quality of Life: How Viewing Shapes Everyday Experience*. New Jersey: Routledge, 1990.

LaRue, Monique. *Between Books* (The Writer's Time) The Antonine Maillet-Northrop Frye Lecture. New Brunswick: Goose Lane Edition, 2010.

Long, Charles. *How to Survive Without A Salary*. Toronto, Warwick Publishing, 1996.

McGraw, Dr. Phil. *Life Strategies*. New York: Hyperion, 1999.

McGraw, Dr. Phil. *Self Matters*. New York: Free Press, 2001.

McKay, Dr. Matthew and Fanning, Patrick. *Self Esteem*. California: New Harbinger Publications, 2000.

Moore, Thomas. *Care of the Soul*. New York: Harper Collins, 1992.

Moore, Thomas. *A Life At Work: The Joy of Discovering What You Were Born To Do*. New York: Broadway Books, 2008.

Myss, Dr. Caroline. *Sacred Contracts: Awakening Your Divine Potential*. New York: Random House, 2001.

Myss, Dr. Caroline. *Why People Don't Heal and How they Can*. New York, Three Rivers Press, 1997.

Myss, Dr. Caroline. *The Castle: An Inner Path to God and Your Soul*. New York: Simon and Schuster, 2007.

Nietzsche, Friedrich. *Thus Spoke Zarathustra*. London: Penguin Books, 1969.

Nietzsche, Friedrich. *Beyond Good and Evil*. London: Penguin Books, 1990.

Pausch, Randy with Jeffrey Zaslow. *The Last Lecture*. New York: Hyperion. 2008.

Peck, Scott. *The Road Less Travelled*. New York: Simon and Schuster, 1978.

Pert, Candace B. *Molecules of Emotion: Why You Feel The Way You Do*. New York: Scribner, 1997.

Pollan, Stephen. *Die Broke*. New York: Harper Business, 1997.

Ruiz, Don Miguel. *The Four Agreements*. California, Amber-Allen, 1997.

Schulz, Dr. *Mona Lisa. Awakening Intuition*. New York: Three Rivers Press, 1998.

Tharp, Twyla. *The Creative Habit: Learn It and Use It For Life*. New York: Simon and Schuster, 2003.

Woodman, Marion. *Addiction to Perfection: The Still Unravished Bride*. Toronto: Inner City Books, 1982.

Zinn, Jon Kabat. *Full Catastrophe Living*. New York, Delacorte Press1990.
Zinn, Jon Kabat. *Wherever You Go There You Are*. New York: Hyperion, 1994.
Zukav, Gary. *The Seat of the Soul*. New York: Simon and Schuster, 1989.

Internet Books and Articles
Ammon-Wexler, Dr. Jill. *Why Optimism Fuels Success*. Canadaone.com 2006.

Petty, Dr. Richard. "Nodding or shaking your head may even influence your own thoughts, study finds" (Ohio State University Research News http:// researchnews.osu.edu/archive/headmvmt.htm)

Schueler, Gerald J. Ph.D and Schueler, Betty J. PhD. The Chaos of Jung's Psyche, an online book www.schuelers.com

Wilbur, Ken, *The Spectrum of Consciousness* (1977) <http://books.google.ca>

Audiotapes, Cd's , Dvd's
Batchelor, Stephen. *Buddhism Without Beliefs*. Sounds True: 2001.His Holiness the Dalai Lama, The Art of Happiness. Simon and Schuster Audio, 1998.

Dyer, Dr. Wayne. *Your Ultimate Calling; Change Your Thoughts—Change Your Life Living the Wisdom of the Tao*. Hay House: 2007.

Gawain, Shakti. Meditations. California: New World Library,1997.

Jeffers, Susan Dr. The *Fear-Less* series by Susan

Jeffers *Inner Talk For Peace of Mind and Inner Talk for a Confident Day.* Hay House: 1990.

Kabat-Zinn, Dr. Jon. *Mindfulness Meditation* Practice Tapes (P.O. Box 547, Lexington, MA 02173)

Myss, Caroline. *The Energetics of Healing.* 2 videotape set; USA: Sounds True, 1997.

Williamson, Marianne. *On Intimacy and On Dealing with Anger.* New York: HarperCollins, Harper Audio 1993.

Other

Gauding, Madonna. *Meditations for Every Day.* London: Octopus Publishing, 2007. cards

www.ingramcontent.com/pod-product-compliance
Lightning Source LLC
Chambersburg PA
CBHW051950090426
42741CB00008B/1330